Indian Migration to the Gulf

This book explores issues of rights, issues, and challenges faced by Indian migrant workers in the GCC countries. It focuses on the struggle of migrants in the state of origin and destination states and how the process of migration shapes the identity and existence of migrant workers. The essays in the volume focus on policy, rights, issues, and challenges faced by migrants as well as the long-term challenges posed by the COVID-19 pandemic.

With contributions from academics and policymakers, this book will be of interest to scholars and researchers of migration and diaspora studies, public policy, and South Asian Studies.

Anisur Rahman is presently heading the UGC Human Resource Development Centre of Jamia Millia Islamia Central University, New Delhi, India. He is a professor of Gulf Studies and has contributed rigorously to Migration and Development especially that of Gulf Migration.

Sameer Babu M is an Associate Professor at Jamia Millia Islamia in New Delhi, India, in the Department of Adult and Continuing Education and Extension. He has been awarded the esteemed Shastri Mobility Grant to Canada. He focuses on migrant issues and education, as well as MOOC development, classroom psychology, tool development, and innovative pedagogy in higher education.

Ansari PA is currently working as a Postdoctoral Fellow at Jamia Millia Islamia, New Delhi, India. He had completed his PhD in Human Rights from Aligarh Muslim University on the issues and challenges of migrant workers. He is currently working as an Associate Editor of the Journal of Policy and Governance (JPG), based in Quebec, Canada.

Indian Migration to the Gulf

Issues, Perspectives and Opportunities

Edited by Anisur Rahman,
Sameer Babu M, and Ansari PA

Routledge
Taylor & Francis Group
LONDON AND NEW YORK

First published 2023
by Routledge
4 Park Square, Milton Park, Abingdon, Oxon OX14 4RN

and by Routledge
605 Third Avenue, New York, NY 10158

Routledge is an imprint of the Taylor & Francis Group, an informa business

British Library Cataloguing-in-Publication Data
A catalogue record for this book is available from the British Library

ISBN: 978-1-032-30764-0 (hbk)
ISBN: 978-1-032-43912-9 (pbk)
ISBN: 978-1-003-36937-0 (ebk)

DOI: 10.4324/9781003369370

Typeset in Sabon
by Deanta Global Publishing Services, Chennai, India

Dedicated to Migrants Working for Development of the Gulf Countries and India

Contents

Figures

Tables

Contributors

Waseem Ahmad is currently an ICSSR Doctoral Fellow at the Centre for West Asian Studies, Jamia Millia Islamia, New Delhi, India. He completed his MPhil in West Asian Studies (Political Science) from Aligarh Muslim University. He has published several research papers in reputed journals, and has presented his findings in national and International Conferences. His area of interest includes International Relations, Soft Power Diplomacy, Peace and Conflict, Migration and Diaspora.

Ansari PA is currently working as a Postdoctoral Fellow at Jamia Millia Islamia, New Delhi, India. He had completed his PhD in Human Rights from Aligarh Muslim University on the issues and challenges of migrant workers. He is currently working as an Associate Editor of the Journal of Policy and Governance (JPG), based in Quebec, Canada.

Muhammad Azhar is Professor (Economics) at the Department of West Asian and North African Studies, Faculty of International Studies, Aligarh Muslim University, Aligarh, India. Before Aligarh, served as Reader at the Academy of Third World Studies, Jamia Millia Islamia, New Delhi. Prior to Jamia worked as Research Associate at the Gulf Studies Programme, Jawahar Lal Nehru University, New Delhi.

Shahid Bashir is working as an Assistant Professor of Economics in the Department of Data Science, Christ University, India. He received his Doctorate in Economics from the Department of Economics, Central University of Kashmir. He is the recipient of the University Gold Medal from the Central University of Kashmir and the Maulana Azad National Doctoral Fellowship from the University Grants Commission, New Delhi. He has qualified UGC-NET in economics four times consecutively.

Javed Charan is a doctoral research scholar at the Centre for Russian and Central Asian Studies, Jawaharlal Nehru University, New Delhi, India. His research focuses on the Indian Diaspora in Russia and Central Asia. Through the lens of cultural diplomacy and soft power, his work provides a multidisciplinary approach to comprehending the Indian Diaspora's connections to India's foreign policy.

Bhupesh Gopal Chintamani completed his PhD in Economics from Gokhale Institute of Politics and Economics, Pune. He is currently associated as Assistant Professor, Symbiosis Law School (SLS), Symbiosis International (Deemed University) (SIU), Vimannagr, Pune, Maharashtra, India. He has previously worked as Senior Research Officer at Vaikunth Mehta National Institute of Co-Operative Management (VAMNICOM) Pune and Visiting Faculty of economics at Gokhale Institute of Politics and Economics and Symbiosis School of Economics, Pune.

K Deepa is a Librarian at the Centre for West Asian Studies, Jamia Millia Islamia, New Delhi, India. Earlier she worked as a Documentation Assistant with the Centre of Social Medicine and Community Health, Jawaharlal Nehru University, New Delhi, India. Her area of research includes contemporary studies on India–West Asia relations. Contributed book chapters to several books and presented papers in a number of national and international conferences in India and abroad.

Muhammed Fazal is a doctoral research scholar at the Centre for Studies in Economics and Planning, School of Social Sciences at the Central University of Gujarat, Gandhinagar, India. He completed his Graduation and Post-Graduation in Economics from the University of Calicut. He completed his MPhil in Economics from the current Centre at the Central University of Gujarat.

K Jafar is currently working as Assistant Professor at Madras Institute of Development Studies Chennai, India. Before joining MIDS, Jafar worked as Assistant Professor at TISS Hyderabad and CSD Hyderabad and worked with APU Bangalore and CDS Trivandrum. He completed his Postdoctoral research at CSD Hyderabad and doctoral research at the National Institute of Advanced Studies Bangalore. His research broadly follows the development with a focus on its link with education, labor migration, financial inclusion, local planning, informality, IPRs, and gender.

Jyothi KK is presently working as Assistant Professor of Economics at Sreeneelakanta Government Sanskrit College, Pattambi, India. She is doing her PhD at the University of Calicut on the topic, "Changing Pattern of Housing in Rural Kerala: A study of Palakkad District". Her area of specialization is Rural Economics.

Lekshmi S Kaimal is currently working as Assistant Professor at CMS College Kottayam (Autonomous) Kerala, India. She completed her doctoral research at Mahatma Gandhi University Kottayam on "Consumerism and Consumption Pattern among IT Professionals in Kerala". Her area of research includes consumerism, migration, education and development.

Atinder Pal Kaur is currently working as Assistant Professor (Sociology) in the Department of Economics and Sociology at Punjab Agricultural University, Ludhiana, Punjab, India. She completed her PhD from Panjab University, Chandigarh with UGC-JRF. Her research areas are broad: International-internal migration, gender and development, transnationalism, labor migration. Her recent publication is Migration a road to Empowerment? Agency, resources and left behind women in Punjab, India. Asian Journal of Women Studies, 28(2), 167–185.

Md. Chingiz Khan is a PhD Research Scholar at Jawaharlal Nehru University's Centre for Historical Studies, New Delhi, India. He has written significantly on the medieval and early modern history of North East India and received numerous national honors, including the "NAMASTE Governor Acharya Award (2018)" in recognition of his academic credentials for research work related to North East India issues. He was appointed as the subject expert of the review work of the textbook, "Themes in Indian History for Class XII with local components/elements", published by the Council of Higher Secondary Manipur (COHSEM), Government of Manipur in 2020.

Baby Kizhakkekalam is presently working as Associate Professor of Economics at Govt. College, Chittur, Palakkad, Kerala, India. She had her PhD from Department of Economics Bharathiyar University, Coimbatore, Tamandu on the topic Household Behaviour and Economic Analysis of Solid Waste Management. Her area of specialization is Environmental Economics.

Mohsin Majeed has done an MPhil and a PhD in Economics from the Department of Economics, Central University of Kashmir, India. His research specialization lies in the areas of development economics and macroeconomics. He has his Post Graduation in Economics from the University of Kashmir.

Mousam is currently working as Assistant Professor of English at Government College, Malsisar, Jhunjhunu, Rajasthan, India. She completed her PhD in Comparative Literature from Central University of Gujarat, Gandhinagar. Her PhD research focuses on crime biographies of the USA, UK and India. Her research interests include Crime Narratives, Diaspora and Migration, Criminal Biographies and Autobiographies.

Nitesh Narnolia is currently working as an Assistant Professor of English at Government Girls College, Churu, Rajasthan. He completed his PhD from the Centre for Diaspora Studies, Central University of Gujarat,

Gandhinagar. His research interests include African American Literature, Slave Narratives, Postcolonial and Subaltern Studies, Race and Ethnic Studies, Transnationalism and Diaspora.

Naziya Naweed is a doctoral research scholar at the Centre for West Asian Studies, Jamia Millia Islamia, New Delhi, India. Her research focuses on the Indian Diaspora as a factor in India's foreign policy toward the GCC. Her writing takes into account an interdisciplinary perspective to understand the Indian Diaspora linkages with foreign policy through the prism of Remittance, Soft Power and Diplomacy.

Ani Merly Paul is currently working as Assistant Professor at CMS College Kottayam (Autonomous) Kerala, India. She is currently pursuing her PhD. Her area of research includes migration, education, and development.

Anisur Rahman is currently Professor and Director, UGC-Human Resource Development Centre, Jamia Millia Islamia, New Delhi, India. He holds Masters in two disciplines: Economics (AMU) as well as Sociology, MPhil and PhD (JNU). Before he joined Jamia Millia Islamia in New Delhi, India in 1999, he worked at the Institute of Applied Manpower Research, Planning Commission, Government of India. His area of interest includes South Asian Migration and Diaspora, Gulf Social Demography, Issues of Higher, Academic Leadership, Education and Minorities. He has published eight books and over 50 Research Papers in Reputed Journals in India and abroad including his contributions as chapters in edited books by well-known scholars. Dr Rahman has presented over 70 research papers in several conferences/seminars/workshops in India and abroad. He has visited several countries like the USA, the UK, France, Germany, the Netherlands, Sweden, Denmark, Switzerland, Hong Kong, Saudi Arabia, and the UAE. He has been the Visiting Professor at FMSH, Paris, and visited Paris, France under the Indo-French Social Scientist Exchange Programme thrice for research in 2010, 2013, and 2015. He has delivered over 150 invited talks at different institutions of higher learning in India and abroad. He is also a member of several academic committees, bodies, and editorial boards.

Sameer Babu M is an Associate Professor, at Jamia Millia Islamia in New Delhi, India, in the Department of Adult and Continuing Education and Extension. He has been awarded the esteemed Shastri Mobility Grant to Canada. He focuses on migrant issues and education, as well as MOOC development, classroom psychology, tools development, and innovative pedagogy in higher education.

Muhammed Shabeer T is currently working as an Assistant Professor on contract (Political Science) at Government Arts and Science College Tavanur, Kerala. He completed his graduation in Political Science from

Aligarh Muslim University and Post-Graduation in International Relations and Political Science from Central University of Kerala.

Mohammed Taukeer is associated as a Research Fellow in the International Institute of Migration and Development, Trivandrum, Kerala, India. His interesting area of study is labor migration from India to the Gulf as well as illegal "donkey" migration of South Asian refugees in Greece.

Sonal Thakker is an Associate Professor and Head of the Department of Sociology, Murgaon Education Society's College of Arts and Commerce, Zuarinagar-Goa, India. She obtained her doctorate degree from Goa University. Her research interests and publications have primarily been related to international migration, sex ratio in India, Goan folklore, multicultural literacy, and perspectives on marginalization. She was presented with the best research paper award at the XIIth Karnataka Sociology Conference at Hampi, 2018 for the paper entitled "Migration of Spouses and Coping Strategies of Stay Behind Women".

Preface

Migration and the mobility of people across the world is rapidly growing today. It is estimated that there are about 281 million migrants globally which roughly constitutes of 3.2% of the world population. The Gulf Cooperation Council (GCC) countries is emerging as one of the major sources of the destination for millions of immigrants especially from the South Asian countries such as India, Bangladesh, Sri Lanka, Pakistan, and now Nepal. The six GCC countries together constitute more than 52% of the non-nationals in their population. It has been noticed in the last few decades that made new provisions of immigration policies to protect the welfare of the local national population and control the outflow of remittances to other countries. But this is not happening as it was expected that there would be an impact of immigration policies of GCC countries directly or indirectly on the size, flow, stock, trend, magnitude, and characteristics of immigrants. The size and volume of non-nationals are still increasing. It is also evident that the India–Gulf migration has emerged as the second-largest employment migration corridor in the world. The six GCC states host more than 8.5 million Indians. These Indians in fact constitute almost 30% of total expatriates in the region. The main aim of the book is to discuss the role played by expatriate workers in bringing tangible changes in the Gulf society where they are working. The role of GCC countries has also been examined that provide economic and social security to expatriates. An attempt has also been made to understand the changing dynamic trends along with a socio-demographic profile of migrants in the Gulf countries. How the Indian migrants would be proved to be made more productive would also be discussed in this volume. Hopefully, this volume is found to be quite interesting and relevant to those scholars who have an interest in migration studies, policymakers, and general readers alike.

I appreciate the role of my co-editors Dr Sameer Babu, Associate Professor, Department of Adult and Continuing Education and Extension Education, and Dr Ansari PA, PDF Scholar for their unstinting support in bringing out this volume. We are grateful to all chapter authors of this unique book on Indian Migration to the Gulf. We are also thankful to the library staff of various institutions of higher learning who have helped us by providing appropriate resource materials and literature. We extend our heartfelt thanks to Routledge Publishers for bringing out this book.

Anisur Rahman

Introduction

India is a land of migration. With a history as long as human civilization, the topic of migration is one that is often in the news. More than 275 million migrant workers are dispersed worldwide in 2019, out of which India figures amongst the major migrant-sending countries in the world. People have been migrating due to the influx of various factors, categorized as the push and pull factors. Poverty, unemployment, political repression, human rights abuses, and conflict are the reasons that push more and more people out of their home countries whereas economic opportunities, political freedom, physical safety, and security pull both highly skilled and unskilled workers into new lands. Thus, migration is often seen as a factor in bringing socio-economic change to the place of origin and destination.

The pattern of Indian labor migration can be discerned into two phases, the pre-independence phase, and the post-independence phase. In the first pre-independence phase, indenture labor (the demand for Indian laborers was high in the colonies of West India, South Africa, Mauritius, Malaysia, and Ceylon (now Sri Lanka), kangani/Ministry of labor (South Indian laborers were recruited to Malaysia, Sri Lanka, and Burma), free or passage emigration (of trading caste and classes to South Africa as well as in the East African countries of Kenya, Tanzania, and Uganda) are some of the historical patterns of Indian migration that may be traced. These migration patterns arose as a result of colonial expansion. On the other hand, "brain drain" or voluntary emigration to metropolitan countries occurrences in Europe, North America, and Oceania, as well as labor migration to West Asia, might be examples of post-colonial emigration trends. These trends are the product of postcolonial India's underlying socio-economic contradictions. Large-scale Indian immigration of highly qualified and semi-skilled professionals to Europe and North America began in the late 1960s. The Sikhs were among the first Indian migrants to these countries. These ethnic groups now make up the major ethnic groups in the United Kingdom, Canada, and the United States. The ethnic makeup of Indians in Europe, North America, and Oceania are equally noteworthy. The majority of Indians in the United

DOI: 10.4324/9781003369370-1

States are scientists, engineers, surgeons, teachers, and other educated professionals. On the contrary, labor mobility in the countries of West Asia started in the 1970s, with the increase in oil prices that resulted in the huge demand for labor to meet the growing infrastructural development of the region. The labor demand was met by the labor imported from the counties of India, Pakistan, Bangladesh, and Sri Lanka. The oil boom aided Indians in meeting the Gulf region's infrastructure expansion needs as well as establishing a niche as a loyal labor force that continues to remain in significant numbers in the region.

Concerning India's relation with the Gulf, migratory labor mobility exhibits certain trends; migrants are "contract laborers", without any citizenship rights, thus debarred from remaining permanently in the host countries. Historically, people from India and the Middle East have been exchanging and engaging with one another for thousands of years now. Indian migrants come from a variety of countries all over the world, and the country is also the world's largest recipient of remittances (money sent back home). Due to the oil boom of the 1970s, Indian migration to the Gulf has acted as a vital source of cash for the country, and also served as the economic backbone of high-migration areas such as Kerala, through the transfer of remittances. Migrant laborers from India were employed during this period. However, today the migration trend shows that large labor mobility from Uttar Pradesh, Bihar, and Rajasthan has started to dominate and has replaced Kerala and other southern Indian states.

A long-standing historical trend, Indian emigration to nations such as Bahrain, Kuwait, Oman, Qatar, Saudi Arabia, and the United Arab Emirates has accelerated significantly in recent decades.

A substantial number of Indians leave the nation in search of higher education or employment opportunities. As previously said, the vast bulk of them arrive in countries in the Gulf region. The main reason for this influx of immigrants into the Gulf is the abundance of work possibilities available there, particularly unskilled and support-based positions that are open to persons with limited professional qualifications. Growing remittances from Indian unskilled laborers in the Gulf region were essential in rescuing India's economic predicament.

As a result, remittances from abroad have historically been a significant source of foreign currency in India, and they have the potential to assist the country in reducing its current account deficit. The outflow of emigrants to foreign countries results in an increase in government revenue in the form of fees for visas, departure taxes, international telephone calls, and other levies. All of these institutions had been used by migrant workers, either directly or indirectly.

As a result, in addition to economic remittances, social remittances are also carried between locations via migrants in a variety of ways. Men and women who migrate to different nations bring a variety of ideas back home with them and exchange them between countries.

Numerous changes have been observed in migrants' lives, including an increase in household/family income, sending their children to school, repaying loans, lowering the unemployment rate, purchasing houses, growing savings, and expanding the commercial sector, among others. Globalization and ITC (information communications technology) are playing a significant role in further enhancing migration from India to various regions of the world, with a particular emphasis on migration to the Gulf.

Hundreds of thousands of employees of Indian ancestry are forced to fend for themselves in the Gulf in the absence of legitimate documents and employment security. Denied access to healthcare, human rights, and correct legal status, their daily struggle to survive and earn a living must be publicized/documented in order to put pressure on the system to implement necessary reforms.

Researchers, policymakers, and academics have been driven to place a high priority on this topic because of the significant economic contribution that Indian migrants make in these countries. Cross-border migration, especially international migration, always has a two-way effect on the places where it originates and where it ends.

Due to economic slowdowns, shifting oil prices, and changes in Gulf labor policies, the outflow of Indian migrants to the region has slowed, while return migration has surged.

This edited volume, consisting of 18 chapters, is structured under four wider sections, viz. sociocultural appraisal of Gulf migration, economic implications of Gulf migration, Gulf migration: A regional perspective, and Gulf migration: Gender and literature.

Chapter 1, titled Indian Diaspora in the Gulf: Impact and Advantages written by Javed Charan. A considerable amount of migration from India to Gulf countries began during the 1973 oil boom, which resulted in greater oil income and supported large-scale commercial enterprises in the Gulf region. Along with the complex parts of cultural heritages, those individuals gained access to a new but previously existing instrument that can facilitate productive discourse among people in their respective socio-religious contexts. The Indian government aided the Indian diasporic community's soft power by making various adjustments to its foreign policies that always address concerns affecting PIOs and OCIs. This framework will provide some new aspects, such as narrative frames drawn from these cultural heritages, to analyze the association and involvement that the Indian Diaspora population still experiences while living outside of India.

Chapter 2, written by Ansari, Anisur Rahman, and Sameer Babu M, discusses the COVID-19 and its Impact on Gulf Returnees: A Study of Kerala, India. It is their contention that migrant laborers appear to be employed in every sector of the Gulf economy as a result of the high wages and growing demand for physical labor jobs. This paper also makes an attempt to look into and analyze the government's response to the COVID-19 situation. Kerala's approach to the pandemic has been both innovative and noteworthy. Despite this, a considerable number of immigrants are employed in the informal or unorganized sector in the Gulf region. The return migrants, who were once an important component of Kerala's economy, have now been relegated to the periphery of society. Because they are not organized, they are still unable to speak on their behalf for improved working conditions or for their rights to be respected. It is difficult for Gulf migrants to lead a regular life after they have left the region without the aid of their extended relatives or the government. Many of these migrant workers encounter similar socio-economic challenges after they are no longer considered the primary breadwinners in their families. All that is addressed in this research is the social and economic life of these migrants, who are no longer considered citizens of the country by the government and society and are therefore no longer a part of its social and cultural framework.

Chapter 3, written by Mohammed Taukeer, addresses the Nature, Process, and Consequences of Migration: A Case Study of Migration from India to the Gulf. In both internal and foreign labor migration, Uttar Pradesh and Bihar are the top two states. In addition to internal migration within India, both these states have recently seen international migration emerge as a viable source of income for laborers who are already involved in internal movement within India in order to supplement their income. Gulf migration is a relatively new phenomenon in both Indian states, although internal migration is a key source of income for a large proportion of the populations in both states. The chapter investigates the nature, mechanism, and effects of Gulf migration from Uttar Pradesh to the Gulf of Mexico in order to understand these implications. According to the information gathered from returned migrant laborers at the source, the chapter investigates the process, determinants, and impact of migration from Uttar Pradesh to the Gulf. It also discusses the working and living conditions of migrant laborers in both domestic and international destinations, as well as the working and living conditions of migrant laborers in these destinations.

Chapter 4, written by Ani Merly Paul and Lekshmi S Kaimal, is on highly skilled Indian professionals working in the Gulf region. As the world's greatest exporter of migrant labor, India is widely regarded as the world's most productive. In India, international migration is considered to be one of the most important aspects of the country's economy. Kerala's economy is heavily reliant on remittances, particularly those coming from the Gulf region. Because of changes in educational and demographic variables, migratory patterns have shifted. The emigration of highly qualified professionals is expanding on a daily basis. Education-oriented youngsters were given new opportunities and greater employment possibilities as a result of globalization and liberalization policies that opened up new horizons for them. The emigration of unskilled laborers from the Gulf region dominated the Gulf boom of the 1970s. A significant influx of educated and competent professionals into the various Gulf countries occurred with the dawning of the new millennium. The emigrated trained professionals found greater comfort and financial stability in the Gulf region, which resulted in a change in their way of life. The emigration proved to be beneficial in that it raised their standard of living while also improving their economic standing in their home country.

Muhammed Shabeer outlines the significance and contributions of the Kerala Muslim Cultural Centre (KMCC) in Chapter 5. He goes on to say that the Gulf Cooperation Council (GCC) is home to the largest Indian expatriate group. Following the oil boom, the Middle East became a new and popular destination for semi-skilled and unskilled labor. One of a country's most valuable assets is its diaspora. According to the Kerala migration census 2018, there are over 2.1 million Keralites emigrating worldwide and 24 lakh Keralites working in the GCC, with remittances totaling about 85,000 crore rupees. Frontal diasporic organizations exist for India's different political parties: The INC (Indian National Congress) is divided into two groups. (1) OICC (Overseas Indian Culture Centre), (2) Priyadarshini Cultural Centre, (3) (5) Priyadarshini. The CPI-M (Communist Party of India (Marxist)) has Navodaya as its expatriate organization, the PDP (People's Democratic Party) has PCF and the SDPI (Socialist Democratic Party of India) has Fraternity Forum, the INL (Indian National League) has INCC (Indian National Cultural Centre), but the IUML's (Indian Union Muslim League) has KMCC. To promote social development, political parties are utilizing their ability to build diasporic organizations. The KMCC (Kerala Muslim Cultural Centre) is the IUML's (Indian Union Muslim League) frontal diasporic organization, and it continues to be the largest among expatriate organizations worldwide. The KMCC's primary goal is to engage in high-level philanthropic activities. Above all, the diasporic diaspora has demonstrated exceptional solidarity for Kerala in the aftermath of the recent floods. The author investigates the function of diasporic organizations in philanthropic activities and the building of social capital.

Chapter 6, written by Bhupesh Gopal Chintamani, is about the relationship between India and the Gulf Cooperation Council countries. Labor migration is an unavoidable part of life in the contemporary world, and India has traditionally been a labor-sending country due to the abundance of labor available in the country. For decades, India has supplied competent and trained skilled professionals to the Gulf Cooperation Council (GCC) countries in a globalized world. More precisely, more than eight million Indians live and work in the Middle East (MEA, 2018). These expats send a considerable portion of their savings and income back to their families in their home countries, not only to support the family's sustenance but also to promote welfare among the household's members at the grass-roots level. This chapter is an attempt to examine the role of the Gulf Cooperation Council in the Indian economy in depth, both in terms of emigration and remittances. MEA data is used in the context of emigration to reinforce the historical incidence between India and the Gulf Cooperation Council in terms of future opportunities. The author argues that there is a structural shift in the ECR profile of Indian states, such as Kerala's role in the India–GCC connection, which is not a new phenomenon; Uttar Pradesh and Bihar will soon be the leading states in terms of ECR migration and inward-remittances into the country from the GCC region.

Anisur Rahman and Waseem Ahmad write in Chapter 7 that about nine million Indians working in Gulf countries are the primary source of remittances and foreign cash for India. In 2018, India got $80 billion in foreign aid, with the Gulf accounting for a sizable portion. The contribution of Indian communities is well recognized, as they are not only earning a significant quantity of foreign cash but also assisting in the reduction of unemployment in their own country. Apart from remittances, there are a number of incentives and initiatives in place to encourage these populations to invest in India. Furthermore, they are permitted to bring gold back into the nation. These are all contributing variables that have a positive impact on India's benefit. They play a critical role in the lives of migrants and their families in particular, as well as in the country's overall growth. On the other side, they are as important to the Gulf because of their significant economic contribution. As a result, the chapter's major goal is to investigate how they are strategically essential and how they might boost our bilateral relations. A map showing annual outflows of Indian migrants to the Gulf is attempted. The number of remittances sent to India, as well as the impact of the Indian Diaspora on India and the Gulf countries, is analyzed. In order to understand the policy change that is required for them, their working and living conditions are also described. In order to handle existing and future issues, the chapter also discusses India's and the Gulf countries' migration policies. Finally, how diaspora communities are growing as a soft power for both sides' mutual benefit will be examined.

In Chapter 8, Muhammad Azhar examines the family tax, Indian expatriates, and the Saudi economy. Saudi Arabia has implemented a new "family tax" or "dependent tax" on the dependents of expatriate workers in the country since July 2017. Expatriate workers must pay 1200 Saudi Riyal for each dependent per year. This tax would rise by SR 1200 per year until 2020, when it would reach SR 4800 per year per dependent, significantly raising the rigor of family tax. It appears that the application of the family tax in Saudi Arabia had two goals in mind. The initial goal was to find an alternative source of funding other than oil and to raise funds for government spending. The second goal was to discourage expatriates from staying in Saudi Arabia by increasing the cost of doing so. It may also result in greater job prospects for Saudi citizens, according to Saudi policymakers. The number of Indian expatriates in Saudi Arabia is believed to be around 3.2 million. Saudi Arabia has the highest concentration of Indian passport holders outside of India of any country (Azhar,2017). The number of dependents of these workers is in the millions. The implementation of a family tax in Saudi Arabia would undoubtedly make the stay of these dependents problematic.

In Chapter 9, Shahid Bashir and Mohsin Majeed make an attempt to empirically analyze the remittance-growth nexus in India using a most recent sample, which they found to be insufficient. The Indian economy stands out as a particularly good candidate for such an examination because the country has seen an increase in remittance inflows over the previous decade. Also included is a synoptic summary of remittance inflows from the Gulf countries, which may be found in Chapter 2. For the purpose of investigating the remittance growth nexus, the authors used the ARDL bounds testing approach. Several studies have demonstrated that remittance transfers help to stimulate the economy of India, both in the short and long term. Further research has found that external debt has a detrimental impact on economic growth, as has been documented. There was no statistically significant association between inflation and economic growth, according to our findings. The policy ramifications of our findings indicate that India should implement policies to stimulate inward remittances from the developing world. This can be accomplished by offering a greater rate of interest on non-resident deposits in order to spur the growth of inbound remittances into the country. Furthermore, the costs of international remittance transfers should be kept to a bare minimum.

Muhammed Fazal's Chapter 10 is titled "COVID-19 Crisis and Migration: Impact on Kerala Economy". He goes on to say that Gulf migration and remittances have been beneficial to Kerala's economy for more than 50 years, as they have provided the foundation for the state's progress in all areas as well as prosperous support during its difficult times. Everyone assumed it would be a stable economic pillar. The chapter argues that Gulf remittance or emigration is not a long-term economic pillar for Kerala because the impact of the COVID-19 crisis differs from the earlier effects of global crises and calamities in the state; and the social remittance acquired and exchanged by migrants is a treasure for returnees to be resettled by the government. The impact of COVID-19 on Kerala's economy, as well as its influence on return migrants and guest laborers, are discussed, as well as methods to use social remittance for their resettlement. The study draws on data from the GoK dashboard to examine COVID-19 statistics in the state; the Kerala Migration Survey to examine migration, remittance, and return migration trends; and a variety of recent papers and news stories to aid in the analysis and assessments.

Atinder Pal Kaur's Chapter 11 is titled "Migration from Punjab to the Gulf Countries: Punjabi Migrants and Social Change in Left-Behind Families". Already, when the British invaded Punjab in 1849, Punjab had a long migration history. Following this, Punjabis began migrating to many areas of the world as indentured laborers, most notably to British colonies and as army men. The migration to Gulf countries occurred later, during the 1973 Gulf oil boom, when demand for laborers to work on Gulf-building projects and factories surged dramatically. As a result, migration from Punjab to the Gulf nations as unskilled laborers increased. The chapter is divided into two sections: (a) a historical overview of Punjabi migration to Gulf states; and (b) a look at developments in left-behind families from an economic to social perspective. The work is theoretically ethnographic and narratorial in nature. Qualitative approaches were used to collect empirical data for this study in the Doaba region of Punjab. According to the chapter, migration began in 1975 and has since become a rite of passage. Individuals are driven to improve their level of living and economic prospects; the Gulf countries have become a conduit for migration.

In Chapter 12, K Jafar discusses the experience of **Mobility on the Margins: The Experience of Migration and Development in Kerala.** It is also stated that the development experience of the southern Indian state of Kerala has been much explored because of its distinctive characteristics. As two separate phases of development, the "Kerala model" of development and "virtuous growth" can be utilized to better understand how education plays a vital part in the process of migration and remittance-driven development that Kerala has witnessed in recent decades. Several academics have documented the positive benefits of labor migration, particularly in terms of initiating upward socio-economic mobility in the recipient country. In general, these narratives portray Kerala's migration as a 'successful model' for local development; nevertheless, they tend to overlook the uneven impact of migration on marginalized groups of society as well as departures from the larger model of migration. The author attempts to draw attention to certain micro evidence related to the pattern of migration across vulnerable groups, as well as the exclusive nature of this broader model and its implications for migration-led growth in the state.

Sonal Thakker investigates the "culture of migration" that occurs in some societies in Chapter 13; that is, the sociocultural environment is a significant predictor favoring male movement in some societies. A male is expected to be a "provider", and his adolescent years are fraught with socio-economic pressure to do so. The technique used in this chapter is mostly based on an examination of secondary data gleaned from a comprehensive review of the literature on the sociocultural elements that have a significant impact on men's mobility. The urge to establish their "masculinity" motivates young males who have grown up in a cultural setting that values migration. He/she conducted an examination of such instances in which migration is the norm. Families in Goa are also acclimated to the absence of males who work primarily in the Gulf, and women appreciate their migrant husbands for performing the role of family breadwinners.

The Pangals' trek to the Gulf is depicted in Chapter 14 by Md. Chingiz Khan. For a long time, the Pangals, Kukis, and Nagas have all been settled. Pangals live in the valleys. Among Manipur's indigenous populations, this community is among the most educationally, economically, and socially disadvantaged, despite their significant contributions to the state's affairs. They make up 8.32 percent of the overall population, according to the 2011 census. Many Pangals have been moving and establishing in Gulf nations such as Saudi Arabia, Kuwait, Qatar, the United Arab Emirates (UAE), and Oman in search of a better way of life. Despite the fact that the Pangals began migrating in the late 1960s, the rate of movement has now surpassed that of the previous decades. Even some Pangals, estimated to number in the tens of thousands, were able to obtain permanent residency in Saudi Arabia. Some of them serve as lecturers in Saudi Arabian universities, while others work in the information technology and medical fields. The following are some of the key questions: What drove Pangals to migrate to different parts of the Gulf, mainly Saudi Arabia? Apart from Mecca, Medina, and Dubai, did they focus on other nearby areas? What motivates them to act in this manner? What prompted the Pangals to relocate to these locations? Do they encounter any difficulties or hurdles when working in such cities? What are the social and economic challenges that Pangals face in the state, with a particular focus on job-related activities prior to being relocated to Gulf countries? What are the consequences of the Armed Forces Special Powers Act (AFSPA) of 1958 for Pangals who have migrated and settled in other Gulf countries? This chapter is based on multiple interviews with Gulf workers. This chapter delves into the history of Pangal migration to various Gulf countries in search of labor.

In Chapter 15, Baby Kizhakkekalam Jyothi KK discusses migration in Kerala, with a particular emphasis on the potential and challenges associated with return migration. When remittances decline, investment in land, construction of houses and other buildings, consumption, education, and health suffer. Repayment of bank loans suffers as a result, particularly in districts where there is a significant concentration of emigration. It is necessary to deal with serious economic suffering for thousands of households that are totally dependent on Gulf remittances for their subsistence. The districts with a high concentration of emigration will be the hardest hit by a downturn in the economy. Malappuram, Kannur, Kasargod, Thrissur, Kottayam, Alappuzha, Pathanamthitta, and Kollam are among the districts that are most at risk of experiencing a recession in the near future. It is expected that about half of the return emigrants will be absorbed into the Kerala labor market. According to the Kerala Migration Survey conducted in 2018, around 2.1 million emigrants from Kerala dwell in countries all over the world. In addition, approximately 90% of Keralite migrants who travel to the Gulf do so on temporary employment contracts, and they must return home when their contracts expire, according to the government. Furthermore, it is estimated that remittances account for nearly 36% of Kerala's state gross domestic product. This is a nearly 13-fold increase above the proportion of remittances received by the Indian Union. This dependence is demonstrated by the flow of Gulf remittances and their contribution to the state's economy, which illustrate the state's reliance on remittances.

Naziya Naweed addresses **Indian Female Migrant Workers and Human Rights Violations in the Gulf: A Case Study of Kuwait** in Chapter 16. Human rights violations are frequently perceived as a threat to people's individual identities. Women have traditionally been on the receiving end of societal hierarchy due to their sex, and they face tremendous constraints. The situation of Indian women is no different from that of women all across the world. However, attractive work opportunities around the world have enticed people to rise above their difficulties. Similarly, the discovery of oil in the Gulf region and the resulting feasible job prospects drew skilled workers from all over the world. With a considerable proportion of the female labor force, the wave of Indian migration to the Gulf region, both skilled and semi-skilled, began quickly. The Kuwaiti diplomatic mission and embassy can play an essential role in highlighting the issue of female migrant workers. As a result, the restrictions, exploitation, and prejudice suffered by female domestic workers in the region are notable, posing an issue for the host country and raising worries for the Indian government's population. As a result, the paper emphasizes the steps undertaken by the Indian government to mitigate their vulnerabilities from time to time. The report also included some modest proposals/recommendations for policy-makers to enhance the situation of Indian female migrant workers.

In Chapter 17, K. Deepa reviews studies on migration to Gulf countries. Indians have moved to many parts of the world throughout history for a variety of reasons. For their livelihood, a considerable number of Indians have relocated to West Asia, mainly the Gulf States, and now make up a significant portion of the Arab population. They work in every aspect of society, from white-collar employment to manual labor. The Indian Diaspora in the Arab Gulf States has been around for about a century. The numbers have risen steadily over the last 45 years and are now settling into a predictable pattern. Not only because of their competence, but also because of their sense of discipline and law-abiding, peace-loving attitude, Indians are one of the most preferred communities in the Gulf region. Many Gulf countries have completed the infrastructure-building phase, which necessitated a significant amount of manual labor. They are increasingly concentrating on knowledge-based sectors as well. This improved white-collar workers' job opportunities in the Gulf region; another change in the pattern of Indian workers migrating to Gulf countries is the geographic expansion. India is the world's largest beneficiary of remittances, particularly from the Middle East. Gulf remittances overtook North American remittances as India's biggest source of remittances in 2008.

Nitesh Narnolia and Mousam write in Chapter 18, **"Indian "Guest Workers" in the Gulf: Discussing Deepak Unnikrishnan's Temporary People"**, that the Gulf region has long been a popular destination for Indian labor migrants. It has provided Indian employees with both financial stability and the uncertainty of returning home, as these migratory workers are known in the Gulf as "guest workers". Indian migrants have expressed dissatisfaction with their current situation. The Gulf has long been thought of as a place where citizenship can never be achieved, no matter how long one lives there. In his debut novel, *Temporary People* (2017), Deepak

Unnikrishnan depicts the living conditions of Indian migrants in the Gulf. Through a review of Unnikrishnan's novel *Temporary People*, this course aims to evaluate the difficult lives of Indian labor migrants in the Gulf (2017). The chapter looks at the history and current tendencies of Indian labor migration to the Gulf, as well as how the selected novel fits into those trends. It also discusses how the Gulf has brought the opportunity for Indian workers and economic stability to the working class, while simultaneously causing problems for migratory workers who encounter hardships in their daily lives.

The editors thank all the contributors for their significant academic contributions. We state that the viewpoints of the writers are not that of the editors and the editors will not be accountable for the plagiarized content (if any) found in any portion of this edited book.

The Editors

Part I

Sociocultural Appraisal of Gulf Migration

1 Indian Diaspora in the Gulf

Impact and Advantages

Javed Charan

Background

Migration has been taking place since the earliest age of civilization. New economic opportunities, political instability, to prevent hostile conditions, and other factors are involved in this. Migration involves people of different communities migrating from their original place carrying with them their rich cultural heritage as well as norms they had been following for decades. It could be said that in some way they maintain their association with their homeland.

The Indian Diaspora is spread all over the world. The US top the list being the single largest host nation of Indians. But if we talk about Gulf Cooperation Council (GCC) countries, together they accommodate the largest portion of the Indian Diaspora. In different parts of the globe, it is a composition of descendants or ancestors who, due to trade and emigration, settle down. Emigrant groups like business entrepreneurs, political exiles, bonded labourers, and tradesmen, among others, can trace their ancestry (Cohen 1997). Many Indian groups have upgraded themselves to skilled workers (in the fields of transportation, manufacturing, and construction) from plantation labourers. They have gone through many phases all over the world to make their name as "knowledge workers", IT professionals and prominent figures in academics, medical services, science, and the law profession. Numerous illustrious figures have proven themselves in the field of literature, film, and the arts in general.

Theoretical and Historical Framework of Diaspora

The term "diaspora" is taken from the Greek language which literally means "to scatter", "to spread", or "to disperse" (Baumann 2000). The real context behind the word is related to the dispersion of Jews following the Babylonian exile in 586 BC. This event resulted in Jewish communities scattered in exile out of Palestine. In the present world context, the term is widely used for any group of people who are migrating or being dispersed.

DOI: 10.4324/9781003369370-3

India and the Indian Diaspora

If we talk about India in this context, in the year 2000, just two decades ago set up the first High-Level Committee on Indian Diaspora by the Government of India. It was Dr L. M. Singhvi, MP, under whose leadership it was constituted. He noted the phenomenon of "communities of migrants living or settled permanently in other countries, aware of its origin and identity and maintaining varying degrees of linkages with their mother country" (Singhvi 2001).

In the era of globalization, the phenomenon of migration affects all states and nations. It has somehow elevated the standard of living in both places of origin and destination countries. In the past few years, it has been seen as a preferential policymaking matter by various governments and political groups all over the world. On the other hand, many diasporic groups or communities have been playing an important role in both international as well domestic contexts. With about 31 million Indian people residing in different parts of the world, "India is one of the most influential diasporas of the world. The Indian Diaspora consists of People of Indian Origin (PIOs) and Non-Resident Indians (NRIs)" (Azeez and Begum 2009). They have demonstrated the diversity of Indian society throughout the world. It has been reflected in many destination countries where people have been living for a very long time and of course, it is due to the fact that they belong to Indian origin. The multicultural dynamism, the cultural practices and commitments, and sociopolitical achievement in maintaining a link between their homeland and the destination country have remained a significant feature of the diaspora.

Since the 1950s, Indians residing abroad have been noticed for their educational brilliance, and professional skills, and recently with the boom of the IT sector as a very specialized skill (Messner 2009). They have also been appreciated for their quality of adaptability and yet maintaining strong ties with the mother country. The Indian diaspora has become highly mobile and dynamic because the globalizing world is changing every day. Indians have not only been considered an asset in destination countries for their skills and expertise but also considered valuable for their multicultural and linguistic diversity and in maintaining their linkage with the homeland (Leonard).

Essential Diaspora: Benefits of India

Among many global powers of the world, India has the advantage of having a leading diaspora in the Gulf countries. They are the largest workforce in the region and for functioning in the GCC countries they are considered essential. Until September 2019, nearly four million Indians were residing in Saudi Arabia; this is a good example. The Indian diaspora has even constituted major populations in many GCC states, which is nearly 30% of the total population which hosts around three million Indians (Wilson 2004). The white-collar professional workers amount to around 17–20%. Indian emigrants have not only supported the economy of the destination country but strengthened the image of India.

Indians are mostly peaceful, accommodative, tolerant, and harmonious by nature. To extract and export their energy resources they are an integral part of GCC states and are thus considered an advantage for them. This advantageous condition opens the door for India's strategic control and provides it with a strong negotiating position with the GCC states. Disruption of Indian labour from GCC states would not only affect India due to reduced remittances but on the other hand, for GCC states it would harm the very ability to function which could become a major security risk for politically and internally unstable regions (Kapiszewski 2006). Not to mention, it would have greater negative impacts both economically as well as politically on GCC states than on India as India has a much larger economy that is very capable of absorbing such a sudden shock and so recover on time. Though GCC states have tried to mitigate this threat of India's so-called advantage they are yet to find any suitable alternative to this.

Gulf Cooperation Council

In the world, the Gulf Cooperation Council (GCC) is the major migration haven for Indian workers. As per the record, around eight million workers from India are engaged in the region. The GCC consists of Bahrain, Kuwait, Saudi Arabia, Qatar, Oman, and the United Arab Emirates and migration to these countries is not new.

Saudi Arabia is the largest in the area among GCC countries. Not to mention, UAE is the biggest trade partner with India. The discovery of crude oil took place in the year 1930 in the Gulf region and at that time it was relatively small. It was during the period from early 1970 to1973 when the migration towards the Gulf region became more conspicuous (Fasano and Goyal 2004). This was due to the oil boom in the world market which led to a rapid increase in labourers for infrastructural development projects to cope with the rising demand for crude oil.

The migrant workers were attracted mainly from Southeast Asian countries to the GCC countries across the globe, such as Sri Lanka, Malaysia, Bangladesh, Indonesia, India, Pakistan and so on and only due to the fact that these countries had the cheapest labour in the world (Kapiszewski 2006).

Remittance and India

India, fortunately, grabbed the opportunity in the Gulf region. In the Middle East countries, India is the largest labour-contributing country. Mostly, Indians choose to work in semi-skilled/skilled or unskilled professions. For the homeland, they are an important source of remittances (Pandhe 2008). In the latest data from the World Bank containing remittances, India tops the list among the top 20 countries. India sent back an incredible USD 78.6

billion in the year 2018 and maintains the world's top position. Apart from India other noticeable countries are Egypt (USD 28.9 billion), Mexico (USD 35.7 billion), China (USD 67.4 billion), and the Philippines (USD 33.8 billion). In the flow of remittances, from the last three years, India has been a consistent performer because the data shows USD 62.7 billion in 2016 to USD 65.3 billion in 2017. According to the World Bank, "Remittances grew by more than 14% in India, where a flooding disaster in Kerala likely boosted the financial help that migrants sent to families. In 1999–2000 Kerala's per capita income reached 49 per cent above" (Kannan and Hari 2002).

The Global Knowledge Partnership on Migration and Development (KNOMAD) head and the lead author Mr Dilip Ratha said regarding appropriate action to lower the costs of remittance,

> Remittances are on track to become the largest source of external financing in developing countries. The high costs of money transfers reduce the benefits of migration. Renegotiating exclusive partnerships and letting new players operate through national post offices, banks, and telecommunications companies will increase competition and lower remittance prices.
>
> (Ratha 2005)

Remittances have played an important role for those workers those who were suffering from poverty and not involved with any economic activity in India before emigration. According to Shah, they mainly emphasized Gulf-specific factors, which explains why a high percentage of Indian workers' income is sent as remittance to India (Shah and Narsa 2010). Indian Diasporas are engaged in various areas of expertise. In India there are mainly four states which are the leading emigrant states, those are Uttar Pradesh, Bihar Tamil Nadu and Kerala, for which there are details in the official database and various surveys. There are more states which also following the trend and contributing to the rising numbers of Indian emigrants overseas as well as boosting the economy through remittances, those are West Bengal, Andhra Pradesh, Karnataka, Jammu and Kashmir.

Remittances: In Perspective of Indian Migrants

The globalization world is getting smaller and smaller and very much interconnected. This interconnectedness has brought different types of social, political, cultural, and economic dimensions. As we all know, the term "globalization" is mainly the process of foreign investment, trade, labour, the process of integration of services etc. It can be said that every country in some way or other is affected by globalization (Haas 2005). Migration also played a vital role in the process of globalization. Since globalization began people moving from one country to another has increased significantly. Rapid developments in the transport, information and communication technology sectors have simplified the process of migration of people to different countries. The Indian migrants in developed countries withdraw their dollar deposits from Indian banks abruptly (Kahdariya 2011).

Since the technological and transportation, people of any country in the world get aware of the job opportunities for workers in any field. Since the adoption of a policy of liberalization in India, the Indian government is trying to encourage Indians to work overseas. According to the MOEA reports, around 25 million Indians maintain connections in their homeland country and also reside outside India. Temporary or contract workers working in GCC countries are a major segment of this diaspora population. They constitute a nearly whopping six million population. In the Gulf countries, a shortage of workers is the biggest problem, particularly in different kinds of projects such as recreational infrastructure, the construction industry, and above all oil refineries (Myron 1982). They demand immigrants from different parts of the world to fulfil the shortage of workers in their countries.

Most of the workers belong to South Asia and India. The largest workforce engaged in the Gulf countries is Indians (Koshy 2008). Their engagement is in diverse types of work. Poverty and high unemployment is the major reason for migration from different states of India, the government has provided limited financial support and allied agencies, less income, lower living standards, fewer job vacancies in all sectors etc. The rural area and villages of India have especially been affected. Both sending as well as receiving countries are contributed by the Indian workforce for their development (Shah 2010). They have contributed significantly to the country they moved to. These are indicators of the development of food, health, housing, and educational standards that are evaluated at the national, micro and household levels. At the community level also significant changes are to be seen.

Emigration to GCC countries: Trends and Pattern

It is stated in the article previously that 5000 years ago Indian immigration to the Gulf countries started. Before the 1980s, there were not many systematic records available of Indians migrating into these countries or any other countries by the Census of India or any other government agencies. The Indian government was mostly dependent upon the different authors or researchers sampled and the work done in respective countries (Nair 1998). It was 1983 when information collection was started. Indian emigrants' records were stored by the government living in other countries. The Ministry of Overseas Indian Affairs (MOIA) 2012, is the nodal government agency to look after matters in this regard. This ministry also looks over the matter of workers safeguarding the interest of those who are abroad and also providing them safety in case any disaster occurs in the destination country.

Protector General of Emigrants (PGE)

In the Protectors of Emigrants (POEs), there are eight offices that give emigration clearance, which is provided to all workers seeking contractual employment in the Gulf or anywhere else under the Emigration Act, 1983. Due to the Protector General of Emigrants (PGE), the recruitment of Indian citizens for employment there is no agency or establishment can undertake in abroad, under MOIA, the act mandates.

New Delhi is the headquarter of the Protector General of Emigrants (PGE). There are eight offices of the Protector of Emigrants which operate under the PGE. To provide facility to the applicants, the grant of emigration clearance has been decentralized, according to MOIA. Including New Delhi, the other seven offices of the Protector of Emigrants are established in Chennai, Kolkata, Thiruvananthapuram, Hyderabad, Cochin, Chandigarh and Mumbai. Records are kept under the Emigration Act 1983 while leaving India it's compulsory according to this act to do an emigration check. An emigration check (EC) is divided into two parts and Emigration Check Not Required (ECNR) are divided for workers. Under the first category, semi-skilled and unskilled workers are included by the Government while the second category comprises skilled workers, professionals, and business persons. These categories are mainly based on occupation. Recently, 17 categories of skilled workers were exempted from emigration clearance. The period of 1983 is quite unreliable because at that time the procedures and rules regulations, mainly the emigration clearance and employment-related recruitment of workers abroad were not well regulated. Hence government clearance recorded data is only provided for the person whose emigration is clear.

Oil Boom Decade (1973–1982)

It was the Oil Boom Decade of 1973–1982 when the massive migration to the Gulf countries from India took place. The very first oil boom came during the 1970s and continued until 1982 for almost a decade. GCC countries made huge profits in this decade with oil exports. The revenues were spent on large-scale economic activities.

According to Winckler,

> Gulf countries uses their oil revenues for other purposes. Their income was used for the development of infrastructure including energy stations. Organizational and power apparatus were also upgraded and developed. Agriculture sectors were also improved. The government also used the extra revenue upon the social services, including health care and education.
> (Winckler 1997)

Due to a large amount of oil found in the years 1973–1982 the fastest-growing region of the world was the desert economy which was converted due to the massive flow of oil revenues. After the end of the boom, a world-wide crisis emerged. Prices of oil went down, which resulted in a loss in oil revenues. The large act of the economy plunged too far from the high levels achieved earlier (Al-Kibsi 2007).

Different Phases of Emigration following the 1990s

It is exceedingly difficult in the Gulf countries to discover the pattern and trends of migration. Before the 1990s, the systematic records of the movement of people were a failure. Since 1990, any citizen leaving work in any country that obtained ECR was traceable based on statistical data of Emigration Check require (ECR) (1990–2011). There are broadly five phases where we identify the Indian Emigration towards the GCC countries. This identification will come out through the data or the systematic records related to the emigration.

First Phase (1990–1993): In these three years an inclined trend of the labourer in the GCC countries of Indian migrants was observed widely. For numerous infrastructural projects the GCC countries broadly demand foreign workers under a low immigration control policy. Most of the Indian migrants came back due to the political crisis during the Gulf War in late 1990.

Second Phase (1993–1997): This phase is also known as a partial constant trend because there had been consistent trends noticed during this period of people emigrating towards the Gulf countries. Social services like hospitals, educational institutions, services sector, banking etc. were upgraded by using oil-generated revenues. During this period on average annually 3,84,000 workers get work permits in the Gulf countries on a contractual basis.

Third Phase (1997–1999): This phase is called a declined trend. Some of the destination countries especially Saudi Arabia and Kuwait adopted a restrictive immigration policy. To control the non-national or non-Arab population through localization this measure was implemented. During this period on average, 3,23,000 workers get work permits in the Gulf countries on a contractual basis. During this period some of the projects finished. This period witnessed the saturation of the labour market in the Gulf countries. To control the overflow of remittances local labourers were recruited.

Fourth Phase (2000–2008): This phase is very important because in this phase many changes took place in terms of the prices of oil increased. Therefore after getting the revenue used in the infrastructure projects. Middle East countries like UAE demanded unskilled and semi-skilled workers for their projects. For the promotion of international migration, the Government of India set up many migration posts for different states in India. During this period an average of 4,71,000 workers get work permits in the Gulf countries on a contractual basis.

Fifth Phase (2009–2011): This phase is also known as a declining trend after a fairly good outflow of Indian emigrants to GCC states witnessed during 2008, this period saw a declining trend to GCC countries. If we compare it to the previous decade it was still high. In this period, an average of 6,26,000 workers get work permits in the Gulf countries on a contractual basis. During this phase workers from Southeast Asia got emigrant clearance. For example, Malaysian workers increased slightly compared to others. During all these phases, the demand of workers from the Asian labour market specific types of workers in GCC countries, and the flow of emigration was determined.

Regional Distribution of Indian Diaspora

In the world as per the Ministry of Overseas Indian Affairs (MOIA), under the GCC countries are Oman, Bahrain, the UAE, Saudi Arabia, Kuwait, and Qatar. These are the best migrant country corridors on an international level. From India, they mostly attract South and Southeast Asian countries' migrant workers.

GCC were also attracting migrant's workers from south and south East Asian countries apart from India. The Indian diaspora had the largest population among all the migrant communities living in the GCC. After China, India makes up the world's largest diaspora. Migrants work in a variety of occupations. Out of a total population of 30 million Indian migrants, approximately 6 million are Indian migrant workers. The majority of Indian migrants work in the six GCC countries. They primarily get employment in these three kinds of job sectors:

1) White-collar jobs (doctors, architects, accountants).
2) Semi-skilled workers or blue-collar jobs (drivers, artisans, craftsmen).
3) Unskilled labourers in different locations such as shops, stores, construction sites, farmlands, household maids, domestic workers, and livestock ranchers.

In the first category, most of the Indian immigrant workers or skilled labours in the Gulf countries engage in this sector – around 30% of the total. The rest of the Indian immigrants – around 70% – come under the second and third job categories (Khadariya 2010). For Indian migrants, the most popular destination is the United Arab Emirates (UAE) and the Kingdom of Saudi Arabia (KSA), 60% of the total Indian migrants work in these two countries.

Movement of People

India has more than 1.3 billion population. In the world, in terms of population size, India is ranked second after China. Due to its large population, India is also facing a high rate of unemployment. Due to its high birth rate, the Indian working-age group comes under 15 to 54 years old and has the 60% largest working-age group population in the world. But there is a significant gap between the population growth rate and the job opportunities' growth rate. The demographic difference plays a vital role and provides an opportunity for Indian migrants to come and work in the Gulf countries. Hence, mostly thinks in the context of migration Indian workers have less skill. If we analyze, the Gulf countries give employment to the Indian migrants on a prior basis.

India has the highest working-age group population. It is also called Demographic Dividend. Most of the Indian population engaged in disguised employment is one of the biggest problems of the Indian economy. As noted by Tattolo, openness is because they are "less expensive to employ, easier to lay off, efficient, obedient and manageable" (Tattolo 2003). On the different side, GCC countries are still facing a shortage of working population for their industries Around six lakh Indians were getting the job from this region. Thus, India can play a significant role in the labour market. The unemployment rate in Kerala state has reduced by about three per cent because of migration, concluded by a Kerala Migration study of 1998 (Kanna and Rajan 2002).

Approximately, in the Gulf region six lakh Indians are getting employment, as per the estimation annually which is a huge number considering unemployment in India. Thus, India can play a significant role in the labour market. "Migration in Kerala played a vital role in unemployment because the rates have reduced around 3% which is huge, concluded by a Kerala Migration study of 1998" (Zachariah 2001). In the GCC countries, those workers who come for jobs or unskilled labour were not allowed to take their families to those countries due to the incipient diaspora. Therefore this is the main reason for not getting a permanent job in these countries.

Other Dimensions

Returning to one's own country brings fortune in many ways – whether permanent or temporary. These Gulf countries give workers valuable knowledge and useful contacts which help them to grow in economic terms from overseas (Jain 2007). There they enhanced their knowledge and skills, therefore, they can provide these skills to others as well which is an asset for their own country. Migration plays a vital role in terms of job perspective, though this migration the people from a village or city, native or relative make a chain within the country thus, social networking also comes into play. Ramamurthy used other important determinants like the exchange rate, wage rates, number of workers abroad, number of years working abroad, employment status of family members back home, marital status, etc. (Ramamurthy 2003). It is observed that most of the emigrant workers come after completing their projects over there and don't want to go again to the same destination country after earning money from that country. Most of them use their savings in different ways like opening new businesses/enterprises, thus creating job opportunities for others. This trend plays a vital role in the domestic economy as well as in the local labour market.

Through the migrant workers, there are other dimensions to see the development process. For instance, bilateral trade is flourishing strongly as the UAE is the largest trade partner of India. Since 2011, the volume of trade has had a mixed nature, but the UAE is the largest trading partner of India among GCC countries. The Indian diaspora working in GCC countries plays a significant role in expanding business ties (Naithani and Jha 2010). In GCC countries a significant number of Indian workers are involved in the white-collar job and thus support the bilateral trade negotiations. Therefore in the GCC countries, India is the second largest trading partner after Japan.

The above evidence indicates that the development of any national economy is co-related to migration as it plays a crucial role in achieving many economic goals for the origin country and vice versa. With the emergence of a speedy mode of transport and new information technology (ICT), the movement of people is an essential feature of globalization and it further strengthens bilateral trade. Earlier phases of globalization in economic history would also suggest that the labour movement has been much more beneficial in relation to the movement of goods, services, and capital (Williamson 1998). The positive aspects of migration and development are huge for both the origin and destination country. There are plenty of different primary studies done by academicians which show the positive changes brought by the emigrant workers working overseas while comparing the non-migrant workers who work in India. In India most workers are from peripheral regions; those workers in the Gulf region contribute 70% of the Indian workforce, and the majority live in poverty before migration. As mentioned above, we see how Indian migrants in GCC countries support the Indian economy (Fasano and Goyal 2004).

There were many variations shown in the living and lifestyle of the migrants. For example, at the family level or household level, money earning has increased. Now their children attend school and live a regular life. Furthermore, now they buy their own houses. The savings are also increasing. The growth of the commercial sector is also an outcome of it. But we must not overlook the problems which were dealt with by the migrants at the place of origin and destination countries. According to the reports, in the Gulf countries, the working environment as well as the living conditions are very harsh. In the case of domestic workers, human rights violations are increasing rapidly. The world is swiftly moving towards globalization. Globalization is facing challenges to keep it more "fair". More opportunities will be created for all of the functions of globalization that run in a "fair" manner (Cohen 1997). There would be lots of gains due to globalization and will be shared equally and relatively. The major role will be played by bilateral agreements and cooperation to convert this into reality. Interests of all types of workers are protected by the policies. Those unskilled workers should be given more attention. The labour laws made should be properly implemented and the interest of the workers should be protected by the government.

India's Advantages in the Gulf

The three major areas by which India can utilize to build stronger relations with GCC states.

1. The country appreciates a munificent image in the eyes of Middle Eastern governments, and also taps a significant soft power in the region of India which can lead to smoothing the way for stronger relations.
2. The Indian demographic size and diaspora in the region have given India significant influence in the Middle East.
3. The primary backer the United States has supported India to enjoy good relations with the GCC states.

Analysis

The Indian government was very late to realize the matter of migrants which is evident by the formation of the High-Level Committee on Indian Diaspora in the year 2000. Unofficially many Indians migrated to GCC countries and come back. But this event did bring fortunes to people. People not only went there and worked but also went on to become the largest workforce in the Gulf region. They also brought hard-earned money back to India and as per the World Bank, India has been ranked first in the world's highest remittance-receiving countries for quite some time now. Due to the high engagement of people, the Indian govt. also took steps to protect its people working overseas and Protectors of Emigrants (POEs) is an example of it. Per capita income and standard of living have also gone up. Thus, it is observed that job opportunities in GCC countries not only reduced the stress on the Indian economy but further strengthened it.

Conclusion

The Diaspora of Indians has contributed a lot to the country; for instance, the expansion of industrial relations, education, technology, trade, education, bilateral relation, commerce, trade and so on. They have played a significant role when it comes to understanding how they play their role in the host countries and after that what they give back to the nation. In the working environment, some of the qualities required are honesty, dedication to work, and adaptability which are admired across the globe. Therefore, there is a prominent status of the Indian Diaspora abroad. They always were willing to donate munificently for development causes in India.

In the globalized world, this story is worthy of attention. Therefore, the diaspora plays a vital role when it comes to settlement in an ongoing role and makes the position for itself in most of the countries it calls home. The endeavours and achievements of them through the years, the roles of its members and their contributions to contemporary society are commendable.

References

Al-Kibsi,G., Benkert, C., & Schubert, J. (2007). Getting Labour Policy to Work in the Gulf, *McKinsey Quarterly*,Retrieved from the EBSCO database.

Annual Reports, Various years, Ministry of External Affairs (MOEA), Government of India.

Azeez, A., & Begum, M. (2009). Gulf, Migration, Remittances, and Economic Impact. *Journal of Social Sciences*, *20*(1), 55–60.

Bauman, Z. (2000). *Community: Seeking Safety in an Insecure World*. Cambridge: Polity Press.

Cohen, Robin (1997). Diasporas, the nation-state, and globalization. In WangGungwu (ed.) *Global History and Migrations*. New York: Westview Press, Harper Collins Publishers, pp. 117–143.

Composition of Gulf Cooperation Council, Source: https://i.imgur.com/NsAUohI .pngWorld Bank, La Documentation Française, UNICEF.

Diaspora Hotspots.Source :Tumbe (2018). India Moving; Ministry of External Affairs 2018, https://www.mea.gov.in/oia-publications.htm

Fasanò, U., & R. Goyal(2004). Emerging Strains in GCC Labour Markets, Paper presented at the 24th Annual Meeting of MEE A, January 3–5.

Hein De Hass (2005). International Migration, Remittances and Development: Myths and facts. *Third world Quarterly*, 26(8), 1269–1284.

India-Middle East Bilateral Trade, Source: ISME, Bangalore, https://images.app.goo .gl/SVt8eWtyuCDmKUM99

KahdariyaBinod (2011). Bridging the Binaries of skilled and Unskilled Migration from India, Dynamics of Indian Migration; Historical and Current perspectives, Edited By S. IrudayaRajan, Marie Percot (pp. 273–274). New Delhi: Routledge.

KannanKp, Hari KS (2002). *Kerala's Gulf Connections: Emigration Remittances and their Macroeconomic Impact 1972–2000*. Working paper no 328, CDS.

Kapiszewski, Andrej (2006). Arab versus Asian Migrant workers in the GCC Countries, UN Population Division, UN/POP/EGM/200

Khadariya,Binod (2010). *Paradigm Shifts in India's Migration Policy towards the Gulf, Middle East Institute Viewpoints*.

Koshy, Susan, & R. Radhakrishnan (2008). *Transnational South Asians: The Making of a Neo- Diaspora*. Oxford: Oxford University Press.

List of Top Remittance Recipients of the world, https://www.worldbank.org/en/news/press-release/2019/04/08/record-high-remittances-sent-globally-in-2018

Messner, Wolfgang (2009). *Working with India: The Softer Aspects of a Successful Collaboration with the Indian IT & BPO Industry*. Berlin & Heidelberg: Springer-Verlag.

Myron Weiner, (March 1982). International migration and development: Indian in Persian Gulf. *Population and Development Review*, 1, 1.

Nair, P.R. Gòpinathan, The process of migration. In *Indian Migration to the Middle East: Trends, Patterns and Socio-Economic Impacts*, B.A. Prakash (ed.). 42. Rohtak: Spellbound Publications.

P C Jain (2007). An Incipient Diaspora: Indians in the Gulf Region. In PC Jain (ed.), *Indian Diaspora in West Asia*. Delhi: Manohar, p.181.

Pandhe, M. K. (2008). Migrants workers in globalised economy. *People's Democracy*, XXXII (20), May 25, p. 1.

Population Pyramid of India, Source: https://www.populationpyramid.net/india /2019/

Ramamurthy, Bhargavi (2003). Migration and Labour Source Remittances, and the Labour Market. In *International Labour Heroes of Globalisation, Sida Studies No.8*, Stockholm.

Ratha, Dilip (2005). Remittances: A lifeline for development. 42(4).

Shah, M. Nasra (2010). Building State capacities for managing contract worker mobility: The Asia-GCC context. In *World Migration Report 2010*. Geneva: IOM.

Singhvi, L. M., et al. eds (2001). *Report of the High Level Committee on the Indian Diaspora*. New Delhi: Ministry of External Affairs.

Tattalo, Giovanna (2003). Arab labour migration to the GCC States, Working Paper.Mimeo.

Winckler, Onn (1997). The immigration Policy of the Gulf Cooperation Council (GCC) States. *Middle Eastern Studies*, *33*(3), 480–98.

Williamson, Jeffrey G. (1998). Globalisation and the Labour Market: Using History to Inform Policy. In Aghion and Williamson. *Growth, Inequality and Globalisation*. Cambridge.

Wilson, Rodney. (2004). *Economic Development in Saudi Arabia*. London, New York: Routledge Curzon.

Zachariah, K.C. et al. (2001). Impact of migration on Kerala's economy and society. *International Migration*, 39(1), 63–87.

2 COVID-19 and its Impact on Gulf Returnees: A Study of Kerala, India

Ansari PA, Sameer Babu M, and Anisur Rahman

Introduction

There has been a worldwide Covid-19 pandemic since December 2019. Restrictions and quarantine have been used in the majority of countries. Covid-19 has spread to more than 215 nations around the world. Covid-19 has brought with it plenty of topical issues ranging from health and transportation to economics and finance to emigration and transfer in various spheres of society (Khan et al. 2021). India, a developing country with high levels of labor emigration, has seen a significant drop in the number of its citizens moving to the Gulf Cooperation Council (GCC) countries due in large part to the outbreak of the Covid-19 epidemic (Rajan 2020, Abella and Sasikumar 2020). Indian emigrant employees and major recruiters in the Middle East have expressed a wish to return home, as reported in the press. According to the World Migration Report 2020, India is home to a large number of foreign nationals (Ullah 2021). Almost 6% of the 272 million overseas migrants are Indians, and three million of them come from Kerala. Migrants in the Gulf were fleeing for their lives as non-essential industries were being shut down one by one by the countries in the region. The number of Covid-19 cases has risen, mainly in Kerala, as a result of a large number of births in 2019–2020. More than 15 lakh Gulf migrants returned to Kerala in 2020 as a result of Kerala's international migration network's Covid-19 issue (Isaac and Sadanandan 2020). Understanding the patterns of movement and return of Gulf expatriates from Kerala is the focus of this chapter.

Review of Literature

International migrants from India make up about 17.5 million people, according to a United Nations report released in 2019. India has been the largest beneficiary of remittances sent by overseas workers since the mid-1990s (World Bank 2020). For the country, NRI remittances constitute a feasible source of development funds, particularly in the state of Kerala (Connell and Brown 1995; *The Economic Times* 2020).

DOI: 10.4324/9781003369370-4

Unskilled, semi-skilled, and skilled workers make up the bulk of the Indian migrant population in the Gulf (Diop, Le & Ewers 2016; Dustmann & Weiss 2007; Firstpost.com. 2020; Hausmann & Nedelkoska 2018). In several reports, it is claimed that poverty is a driving factor in the movement of unskilled labour (Edumundo et al. 2011). Unemployment upon graduation (Zachariah et al. 2002; Zachariah & Rajan 2004; 2010), the influence of family, and the desire to get administrative posts are some of the causes for the influx of semi-skilled workers in Kerala. In recent decades, Kerala has seen an increase in the outflow of highly educated people resources, including but not limited to physicians, engineers, and academics, to Gulf countries (Nair, Rajan 2006; Prakash 2000; Rahman 2009; Rajan 2004; Reshmi 2008; Shekhar 1997). Low wages and increasing unemployment uncertainty in the home country are two factors that drive unskilled labour migration to the Gulf (Osella & Osella 2003 and 2007), as well as shrinking productive lands (Ammassari and Black (2001), Fazal 2000) and poverty, the burdens of dowry systems, and heavy marriage expenses (Rajendran 2018), expensive housing loans (Bhattacharya 2008), medical expenses, and unaffordable education for children (Bhattacharyya 2008), among others (Wright 2020; Stawicki et al. 2020).

India's Emigration Certificate Requirement (ECR) and expedited passport services have further boosted the flow of Indian employees into Gulf countries since 2012 (Martin 2012). Few of the characteristics often associated with unskilled workers apply to the semi-skilled sector. Many other factors contribute to the marginalization of women, such as caste or income-based quotas on employment, a lack of acknowledgement from family members, a desire for independence or religious confirmation, and a lack of interest in menial occupations in home cities (Bijral 2015; Mohan 2017).

The highly skilled workforce's migration to the Gulf, especially to the GCC countries, Saudi Arabia, Qatar, and the United Arab Emirates (UAE), was motivated by the following factors: Fluency in both English and Arabic, cultural and religious adaptability, desire for better living, medical insurance, a wish to be active movers in the family, job flexibility, and a chance to achieve unfulfilled aspirations (P A Ansari, 2020; Osella & Osella 2006 and 2000; Hiller and McCaig 2007). The pursuit of professional goals and the ability to contribute to the family's financial well-being are other important considerations, as are aspirations for a higher social position and a more comfortable way of life abroad. As a result, many professionals see relocation from the Gulf as a path to personal growth and uniqueness (Ansari 2016, Ansari & Osella 2019).

Indian Expatriates Tend to See the Gulf as a Second Home

For these return migrants, unlike other immigrants, Gulf Indians are plagued by a constant sense of ambiguity and uncertainty about their futures. Despite these discrepancies, Indians have long seen the UAE as a potential location for employment and business. More than two decades have passed since many Malayalees who first arrived in the UAE on a temporary visa decided to remain. Migrants from middle-income countries who get professional employment, as well as rich Malayalees who have experienced tax-free income growth, consider the UAE home (Iyer 2017).

Non-resident Indians (NRIs) cite worries about infrastructure, power shortages and congestion, poor hygiene and enforced Indian family customs as some of the reasons they do not want to come back to India (Gowricharn 2020). The epidemic, on the other hand, has altered situations, as well as traits, worries, and values. What's the point of going backwards? The negative growth in the UAE's economy as a consequence of Covid-19's impact on global commerce has increased the danger to UAE government-related enterprises (Mathew 2020). A poll by the Dubai Chamber of Commerce estimated that 70% of businesses in the Emirates would collapse in the consecutive six months because of worldwide lockdowns (Turak 2020).

In a country where 80% of the people are expatriates and more than 150,0000 Indians are prepared to leave the country, the Covid-19 problem might have a larger effect than the financial crisis of 2008–2009, the government acknowledges. According to Fitch Solutions (2020), Abu Dhabi's real GDP growth would drop to only 0.6% in 2020, down from a projected 3.0% in 2019. Companies in the construction, vehicle repair, and cleaning industries, particularly those in financial distress, have either resorted to furlough, terminated their employees, or placed them on unpaid leave. Many low-wage employees had to leave their homes because of this. Members of Indian community organizations fed these street-living labourers (Badam 2020). The unexpected loss of employment by Malayalees in the professional sector also influenced their mental health. Reuniting with relatives in Kerala was a top priority for many who spoke out. For a variety of reasons, the overwhelming majority of Indian expats who have lost their employment abroad think that returning to India is the best option (Rasheed 2017; Khadria & Kuptsch 2013).

Understanding that an individual's actions are influenced by their emotions of insecurity or lack thereof, the scarcity of research on instances such as premature reversal migrations indicates the necessity of this topic within the backdrop of a pandemic.

Impact of Covid-19 on Gulf Return Migration as a Whole

During the Covid-19 crisis, a large number of people returned to their home countries. Most of Kerala's emigration go to Gulf countries. In the UAE, Kerala migrants make up 39% of the population, compared to 23% in Saudi Arabia. Kerala expatriates from Oman and Qatar make up over 20% of the state's population. Most return migrants come from Saudi Arabia, followed by the UAE and Oman as a result of changing labor policies.

As shown in Table 2.1, the top six destinations account for nearly 4% of total of all Covid-19 cases. Most of its influence comes from the Gulf

Table 2.1 Percentage of return migrants by destination countries and non-resident Keralites returned from May 2020 to July 2021

Nations	*Return migrants (%)*	*Non-resident Keralites retuned (May 2020–July 2021)*
United Arab Emirates	**59.3**	8,90,485
Saudi Arabia	11.5	1,73,561
Qatar	9.93	1,47,917
Oman	9.08	1,36,445
Kuwait	3.46	52,032
Bahrain	2.94	44,246
GCC countries	**96.2**	**14,44,686**
Non-Gulf countries	3.79	56,640
Total	100	**15,01,326**

Source: Data were taken from the Department of Non-Resident Keralites Affairs (NORKA); this was reported in *The Indian Express* News, 5 July 2021.

Arab states of Saudi Arabia and Qatar. A total of 8.7 million people had returned by the first week of January 2021, but as of July 3, the number had risen to 15,01,326, per NORKA's most recent data. More than 10 million migrants returned to the state because they lost their jobs. Of the more than 15,000 returnees, NORKA estimates that ten million returned because they lost their jobs, two million returned because their visas had expired, and 84,154 returned because they were minors under the age of ten. A total of 30,704 NRKs, 13,641 pregnant women, and 2,914 husbands of pregnant women make up the rest of the population (Philip 2021). There was a total return migration roughly 70%, largely from the UAE and Saudi Arabia, followed by Qatar (9.53%), Oman (9.08%), Kuwait (3.46%), and Bahrain (2.94%).

Return Migration: Kerala

Migrants in the Middle East are on the lookout for better-paying jobs as the Gulf region comes up restrictions and increased rate of nationalisation in the GCC. There are also several reasons the emigrants are forced to move back to their home states. It turns out that Malappuram is a top destination for people looking to leave or return home, according to the most recent KMS data (2018) (Table 2.2). When compared to the other districts, the UAE and Saudi Arabia have quite large migratory links with Kannur, Thrissur, and Ernakulam like the other districts (worst affected in the GCC region).

Table 2.2 shows the emigration and return movement of expatriates from various districts in Kerala, subdivided per district. Malappuram district (23.9%) has the highest percentage of return migrants in the state, according to the report. Kollam (12.8%), Calicut (11.7%), Ernakulam (7.9%), and

Table 2.2 Emigrants and return migrants to Kerala district wise

Top five districts in Kerala where return migration is highly visible	*Percentage of emigrants*	*Percentage of return migrants*
Malappuram	19.1	23.9
Kollam	11.3	12.8
Kozhikode	7.6	11.7
Ernakulam	7.9	7.9
Kannur	11.8	7.3
Total of the above five districts	**57.7**	**62.9**
Other nine districts[a]	42.3	37.1
Total (Kerala)	**100**	**100**

Source: Kerala Migration Surveys 2018.
[a]Other nine districts include Trivandrum, Pathanamthitta, Alappuzha, Kottayam, Idukki, Trissur, Palakkad, Wayanad, and Kasaragod.

Kannur (7.9%) are the next three most populous cities in Kerala (7.3%). To be precise, only the top five districts were included for this study's analysis.

More than 15 million NRKs are working overseas Indians who have returned to Kerala in the last few months, and Covid-19 has become a bigger problem for them (Chathukulam and Tharamangalam 2021). The large-scale exodus of Keralans from their places of employment and financial security is a significant problem. In the city of Malappuram, for example, one in every three residences is an NRK. It has a population of about 400,000 and receives nearly a quarter of the state's total revenue. However, the inflow of residents returning home is also the biggest – around a quarter, with nearly one-fourth of households returning (Zachariah and Rajan 2011).

Expatriate families in Kerala aren't the only ones affected by migration; migrants' families in Kerala are also heavily reliant on one another to meet their necessities (Osella and Osella 2008, Ilias 2015). State GDP will be directly impacted by this, as will migrants or families who rely on Gulf money. Transfer funds and migrants are intertwined. Kerala's economy relies heavily on remittances, which have grown dramatically over the previous few decades. There will be a loss of money because of the pandemic's economic slowdown. Remittances to Kerala are expected to decrease by 25% since the crisis has worsened, and the survival concerns are mounting day by day (Oommen 2020). Returned migrants are mostly employed either part- or full-time. Over a fifth of return migrants are unemployed, according to studies by return migrants. Self-employment and salaried work bring in only a small amount of money each month for them. One in every four returning immigrants from Gulf countries has not improved their socioeconomic situation as a result of their emigration, according to research. Two-thirds of households have been struggling financially (Rajan 2020).

Similarly, the return of emigrant families brings with it societal tensions and difficulties. Emigration has an impact on the education and development of children, as well as on the emotional well-being of emigrant mothers (Osella and Osella 2008). The formation of children is impacted by emigration. As a result of their exile from society, returning emigrants also feel isolated (Kurien 2002). Immigrant communities with high numbers of immigrant households experienced a mild or moderate economic slowdown during the crisis (2008) and largely by Covid-19 (2020) (Rasgul et al. 2021).

Characteristics of Migrants Who Returned

Men and women of all ages, genders, marital statuses, and educational attainments made up the majority of the return emigrant population. According to Zachariah and Rajan (2012), the number of females returning emigrants grew significantly in the wake of the Covid-19 crisis (Sulaiman et al. 2021). More than 80% of the total migrants are now married; this is a marked change from their first migration. There is a noticeable difference in living standards between highly educated expats and the large numbers of returning migrants with a low level of education. According to religious classification, 44% of Muslims, 39% of Hindus, and 16% of all respondents were classified as Christians, respectively. Policy frameworks for returning emigrants, including information policies, financial assistance systems, and institutional policies are all included in the research: (Sulaiman et al. 2021; Jabir 2014; Ansari, 2021). Even though emigrants return to their homelands with a wealth of new skills, emigration is also beneficial (Skeldon, 2008). Management/control abilities and financial management skills are among the various ways included here. Tendencies and patterns of return migration, geographical comparisons and impediments to returning migrants' assimilation into their communities, as well as issues they face in their home countries of origin are not fully studied (Arowolo, 2000).

Objectives of the Study

- To have a better understanding of the economic and social issues that returned migrants in Kerala confront.
- Covid-19's impact on Kerala's Gulf expatriates from Kerala will be examined.
- To propose the best measures for the welfare of the state's repatriated migrants.

Methodology of Study

In this investigation, both primary and secondary methodologies were employed. Observation methods and interview schedules were used to obtain the primary data, mostly through long-distance telephone interviews. The following original data was gathered in order to document their findings and provide important insights into the reality on the ground.

Covid-19's impact on return migrants' lives in their native state was studied through participant observation. Observation of the family members has been done using the Covid-19 protocols as a starting point. The researcher was also able to gain a better understanding of the difficulties faced by Kerala's return migrants on a socioeconomic level.

Using a scheduled method, the problems and prospects of Gulf return migrants, particularly during Covid-19, were studied using a semi-structured interview schedule. A random snowball sampling was used to identify the first responders and then move on to the other Gulf return migrants. A telephonic survey lasting between 60 and 90 minutes was chosen by the researchers because some of the respondents had been affected by Covid-19. All the difficulties they encountered with Covid-19 were shared openly by the majority of respondents. All three of these topics were covered in a set of questions included in the survey schedule. Wage theft, socioeconomic profiles, Gulf region occupations, concerns and obstacles faced by Covid-19, cause for return migration, and more were all examined in the study. Purposive sampling is the preferred method of sampling.

A non-probability sampling strategy known as purposive sampling has been used by the researcher, in which data are collected and samples are chosen only based on their relevance to the study's problem. The researcher attempts to cover the population sample from the returning migrants owing to Covid-19 engaged in various GCC countries (Saudi Arabia, Bahrain, Kuwait, Oman, Qatar, and the UAE). Protocols used in this study were also used in conjunction with Covid-19. According to the convenience of the respondents, the researcher visited the homes and other locations where they were available and interacted with them in person. Telephonic interviews were conducted with some of the researchers. Only Gulf return migrants affected by Covid-19 were included in the study's sample. Two hundred migrant labourers from the Ernakulam (Cochin) and Malappuram districts of Kerala were selected from the return migrant pockets that were negatively affected by Covid-19.

The Effects of Covid-19 on Gulf Migrants' Lives

Researchers in Kerala focused on how Gulf migrants' lives changed after they returned to the state. For the sake of better understanding how the Gulf return migrant workers are affected, the researcher undertook this study. Purposive sampling was used to identify 200 participants for this investigation. Men and women were recruited in equal numbers from Kerala's migrant communities, particularly in Malappuram and Ernakulam (Cochin), where huge numbers of Gulf return migrants are readily noticeable. The following sections go into detail about the research.

Respondents' Occupations

Since the 1980s, the GCC nations' oil boom and affluence have attracted individuals from all over the world, mainly from India, to Kerala. Numerous Malayalee Pravasis have taken notice of it (Osella and Osella, 2006a). Thousands of talented workers from Kerala moved to the Gulf because of the high earnings and social standing that was equivalent to their home states (Ansari, 2021). Following is a breakdown of the jobs that these migrant workers held while working in the Gulf before returning to their home countries (Table 2.3).

Most of the Gulf migrants lacked proper planning and preparations, only a small proportion of expatriates found the job they dream of, most of them vest in the line of hope and engaged in the job they were offered and carried on with life for decades. However, a glimmer of hope for an improved standard of life and source of income was always an objective for millions of emigrants (Rahman, 2020). As a result of the problems and challenges, there has always been an after-effect. To fulfill their basic requirements, 15% of migrants started opening or establishing a small store or enterprise, even though they had to make a sizeable initial investment in the beginning. Meanwhile, 7.5% of respondents engaged as private company accountants seem to be doing a better job than the rest of respondents, while 13.5% of those surveyed were house and company drivers who have to work very long hours. There were also domestic servants (11%) who look after children and the elderly while their owners are away. Workers in the construction and supermarkets accounted for 12.5% of the total workforce respectively, to earn a living these workers had to work more than 12 hours. This finding is supported by previous research, including Rajan et al. 2020, Sulaiman et al. 2021.

Table 2.3 Occupation engaged by number of expatriates in the Gulf

Occupation	*Districts*		*Total*	*Percentage*
	Ernakulam	*Malappuram*		
Accountant	7	8	15	7.5
Business (small shops/ small businesses)	15	15	30	15
Driver	12	15	27	13.5
House servant	10	12	22	11
Home nurse/nurse	8	8	16	8
Cook	15	10	25	12.5
Electrician	8	10	18	9
Construction	15	10	25	12.5
Supermarket/sales	10	12	22	11
Grand total	**100**	**100**	**200**	**100**

Source: Based on the study conducted during 2021–2022.

First Case Study: Annie, a 37-year-old woman from Ernakulam

> *"As a result of the Gulf Covid-19 shutdown, I was forced to close my firm and return to India in 2019 after having invested ten lakhs in a small business in Kuwait. By my late 30s, I finally made it to Kerala, the land of my dreams and hopes. I was able to acquire and manage container trucks after investing in an initial investment of 20 lakhs. Selfish political players were intervening in an attempt to gain commission, yet after all the expenses of levies, driver charges and tire maintenance, they still were suffering. I was forced to sell it at a loss of nine lakhs. After that, my friends and I started a successful grocery store in the Cochin, Chellanam, region of Kerala. And there, with all my Kuwaiti money, I lost over 11 lakhs. Now I've spent off all of my Gulf savings, I'm forced to rely on my bank funding to cover my family's and my expenses. I have no funds or savings left with me, nor am I'm not optimistic. I'm considering leaving the nation to make more money and pay off my debts".*

Return Migration and Its Causes

Individuals are compelled to migrate to destinations like the Gulf coast because of a variety of factors; the interviews with expats from Kerala who have settled in the Gulf area have revealed several reasons why they left their homeland. The key driving elements listed following may be directly or indirectly linked to any of these reasons; however, other motives are attributed to migrant labour (Table 2.4).

The findings of the study indicated that Covid-19 was the predominant source of Gulf return migration to Kerala. More than 45% of people have

Table 2.4 Reasons for return migration

Reason for return migration	*No of respondents*	*Percentage*
Covid-19 impact (job loss, salary cut, etc.)	90	45
Low wages	20	10
Expiry of contract – did not renew due to Covid-19 economic reasons	10	5
Nationalization	30	15
Poor working conditions	10	5
Issues at home	10	5
Harsh behavior of employer	20	10
Ill health	10	5
Others	–	–
Total	200	200

Source: Based on the study conducted during 2021–2022.

been directly impacted by Covid-19, making it even more difficult for expatriates to get employment back in Kerala. Whereas 10% of the respondents indicated they were unable to save money while working long hours because of extremely low incomes during Covid-19 restrictions in the Gulf. Even 5% of participants agree that the full contract expiration was not prolonged due to Covid-19 restrictions. Around one-fifth of those polled felt their return was motivated by the Gulf's nationalization policies – employers' aggressiveness was cited by 10% of the total of expatriates.

Second Case Study

Male, 34, from Malappuram, Mr Jamsheer

As a native of Malappuram, Kerala, Jamsheer (name has indeed been changed to protect his identity) is an HR manager. Each month, he earned Rs 85,000. All four members of his family rely on him for financial support: His wife, two children, and their respective mothers and fathers. As a result of the negative economic effects of Covid-19, he was laid off.

"*Today, there is no employment for him in Kerala. SBI Veliyankode Branch, Malappuram, stranded him because of his housing debt. To rebuild his apartment, he received a credit of around Rs 30 lakhs, and now I'm experiencing difficulties repaying SBI Bank's Rs 60,000 monthly interest. He's at a crossroads on what to do next. There is no way that I can earn more than 30–35000 rupees per month in Kerala regardless if I can get employment. How can I provide for our family, my offspring, and my parents' health costs*".

Going back to Abu Dhabi is indeed an alternative to him, considering visa requirements as well as other impediments.

Problems and Barriers for Returning Migrants

Migrants who return to their home countries encounter a wide range of problems and difficulties. They may gradually get into debt if they are unable to secure a regular source of income to cover their ongoing expenses. Difficulties experienced by investing in an unfamiliar business, as well as personal and financial obligations like weddings, private education for children, or unexpected medical costs, all enhance a migrant's vulnerability once they return to their home.

Table 2.5 displays the difficulty which Arab returning emigrants experience in their homelands. Covid-19 was the most often cited cause of despair as well as failure by interviewees (50%). They had lost their livelihoods, earnings, well-being, and all of their incomes as a consequence of Covid-19. Almost 15% of those surveyed said that they were particularly concerned about their ability to maintain a better standard of living. More than half of those who have already arrived in the Gulf are concerned about unforeseen

Table 2.5 Issues and Challenges faced by Return Migrants

Issues faced by return Gulf migrants in Kerala	*Number of respondents*	*Percentage*
Issues and problems affected by Covid-19	100	50
Lack of earnings/wages	30	15
Unexpected health issues/other expenses such as education and marriage of children	30	15
Social and financial alienation (loneliness/ indebtedness)	20	10
Lack of social respect	15	7.5
No government support (due to lack of awareness and sensitization)	20	10
Others	5	2.5
Total	**100**	**100**

Source: Based on the study conducted during 2021–2022.

health issues for their offspring, as well as their child's schooling and possible marriage to family members. A total of 7.5% said they would not receive government funding if they return, while 10% said they were socially and financially deprived. However, 10% of those polled thought that after losing their reputation as high-earning members of the family, they would experience a loss of social acceptance both from family and society. When it comes to family and community, a breadwinner is always held in high regard. Even when the Pravasi label has been removed, it is difficult to face society and one's family, and that was something they experienced as well.

To put it simply in the words of Mr Rahim:

Third Case Study: Mr Raheem, a 65-year-old ex-migrant worker

Our lives as Pravasis are much superior to those of return migrants since we were earning members of the Gulf community and owed a respectable existence to everyone who relied on us for Gulf Money. We've now achieved the status of "Ex-Migrants", and no one from our community or extended family is here to celebrate with us; they're all too busy living their own lives. As a scapegoat, we sometimes feel that we've laboured 30 years and are still waiting for the call of death.

Fourth Case Study Vijesh (Name Changed)

He is 45 years old and hails from Kerala, India. Unfortunately, in February 2020, he was making more money than others, with a monthly salary of about

75,000. He was in a coma for six months after being infected with Covid-19 from Oman and was treated at a government hospital in Oman. The cost of his journey amounted to over 2850 riyal. As a result, he was able to return to Kerala with the support of his Egyptian sponsor. A charitable organization covered the cost of 850 riyals. Some of his friends and a charity are now providing him and his family with Rs 10,000 every month. Since Covid-19, charities have lost all their funds and are unsure how they will continue to operate. He was the only breadwinner in the household. His family consists of two daughters, a husband, and a mother. To satisfy their daily requirements, the wife relies only on the assistance of a family member or friend. In addition to this, the family has raised Rs 10 Lakh for his medical needs via charitable and religious organizations in the hope that he would wake up from his coma. At this time, no financial assistance is being provided by the government.

Efforts to Improve Kerala's Gulf Returnees

Suggestions for Gulf return migrant expatriates are discussed in the next section. The respondents face a variety of difficulties and hurdles when they return to their daily routines. For those returning to the Gulf after working in Kerala, the migrants have come up with specific ideas on how they can improve their livelihoods back in the states (Table 2.6).

For instance, 28% of the total of those polled said that a new forum for discussing the difficulties of return migrants, particularly those impacted by Covid-19, would be helpful for the development of policy on returned migrants in the state. With government assistance, specifically for Gulf Return migrants, 17% of respondents feel that establishing new projects would strengthen their economic base, such as initiating young immigrants to partake in the Entrepreneurial Training and Development Programme by highlighting its benefits (ESDP). A total of 25% of all respondents want accessible and compulsory basic healthcare facilities to be made publicly available to returned migrants. Individuals' trust in their capacity to afford medical expenses, rather than depending on family members or charitable organizations for their medical expenses as the result of these activities. With the help of NORKA, non-governmental organizations, and those who support immigrant rights' organizations, it is also attainable. Older physiologically and psychologically challenged returning migrants should receive 10% of respondents' attention in counseling sessions. They have particular problems in adjusting to society's pace with the fast demands. More than a quarter of all expats are in desperate need of new forms of assistance from the government and civil society.

Conclusions and Implications

The effects of emigration and remittances on Kerala's Diaspora are well documented. Many studies are conducted at the state and federal level,

Table 2.6 Society's inclusion and policy-making measures for return migrants in Kerala

Measures for inclusion and suggestions	*Number of respondents*		*Percentage*
	Malappuram	*Ernakulum*	
Creating a new platform to discuss the issues of return migrants, especially those who are affected by Covid-19	30	25	28
Encourage and sensitize young migrants for the Entrepreneur Skills Development Program (ESDP)	15	20	17
Free and compulsory basic medical facilities to return migrants at least to meet their essential medicines (with the support of NORKA, NGO, and these Friends of Migrants Groups)	25	20	25
Counseling sections should be given to old age/physically and mentally returned emigrants as most of them challenging to cope with the changing demands of society	10	10	10
New support system from Government and Civil Society is strongly needed	20	20	20
Total	50	50	**100**

Source: *Based on the study conducted during 2021–2022.*

including the Kerala Migration Surveys, which are conducted regularly, and the majority of the research conducted by the Centre for Development Studies, Trivandrum. It should be highlighted that most of this research focused on the macro level, ignoring micro-level studies that examined the personal and local consequences. The impact of Covid-19 on Gulf migrants returning from the Gulf to Kerala is particularly under-researched. As a result, it seems that studies on the effects of Covid-19 on Gulf return expatriates from Kerala are lacking in the available literature. When researching personal and social shifts at the micro level, researchers uncovered the effects and problems of Covid-19, as well as those of expatriates' broader economic and societal changes.

As a result, the research focuses on the problems, difficulties, and effects of Gulf return migrants in Kerala, as well as the lives of those supporting them (once they are back to their home state). In academic terms, this investigation adds to the growing body of knowledge about Covid-19 in the

Gulf States' Kerala Diaspora – focusing on linking low-end Pravasi and the subjective to transformative processes and their outcomes. Kerala's return migrants are impacted by the pandemic. It is hoped that this research, which seeks to assess the concerns confronted by Gulf return migrants during Covid-19, will contribute to policy initiatives aimed at improving conditions for returnees to their homeland.

References

Abella, M. I., & Sasikumar, S. K. (2020). Estimating earnings losses of migrant workers due to COVID-19. *The Indian Journal of Labour Economics*, *63*(4), 921–939.

Ammassari and Black (2001). *Harnessing the Potential of Migration and Return to Promote Development: Applying Concepts to West Africa*. Sussex Migration Working Papers.

Ansari, P. A (2016). Internal migration: An analysis of problems faced by the migrants in India: A step to the solution. *Political Science*, *6*, 7–9.

Ansari, P. A., & Osella, C. Challenges to stakeholders. 2019, Handbook of Internal Migration: Sage Publications, New Delhi, Edited by S Irudaya Rajan & Sumeetha M, ISBN: 9789353287788.

Ansari, P. A., & Rahman, A. (2021). Covid 19 And Its Implications For Gulf Migrants: Some Reflections From Kerala. *Journal of Psychology and Political Science (JPPS)* ISSN 2799-1024, *1*(01), 35–49.

Arowolo, O. O. (2000). Return migration and the problem of reintegration. *International migration*, *38*(5), 59–82.

Badam, R. T. (2020). Coronavirus: About 130,000 Indians Leave UAE on Repatriation Flights. Accessed July 31, 2020. https://www.thenational.ae/uae/transport/coronavirus-about-130-000- Indians-leave-uae-on-repatriation-flights-1.1043371.

Bhattacharya, S. (2008). Indian Expats Fear Economic Future. Accessed May 30, 2020. https://www. The national.ae/UAE/Indian-expats-fear-economic-future-1.520096

Bijral, Q. K. B. (2015). Affirmative Action: The System of Reservations and Quotas in India. Accessed May 13, 2020. https://thelogicalindian.com/story-feed/awareness/affirmative-actionthe-system-of-reservations-and-quotas-in-india.

Connell, J., & R. Brown. 1995. Migration and Remittances in the South Pacific: Towards New Perspectives. Asian and Pacific Migration Journal 4 (1): 1–33.

Diop, A., Le, K. T., & Ewers, M. C. (2016). Working and living conditions of migrant workers in the GCC. In India Migration Report *2016* (pp. 97–111). Routledge India.

Dustmann, C., & Weiss, Y. (2007). Return migration: Theory and empirical evidence from the U.K. *British Journal of Industrial Relations*, *45*(2), 236–256.

Edumundo, M., L. Jennica, and S. Marcin. 2011. Migration and Poverty: Toward Better Opportunities for the Poor. Accessed 12 March 2020. https://openknowledge.worldbank. org/ handle/10986/2535.

Employment, Wages and Working Conditions of Kerala Emigrants in the United Arab Emirates. Working Paper No.13, CDS

Fazal, S. (2000). Urban Expansion and Loss of Agricultural Land – A GIS-Based Study of Saharanpur City, India. *Environment and Urbanization* *12*(2), 133–149.

Firstpost.com. (2020). The Promised Land Opportunity, Discovery and How Kerala Embraced Migration. Accessed June 12, 2020. https://www.firstpost.com/long-reads/the-promised-landpart-1-opportunitydiscovery-and-how-kerala-embraced-migration-3544633.html

Gowricharn, R. (2020). *Shifting Transnational Bonding in Indian Diaspora*. New York: Routledge.

Hausmann, R., & Nedelkoska, L. (2018). Welcome home in a crisis: Effects of return migration on the non-migrants wages and employment. *European Economic Review*, *101*, 101–132.

Hiller, H. H., & K. S. McCaig. 2007. Reassessing the Role of Partnered Women in Migration Decision-Making and Migration Outcomes. *Journal of Social and Personal Relationships*, 24(3), 457–472. doi:10.1177/0265407507077233

https://indianexpress.com/article/india/kerala/in-pandemic-year-15-lakh-expats-returned-to-kerala-10-4-lakh-of-them-having-lost-jobs-abroad-7388028/

Ilias, M. H. (2015). Malayalee Migrants and Translocal Kerala Politics in the Gulf: Re-conceptualising the 'Political'. *Diasporas of the Modern Middle East: Contextualising Community*, 303–337.

Isaac, T. T., & Sadanandan, R. (2020). COVID-19, Public health system and local governance in Kerala. *Economic & Political Weekly*, *55*(21), 35.

Iyer, A. (2017). Indian Expats Share Why Dubai Is Home for Them. *Khaleej Times*, March 18, 2017. Accessed June 12, 2020. https://www.khaleejtimes.com/nation/dubai/indian-expats-share-whydubai-is-home-for-them

Jabir, M.M. (2014) Reintegration of Return Migrants in Kerala: Policy Initiatives and Challenges *International Journal of African and Asian Studies - An Open Access International Journal*, 4-6, 112–123.

Khan, M., Adil, S. F., Alkhathlan, H. Z., Tahir, M. N., Saif, S., Khan, M., & Khan, S. T. (2021). COVID-19: A global challenge with old history, epidemiology and progress so far. *Molecules*, *26*(1), 39.

Kurien, P. A. (2002). *Kaleidoscopic Ethnicity: International migration and the reconstruction of community identities in India*. Rutgers University Press.).

Martin, P. 2012. Reducing Migration Cost and Maximizing Human Development. In Irena Omelaniuk: Global Perspectives on Migration and Development, GFMD Puerto Vallarta and Beyond. London: Springer.

Mathew, S. 2020. Poses Shock to U.A.E. Economy, Says Moody's. Accessed August 1, 2020. https://www.bloombergquint.com/onweb/moody-s-says-dubai-at-risk-as-virus-poses-shock-tou-a-e-eonomy

Mohan, A. C. 2017. Migration to Kerala: Issues and Challenges. Indian Journal of Research 6 (2): 79–96. Accessed July 3, 2020. https://www.worldwidejournals.com/paripex/recent_issues_ pdf/ 2017/ February/February_2017_1488455290__111.pdf.

Nair, P. R., Rajan, S. I. (2006). *Return Emigrants in Kerala- Welfare, Rehabilitation and Development*. New Delhi: Manohar Publishers and Distributors.

Oommen, G. Z. (2020). Gulf Migration, Remittances and Religion: Interplay of Faith and Prosperity Amongst Syrian Christians in Kerala. In *Asianization of Migrant Workers in the Gulf Countries* (pp. 247–266). Springer, Singapore.

Osella, C., & Osella, F. (2006). Once upon a time in the West? Stories of migration and modernity from Kerala, South India. *Journal of the Royal Anthropological Institute*, *12*(3), 569–588.

Osella, C., & Osella, F. (2006). *Men and masculinities in South India*. Anthem Press.

Osella, C., & Osella, F. (2008). Nuancing the migrant experience: Perspectives from Kerala, South India.
Osella, C., & Osella, F. (2008). Nuancing the migrant experience: Perspectives from Kerala, South India.
Osella, F., & Osella, C. (2000). Migration, money and masculinity in Kerala. *Journal of the Royal Anthropological Institute*, *6*(1), 117–133.
Osella, F., & Osella, C. (2003). Migration and the commodification of ritual: Sacrifice, spectacle and contestations in Kerala, India. *Contributions to Indian Sociology*, *37*(1–2), 109–139.
Osella, F., & Osella, C. (2007). "I am Gulf": The production of cosmopolitanism among the Koyas of Kozhikode, Kerala. From https://eprints.soas.ac.uk/5178/1/ch9_osellas.pdf
P A Ansari. (2020/11/10). Understanding the Socio-Economic Issues and Challenges of Gulf return migrants from GCC Countries: A study of Kerala. *International Journal of Research in Social Sciences*, 10(10), 1–15. Impact Factor: 7.081, ISSN: 2249-2496
Pillai, *Return migration and immigration in Kerala*. Academia.edu.
Prakash, B. A. (2000). Exodus of Gulf emigrants: Return emigrants of Varkala town in Kerala. *Economic and Political Weekly*, 4534–4540.
Rahman, A. (2009). Indian diaspora in the Gulf: Problems and prospects. *Diaspora Studies*, 2(1), 31–51.
Rahman, A. (2020). *Migration and Social Change in the Gulf: A Comparative Study in the Six Gulf States*. Qatar University Publication.
Rajan, S. (2012). Assessment of NORKA-ROOTS and the Applicability of a Similar Organisation to the Other States in India. Migrant Forum in Asia.
Rajan, S. (2004). From Kerala to the Gulf: Impacts of labour migration. *Asia Pacific Migration Journal*.
Rajan, S. I. (2020). Migrants at a crossroads: COVID-19 and challenges to migration. *Migration and Development*, *9*(3), 323–330.
Rajendran, K. (2018). In Kerala, A growing greed for dowry is pushing women into unhappy 'Salem Marriages.' Accessed March 4, 2020. https://scroll.in/article/867856/in-kerala-agrowing-greed-for-dowry-is-pushing-women-into-unhappy-salem-marriages
Rasheed C.K. (2017). *International Return Migration to Kerala: A Socio-Economic Analysis International Multi-Disciplinary E-Journal, Report of the study submitted to Department of Economics*. American University. http://www.norka.gov.in/norka.htm
Rasul, G., Nepal, A. K., Hussain, A., Maharjan, A., Joshi, S., Lama, A., ... & Sharma, E. (2021). Socio-economic implications of Covid-19 pandemic in South Asia: Emerging risks and growing challenges. *Frontiers in Sociology*, 6, 1–14.
Reshmi, R.S. (2008). Labour Migration of Women from Kerala: Socio-Economic Impact on Migrants and Their Families. Unpublished PhD. Thesis, IIPS Mumbai
Shaiju Philip, *Indian Express-News*, In a pandemic year, 15 lakh expats returned to Kerala, 10.4 lakh of them having lost jobs abroad, 6th July 2021,
Shekhar, T.V. (1997). Migration and social change. *Rawat Publication*, New Delhi.
Skeldon, R. (2008). International migration as a tool in development policy: A passing phase?. *Population and Development Review*, *34*(1), 1–18.
Stawicki, S. P., Jeanmonod, R., Miller, A. C., Paladino, L., Gaieski, D. F., Yaffee, A. Q., ... & Garg, M. (2020)..Sulaiman Km Afsal Kalangandan R. B.

BhagatR. COVID-19 and Gulf Return Migration: An Opportunity to Re-Orient Government Strategies March 2021 Conference: Kerala and the World Economy At. Trivandrum: Center for Development Studies

The Economic Times. (2020a). Economy suffers "Unprecedented Collapse" Due to COVID-19: Survey. *The Economic Times*. April 21, 2020. Accessed April 30, 2020. https://economictimes. indiatimes.com/news/economy/finance/economy-suffers-unprecedented-collapse-due-to-covid19-survey/articleshow/75276117.cms.

Turak, N. (2020). 70% of Dubai companies expect to go out of business within six months due to coronavirus pandemic, survey says. Accessed August 1, 2020. https://www.cnbc.com/2020/05/ 21/coronavirus-Dubai-70percent-of-companies-expect-to-close-in-six-months.html.

Ullah, A. A., Nawaz, F., & Chattoraj, D. (2021). Locked up under lockdown: The COVID-19 pandemic and the migrant population. *Social Sciences & Humanities Open*, *3*(1), 100126.

World Bank. (2020). World Bank open data. IBRD.IDA. Accessed 21 January 2020. https://www.worldbank.org/.

Wright, A. (2020). No good options for migrant workers in Gulf COVID-19 lockdown. Middle East Research and Information Project. Accessed June 28, 2020. https://merip.org/2020/04/nogood-options-for-migrant-workers-in-gulf-covid-19-lockdown/.

Zachariah, K. C., & Rajan, S. I. (2004). *Gulf revisited economic consequences of emigration from Kerala: Emigration and unemployment.*

Zachariah, K. C., & Rajan, S. I. (2011). Impact of remittances of non-resident Keralites on Kerala's economy and society. *Indian Journal of Labour Economics*, *54*(3), 503–526.

Zachariah, K. C., & Rajan, S. I. (2012). *The Inflexion in Kerala's Gulf Connection: Report on Kerala Migration Survey 2011.*

Zachariah, K. C., Prakash, B. A., & Rajan, I. (2002). *Gulf Migration Study.*

Zachariah, K. C., Nair, P. R., & Rajan, I. (2018). *Kerala Migration Survey-2018.* CDS Trivandrum.

Zachariah, K.C., & Rajan C. (2010). *Impact Of The Global Recession On Migration And Remittances In Kerala: New Evidences From The Return Migration Survey (RMS) 2009.* Thiruvananthapuram: Centre for Development Studies. Working Paper 432.

3 Nature, Process, and Consequences of Migration

A Case Study of Migration from India to the Gulf

Mohammed Taukeer

Introduction

Both Uttar Pradesh and Bihar emerged as leading states of origin of semi-skilled and unskilled labor migration to the Gulf in the 21st century (Affairs, Ministry of External Affairs, Government of India, 2014–2015). Both Uttar Pradesh and Bihar are two top states in emigration clearance of labor migration from India to the Gulf compared to such trends from Kerala to the Gulf (Zachariah & Rajan, 2012: 36, 241–244). The dynamics of labor migration from North India to the Gulf is caused by both economic and non-economic reasons because of the availability of better jobs with higher wage rates in the Gulf compared to India as pull factors as well as authorized and unauthorized requirement agencies are also leading to labor migration from North India to the Gulf (Sasikumar & Thimothy, 2015: 15).

A recent study about Gulf migration from North India shows that Uttar Pradesh is the top state for labor migration within India with migration from India to the Gulf in the 21st century. Uttar Pradesh surpassed the position of Kerala in emigration clearance of labor migration from India to the Gulf. In Uttar Pradesh, the Lucknow district ranked first in labor migration from Uttar Pradesh to the Gulf. It is also observed that Lucknow district was ranked second in the top 50 districts of India for labor migration to the Gulf (Taukeer, 2020: 124–125). Looking at these consequences, this chapter examines the process, determinants, and impact of migration from the Lucknow district of Uttar Pradesh to the Gulf while also covering Mumbai as an internal destination and the United Arab Emirates as an international destination for observing the working and living conditions of migrant laborers.

Methodology: Sampling, Strategy of Collection of Data, and Analytical Framework

Sampling: Strategy for Selection of Migrant Laborers from Uttar Pradesh, Mumbai, and the United Arab Emirates

I purposively selected the Lucknow district of Uttar Pradesh for examining the processes and consequences of Gulf migration. I purposively selected

DOI: 10.4324/9781003369370-5

180 returned migrant laborers in ten selected villages and two urban towns (15 returned migrant laborers in each selected village/urban town). Among them, 150 migrant households were Muslim and the rest were Hindu, with the same pattern in the rural and urban ratio. I identified the migration-based villages/urban wards through a snowball sampling method as well as identifying returned migrant laborers through stratified random sampling. Both qualitative and quantitative techniques explored the nexus of internal and international migration. The methodology of the research work used the recall situation method for the collection of primary data from returned migrant laborers at a grassroots level through field visit in Lucknow conducted between December 2017 and March 2018. Apart from that, I purposively selected 180 migrant laborers from Uttar Pradesh and Bihar in Mumbai through a field visit in February 2019 as well as 180 Indian migrant laborers through a field visit in the United Arab Emirates in December 2019. I used snowball sampling for the selection of migrant laborers in both destinations. I collected data about the issues of the working and living conditions of migrant laborers through participant observation, distance observation, and informal interviews among migrant laborers in both Mumbai and the United Arab Emirates.

Strategy for Collection of Primary Data from Grassroots to Destinations

I used a QUAL & QUAN approach for the collection of primary data in Uttar Pradesh while I used a QUAL method for the collection of primary data in both Mumbai and the United Arab Emirates according to the nature of the study (Figure 3.1).

Analytical Framework of Findings

Table 3.1 provides the analytical framework for analysis of primary data according to the nature and objectives of the study.

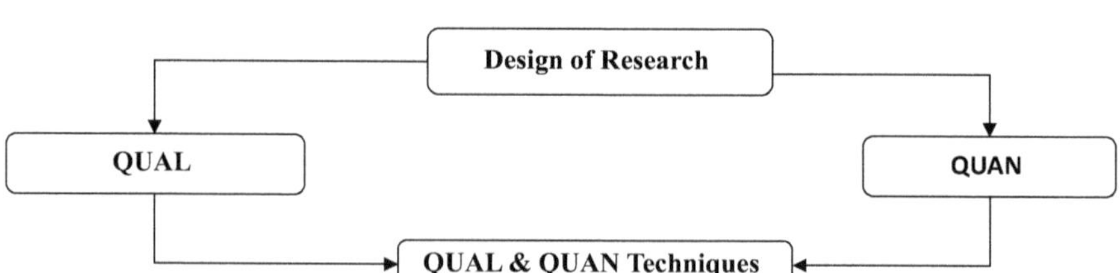

Figure 3.1 Design of Research for Collection of Primary Data. Source: Designed by Author

Table 3.1 Analytical framework for analysis of data

Sl. No.	*Content*	*Approach*	*Respondents*
1	Understanding of Gulf migration	QUAL approach	Returned migrant laborers and migrant laborers in Mumbai and United Arab Emirates
2	Routes of migration	Mixed approach	Returned migrant laborers
3	Process and determinants of migration	Mixed approach	Returned migrant laborers
4	Socio-economic profile	Mixed approach	Returned migrant laborer
5	Impact of migration at origin	Mixed approach	Returned migrant laborers
6	Internal and international migration: similarities, differences, and linkages	Mixed approach	Returned migrant laborers and migrant laborers at destinations

Source: Based on nature and objectives of study.

Findings and Discussion

Understanding Migration

Migrant laborers migrated with the help of a social network system of migration because this minimized the risks of migration within India and abroad. Gulf migration worked as a source of livelihood among migrant households due to a culture of migration to the Gulf. Both Muslim and Hindu migrants were engaged in Gulf migration but Muslim migrants were largely involved in Gulf migration compared to Hindu migrants due to a well-developed social network system of migration in Muslims. In the rural areas, these returned migrants used the word *Pardesh* (destinations); for internal and international destinations they used the term *Pardeshi* (migrant laborer). They used the term *Mulk* for origin while urban migrants used the words of NRIs for the migrants. It was observed that mostly young boys had dreams of migrating to the Gulf because they thought they could access better economic opportunities in the Gulf compared to India.[1]

Pathways of Migration from North India to the Gulf

Both internal and international migration was led by similar economic and non-economic reasons but there were similarities and differences in the process and determinants of internal and international migration. Internal migration within India led to migration to the Gulf countries because this gave the training of skills and experiences of migration to migrant laborers for migration to the Gulf. Migrant laborers gained both economic and non-economic assistance during internal migration in India which led to the dynamics of migration to the Gulf countries. Both internal and international migration were connected but the dynamics of migration from North India to the Gulf was difficult compared to internal migration due to the difficult procedure of documentation of migration to the Gulf. Laborers migrated to the Gulf countries due to the availability of better jobs with higher incomes compared to the labor markets of India.[2]

Process and Determinants of Migration from North India to the Gulf

INTERNAL MIGRATION

Out of the total returned migrant laborers, nearly 58.0 per cent (n=104) of returned migrant laborers were engaged in internal migration before migration to the Gulf countries while the rest of the returned migrant laborers directly migrated to the Gulf. The dynamics of internal migration was led by both economic and non-economic reasons because laborers internally migrated within India for the availability of better jobs with higher wage rates compared to origin as well as for the purpose of gaining skills of occupation for work in the Gulf countries. Both Mumbai and Delhi were the favorite destinations for the less educated, semi-skilled, and unskilled migrant laborers while Bangalore was the favorite destination for educated and professional migrant laborers. Internal migration was characterized by seasonal and temporary migration for migrant laborers because migrant laborers migrated for spells of three to six months of internal migration (Table 3.2).

Table 3.2 Internal migration

Indicators	*Quantitative description*
Numbers of internal migrant laborers	Total 104 returned migrant laborers were engaged in internal migration in out of total 180 returned migrant laborers.
Causes of migration	Nearly 88.0 per cent of the returned migrant laborers migrated due to higher wages in internal migration and rest migrated due to unemployment at origin.
Social network of migration	Nearly 88.0 per cent of the returned migrant laborers migrated with help of social networks and rest migrated with help of unauthorized contractors of migration
Destinations	Nearly 92.0 per cent of the returned migrants worked in Mumbai and Delhi while the rest worked in Bangalore before migration to the Gulf
Occupational structure	Nearly 82.0 per cent of the returned migrant laborers were engaged in blue-collar jobs (tailor, driver, plumber, welder, and electrician) while rest worked as professional (manager and engineer)
Nature of migration	Seasonal and temporary

Source: Field Survey 2017–2018.

INTERNATIONAL MIGRATION

There were the following steps in the dynamics of migration from India to the Gulf:

First Step: Sponsors used to take permission from the immigration authority of the Gulf countries regarding recruiting laborers from India.
Second Step: Sponsors completed the documentation process with help of authorized registered agencies of migration in India for migration from India to the labor market of the Gulf.
Third Step: Migrant laborers completed the documentation process with the help of unauthorized agencies of migration at a grassroots level.

The above three steps were regulated and monitored by a well-developed framework of migration from India to the Gulf countries. There were many stakeholders including sponsors, authorized and unauthorized agencies, and migrant laborers engaged in the dynamics of migration from India to the Gulf.

This movement to the Gulf was led by both economic and non-economic reasons because laborers migrated due to the availability of higher wages in the Gulf compared to India as well as the glamor of jobs in the Gulf which also attracted laborers. Both authorized and unauthorized agencies played a crucial role in the dynamics of migration to the Gulf countries because these agencies provided help to migrant laborers in completing the documentation process (Table 3.3).

Socio-economic Profile of Returned Migrant Laborers

Migration to the Gulf countries was characterized by Muslims because nearly 96.0 (n=173) per cent of the returned migrant laborers were Muslims and the rest were Hindus. Among them, nearly 83.0 (n=150) per cent of returned migrant laborers were from rural areas and the rest were from the urban areas of Uttar Pradesh. Out of the total returned migrant laborers, nearly 88.0 (n=159) per cent of the returned migrant laborers gained training of skills through an informal mode while the rest of the professional returned migrant laborers trained in engineering and management institutions in India before migration to the Gulf (Source: Field Survey 2017–2018).

INTERNAL MIGRATION: AVERAGE PER MONTH INCOME AND REMITTANCES OF RETURNED MIGRANT LABORERS BY OCCUPATION AND SKILLS

There were variations in the structure of per month income and remittances of returned migrant laborers according to the occupational structure of returned migrant laborers in internal migration. Professional

Table 3.3 Description of international migration

Indicators	*Quantitative Description*
Causes of migration	Nearly 75.0 per cent of the returned migrant laborers migrated to the Gulf due to higher wages and the rest migrated due to problems of unemployment at origin.
Social network of migration	Nearly 54.0 per cent of the returned migrant laborers got information through help of their kinship network and rest got through help of authorised migrant agents.
Source of work permit visas	Nearly 87.0 per cent of the returned migrant laborers got visa from help of their kinship network and rest got through recruitment agents.
Economic cost of migration	Average cost of international migration was INR 54,500 per returned migrant laborer.
Source of gaining economic cost of migration	Nearly 87.0 per cent of the returned migrant laborer received financial assistance through help of their kinship network while
Destinations	Kingdom of Saudi Arabia was the largest destination followed by United Arab Emirates.
Occupational structure of returned migrant laborers	Nearly 88.0 per cent of returned migrant laborers engaged in blue-collar jobs (welder, driver, tailor, plumber, and electrician) while rest of the returned migrant laborers were engaged in white collar jobs (manager and engineer) in the Gulf countries.
Nature of migration	Seasonal and contract-based migration.
Tenure of contract migration	Average tenure of migration was 3.0 years per returned migrant laborer in the Gulf

Source: Field Survey 2017–2018.

migrant laborers (managers and engineers) got a higher income compared to semi-skilled migrant laborers (welders, tailors, plumbers, drivers, and electricians). Similarly, professional migrant laborers used to send more remittances compared to semi-skilled migrant laborers in internal migration (Tables 3.4 and 3.5)

INTERNATIONAL MIGRATION: AVERAGE PER MONTH INCOME AND REMITTANCES OF RETURNED MIGRANT LABORERS BY OCCUPATION AND SKILLS

There were variations in the structure of average per month income and remittances of returned migrant laborers in the Gulf countries because professional migrant laborers (managers and engineers) got a higher income compared to semi-skilled migrant laborers (welders, tailors, plumbers, drivers, and electricians). It was also observed that professional migrant laborers used to send more amount of remittances compared to semi-skilled migrant laborers from the Gulf countries to India (Tables 3.6 and 3.7).

Table 3.4 Average per month income and remittances of returned migrant laborers by occupation

Occupational structure of retuned migrant laborers in internal migration	*Average per month income in INR*	*Average per month remittances in INR*
Tailor	23070	17920
Plumber	18750	17500
Driver	23130	17430
Welder	25940	19940
Electrician	25710	22860
Manager	35900	29800
Engineers	40000	25000
Total of average	25100	18640

Source: Field Survey 2017–2018.

Table 3.5 Average per month income and remittances of returned migrant laborers by skills

Skill-wise classification	*Average per month income in INR*	*Average per month remittances in INR*
Semi-skilled returned migrant laborers	23,320	19,130
Skilled migrant laborers	37,950	27,400

Source: Field Survey 2017–2018.

Table 3.6 Average per month income and remittances of returned migrant laborers by occupation

Occupational structure of returned migrant laborers	*Average per month income in INR*	*Average per month remittances in INR*
Tailor	56,100	46,090
Plumber	51,820	42,730
Welders	58,700	51,300
Driver	57,050	46,865
Electrician	67,720	54,440
Engineer	110,670	87,500
Manager	100,100	78,460
Total of average	62,670	51,420

Source: Field Survey 2017–2018.

Table 3.7 Average per month income and remittances of returned migrant laborers by skills

Skill-wise classification of returned migrant laborers	*Average per month income in INR*	*Average per month remittances in INR*
Semi-skilled returned migrant laborers	57,020	47,390
Skilled returned migrant laborers	104,050	81,900

Source: Field Survey 2017–2018.

Impact of Migration at Origin

The Gulf migration created multiple impact with social and economic changes in migrant households because they invested remittances in unproductive items compared to productive items. The impact of Gulf migration created an environment of the culture of migration among the migration-based community in the rural areas of Bihar (Rahman, 2001: 167–168). It also improved the socio-economic status of migrant households in after the Gulf migration scenario compared to before the Gulf migration in the selected rural areas of Uttar Pradesh (Majumder & Taukeer, 2019: 172). Examining these consequences, this section analyzes the socio-economic impact of the Gulf migration in the sample areas of Uttar Pradesh.

Returned migrant laborers reported that they used to send remittances through an online money transfer system from the Gulf to India. These migrant laborers returned with social remittances because they gained the cultural norms, values, and beliefs of the Gulf countries which were reflected in the sociocultural practices of returned migrant laborers and their family members in the sample areas of Uttar Pradesh. It is also observed that both types of migration created multiple impact as well as a culture of migration from the sample areas of Uttar Pradesh to the cities of India with migration to the Gulf due to physical and non-physical impacts of migration.[3]

SOURCES OF INCOME IN MIGRANT HOUSEHOLDS BEFORE AND AFTER INTERNATIONAL MIGRATION

Both internal and international remittances were major sources of income in migrant households but the latter was the predominant source in migrant households after international migration compared to domestic remittances after international migration. Income from other sources like domestic remittances, livestock, and agriculture declined after international migration compared to before international migration (Table 3.8).

Table 3.8 Average monthly income in migrant households in selected sources

Sources of income	*Before international migration*	*After international migration*
	Per cent of total income	*Per cent of total income*
International remittances	0.0	85.0
Domestic remittances	88.5	11.5
Livestock	4.5	1.5
Agriculture	7.0	2.0
Total	100.0 (INR 16,280)	100.0 (INR 109,600)

Source: Field Survey 2017–2018.

Table 3.9 Pattern of investment of remittances in migrant households during last three years

Investment of Gulf remittances by migrant households	*Average invested remittances in last three years in INR*
Investment in education	40,900
Investment in agricultural lands	229,450
Investment in buying motor cars	206,000
Investment in repair of house	358,000
Investment in marriage ceremony	54,000

Source: Field Survey 2017–2018.

THE PATTERN OF INVESTMENT OF GULF REMITTANCES IN MIGRANT HOUSEHOLDS DURING THE LAST THREE YEARS

Migrant households invested remittances in both productive and unproductive items but unproductive items like investment in buying motor cars, house repairs, and marriage ceremonies were more dominant compared to the productive investment of remittances in education and agriculture land. The investment pattern of remittances created an environment of physical culture among migrant households in the sample areas of Uttar Pradesh (Table 3.9).

EXPENDED REMITTANCES IN FOOD AND NON-FOOD ITEMS IN MIGRANT HOUSEHOLDS BEFORE AND AFTER INTERNATIONAL MIGRATION

Migrant households expended domestic and international remittances in both food and non-food items in before international migration and after international migration. Migrant households expended more on non-food items compared to food items before and after international migration. It

Table 3.10 Average monthly expenditure in migrant households

Food and non-food items expenditure	*Before international migration*	*After international migration*	*Growth between before and after international migration*
	Per cent of total	*Per cent of total*	*In per cent*
Transport items	7.5	8.5	176.0
Entertainment items	5.0	5.0	145.0
Communication items	6.0	6.5	148.0
Health items	14.0	14.0	148.0
Education items	15.0	16.0	167.0
Food items	45.0	41.0	110.0
Other items	7.5	9.0	155.0
Total	100.0 (INR 6640)	100.0 (15680)	138.0

Source: Field Survey 2017–2018.

was also found that migrant households expended more on health and education items compared to items of consumer durables like transport, entertainment, and communitarian items before and after international migration (Table 3.10).

Migrant households did not receive economic remittances but also non-economic remittances like cultural values, norms, and beliefs of the Gulf countries which were reflected in the social and cultural practices of returned migrant laborers and their family members. These consequences created a mixed culture of India and Arab in the sample areas of Uttar Pradesh because it was observed that the linguistic patterns of returned migrant laborers were more influenced by the Arabic language because the laborers and their family members used Arabic with their native Hindi language. It was also observed that both economic and non-economic remittances created social and economic transformations among the migrant-based community in the sample areas of Uttar Pradesh. The matter of migration to the Gulf was associated with the sacred space among Muslims because they considered Saudi Arabia as the Holy Land of Prophet Muhammed and they expressed the fact that earning Swift money was with the blessing of Prophet Muhammed.[4]

Working and Living Circumstances of Migrant Laborers at Destinations

It was observed that migrant laborers worked temporarily in both Mumbai and the United Arab Emirates. These migrant laborers worked under *Seth* (the owner) in Mumbai while they worked under *Kafeel* (the sponsor) in the

United Arab Emirates. They faced similar working conditions in both internal and international migration because they tolerated the problems of socio-economic and geographical identities in both destinations. Migrant laborers reported that Arabians recognized them as *Ghulam* (slave laborers) and *Kafheer* (non-Muslim while internal migrant laborers were identified as *Bhaiya* (a geographical identity of North India and *Chedabhai* (individual migrant laborers who lived on rent in Mumbai). It was also observed that there was homogeneity in the socio-economic and geographical identity of South Asian migrant laborers in the United Arab Emirates because they were recognized by their native languages, hence Arabians used to call North Indian migrant laborers "Hindi" and migrant laborers of Kerala "Malyali". Likewise, there were socio-economic and geographical homogeneities among North Indian migrant laborers in Mumbai because they were being identified as only *Bhaiya* regardless of their social, geographical, and economic identities.[5]

There were also similarities in the living circumstances of migrant laborers in both internal and international destinations. Internal migrant laborers lived on rent in *Khholi* (a small room) in the outer areas of Mumbai. The settlement pattern of North Indian migrant laborers was known as *Chall* (planned settlement pattern) in Mumbai but international migrant laborers usually live in labor apartments provided by the sponsor. It was observed that the latter accommodations were in better condition compared to *Khholi* in Mumbai. There were explicit impacts of these migrant laborers at both destinations because North Indian culture was more visible in Mumbai due to the huge presence of North Indian migrant laborers. There was the same story in the United Arab Emirates because South Asian culture was more visible than Arabian culture due to the huge presence of South Asian migrant laborers in the United Arab Emirates. It was also observed that there was a clear impact of South Asian languages, music, movies, foods, and dress style in the environment of Arabian culture in the United Arab Emirates. Therefore, there were close similarities in the working and living conditions of internal and international migrant laborers at both destinations in the perspective of economic and non-economic indicators but both types of migration was connected with matters of livelihood.[6]

These migrant laborers said that *Kafeel* used to mentally exploit them because they used to retain the passport of migrant laborers as well as hold their salaries without any valid reasons. These migrant laborers used to keep Emirates ID issued by *Kafeel* which showed their geographical and economic identity with unique identification number but *Seth* did not issue any type of identity card to migrant laborers who worked in the casual labor market of Mumbai. There was a similar story of the working and living conditions of internal migrant laborers in Mumbai because *Seth* also mentally exploited them. Internal migrant laborers reported that *Seth* did not give regular salaries as well as used to hold their salaries without any valid reason. Therefore, both types of migrants faced precarious socio-economic conditions in both Mumbai and the United Arab Emirates.[7]

Internal and International Migration: Similarities, Differences, and Connections

There were similarities, differences, and links between internal and international migration because internal migration within India worked as transit migration between India and the Gulf; the dynamics of international migration was led by internal migration. Both types of migration were caused by similar economic and non-economic reasons but the dynamics of international migration long-term compared to short-term internal migration. There were differences between both types of migration in the perspectives of the structure of income because international migrant laborers got a predetermined minimum wage rate according to their agreements of contract migration in the Gulf while there were not any proper mechanisms of minimum wage rate in internal migration.

Both types of migration were inter-connected in terms of both economic and non-economic indicators because mostly migrant laborers used to work in blue-collar jobs in both Mumbai and the United Arab Emirates. Internal migrant laborers were recruited by contactors but international migrant laborers were recruited by both unauthorized and authorized recruitment agents with the help of well-developed social network systems from India to the Gulf. In addition, they also faced problems with identity in both Mumbai and the United Arab Emirates but both types of migration were key to the livelihood of migrant laborers and their family members. Domestic and international remittances enhanced the income of migrant households but the impact of international remittances was so sufficient compared to domestic remittances because migrant laborers earned more in the Gulf countries compared to domestic migration.

It was also observed that the impact of international migration was more visible than internal migration because youth desired migration to the Gulf due to the glamor of Dubai but they migrated to Mumbai where they gained training of skills with experiences of migration which led to the mechanism of adjustment in the glamourous life of Dubai. Both Mumbai and Dubai are global cities as well as both destinations attracting migrant laborers from North India because mostly young people stated that both Mumbai and Dubai were dream cities for them. It was also observed that migrant laborers developed a social and mental region of migration from the rural areas of Uttar Pradesh to the Gulf because the culture of migration reduced the geographical boundaries between India and the Gulf. Migrant laborers considered Dubai as Mumbai because they found similar socio-economic conditions in both destinations due to a huge presence of migrant laborers from North India in both Mumbai and the United Arab Emirates. Finally, both internal and international migration assimilated each other in the views of migrant laborers due to the culture of internal and international migration from North India.

Concluding Remarks

On the basis of the above findings, it can be concluded that the dynamics of both types of migration were led by similar economic and non-economic reasons. Matters of livelihood of migrant laborers were based on the migration within India and international migration to the Gulf. Migration determined the social and economic behavior of migrant laborers and their family members because both economic and social remittances created structural changes in social and economic transformations among migrant households in sample areas of Uttar Pradesh.

Secondly, both types of migration were deep-rooted in the economic practices of migrant laborers because they considered migration as a tool of survival as well as the creation of a social region. They had their own perception about migration due to long experiences in the journey of migration. They used to take satisfaction in migration from India to the Gulf because migration was the major source of prosperity for migrant laborers and their family members in Uttar Pradesh.

Thirdly, migrant laborers faced similar socio-economic and geographical identities in both Mumbai and the United Arab Emirates but they tolerated these problems because they had no other option for their livelihood except to migrate.

Recommended Policies

Therefore, there are the following recommended policies regarding ensuring the welfare and protection of migrant laborers at internal and international destinations enhanced utilization of remittances at the origin:

i. There is a need for the implementation of skills-oriented programs like *Pravasi Kaushal Vikas Yojna* at the grassroots level with the collaboration of the State Government of Uttar Pradesh for better utilization of skills in cities of India and the Gulf.
ii. The Government of India should develop a framework to ensure the issues of human rights of migrant laborers in the working circumstances of Mumbai and the United Arab Emirates.
iii. There should be established mapping of social remittances on migration-based communities at a grassroots level because social remittances create social changes in migrant households.
iv. There is a need to give way to migrant households for better utilization of economic remittances in productive items compared to unproductive items.

Notes

1 Information is based on the informal and focused group interview of returned migrant labourers in the sample areas of Lucknow district of Uttar Pradesh on 12 January 2018.
2 Information is based on the informal interview of returned migrant labourers in the sample areas of Lucknow district of Uttar Pradesh on 14 January 2018.
3 Information is based on the informal interviews of returned migrant labourers in the sample areas of Lucknow district of Uttar Pradesh on 14 January 2018.
4 Information is based on the focused group and informal interview of retuned migrant labourers in the sample areas of Lucknow district of Uttar Pradesh on 15 March 2018.
5 Information is based on focused group interview from migrant labourers in Mumbai on 2 February 2019 as well as United Arab Emirates on 2 December 2019.
6 Information is based on the passive observation method among migrant labourers in Mumbai on 6 February 2019 as well as United Arab Emirates on 4 December 2019.
7 Information is based on focused group interview from migrant labourers in Mumbai on 4 February 2019 as well as United Arab Emirates on 8 December 2019.

References

Majumder, B., & Taukeer, M. (July–September 2019). Dual- Step Migration from a Village in Uttar Pradesh: Causes, Process and Consequences. *Productivity*, *60*(2), 162–174.

Rahman, A. (2001). *Indian Labour Migration to Gulf*. New Delhi: Rajat Publication.

Sasikumar, S. K., & Thimothy, R. (2015). *From India to the Gulf Region: Exploring Links between Labour Markets, SkIlls and the Migration Cycle*. Geneva: IOM.

Taukeer, M. (December, 2020). Process and Determinants of Labour Migration from Selected Rural Areas of Uttar Pradesh to Gulf Countries. *Man and Development*, 123–138.

Zachariah, K. C., & Rajan, S. I. (2012). *Kerala's Gulf Connection, 1998–2011. Economic and Social Impact of Migration*. Hyderabad: Orient Blackswan Private Limited.

4 Emigration and Changing Lifestyles among Skilled Indian Professionals in the Gulf Region

A Sociocultural Perspective

Ani Merly Paul and Lekshmi S Kaimal

Introduction

Migration is defined as a move from one defining area to another that is made during a given migration interval and that involves a change of residence. Thousands of people are crossing borders either voluntarily or compulsorily as a part of migration and today such a move is an inevitable part of development in any country. The trajectory of migration is very interesting to study. Migration has become a central concern for today's international relations. It is a major factor in economic and political change. It is an important issue in both domestic and international politics, in both the mother country and host countries (Kaimal & Paul, 2020).

India is considered to be the largest migrant-exporting nation in the world. International migration is considered to be one of the vital features of the Indian economy and India is the world's top receiver of remittances from abroad.

Migration for jobs has often been portrayed as a means to eradicate poverty, especially among poor households. Thus, migration trends have altered the so-called immobile social mobility in terms of better standards of living from a generation of utter hopelessness to a generation who have altered their homes and surroundings as a result of benefits from migration. For instance, the "oil boom" of the 1970s and the migration that followed was predominantly among laborers who were unskilled they opted to work in an environment that was unfavorable and unfamiliar to them, and they adjusted to the scorching heat just with the quest to feed their family.

Since the 1970s "oil boom", migration of Indians to the Gulf regions has played an important role as a valuable source of income and as the main pillar of the economies of high-migration states such as Kerala through the transfer of remittances (Kozhanov, Young, Calabrese, Husari, & Mammadov, 2021). Despite this, Indian migrant workers have made considerable contributions to the economic growth of the Gulf States.

According to the latest estimate made by the Ministry of Overseas Indian Affairs (MOIA), the Indian emigrants constitute 30 million spread around 130 countries. Out of this, almost six million were working in six Gulf

DOI: 10.4324/9781003369370-6

Table 4.1 Indian Diaspora in the GCC countries

Sl. No.	*Name of GCC country*	*Indian Diaspora in million*
1	Saudi Arabia	2 million
2	UAE	1.7 million
3	Kuwait	0.64 million
4	Oman	0.7 million
5	Bahrain	0.35 million
6	Qatar	0.50 million
Total		5.94 million

(Source: Kumar, 2014).

Corporation Council (GCC) countries (Kumar, 2014). These emigrants were mainly employed in three categories of jobs: (1) White-collar jobs (medical, engineering, and banking professionals); (2) Semi-skilled workers or blue-collar jobs (craftspeople, taxi drivers); (3) Unskilled laborers engaged as manual workers in construction sites, shops, and households (Kumar, 2014).

The first group of workers or skilled laborers nearly includes about 30 percent of the total Indian migrants in the Gulf countries. The second and third categories together constitute 70 percent of the total Indian migrants (Kumar, 2014). Within the GCC countries, the Kingdom of Saudi Arabia (KSA) and the United Arab Emirates (UAE) are the most widespread destinations of Indian emigrants which together contributed more than 60 percent of the overall distribution of Indian emigrant workers (Kumar, 2014) (Table 4.1).

Migration of Skilled Professionals in Kerala: An Overview

Kerala, unlike other Indian states, has been a trendsetter. Kerala experienced an awakening in all realms with the coming of missionaries and the repercussions were felt among various sections of the society and various social awakenings like the Sree Narayana Dharma Paripalana movement (SNDP), the upliftment of Ezhava caste in Kerala, and the Ayyankali social awakening was witnessed. The universalization of education in Kerala had a trickledown effect hence attitudinal change due to education was felt and experienced by the people of Kerala earlier than in the other states. This changed the social fabric of Kerala society since it always stands apart from the rest of the states not only in terms of education but also socially and culturally even in the health sector. The educational sector in Kerala has adapted to the real-time needs of society. Hence, Kerala has emerged increasingly developing towards a hub of the skilled workforce (Planning Board). The education system in Kerala is modeled toward skills development and vocational training. The state's skilled professional workers are preferred by employers from different parts of the world.

Kerala's remittances from abroad have gained attention as a major source of growth. The economy of Kerala is very much dependent on remittances especially from the Gulf. Migration trends changed due to educational and demographic variables. In the modern era, the emigration of skilled professionals is accelerating by the day. With the automation and development of the global manufacturing sector, Kerala's young population got opportunities to pursue new career aspirations because of the strengths concerning school and higher education prospects. Kerala is a state which is considered able to supply a large number of professionally qualified candidates in all fields worldwide. These quality education prospects enable the state to deal with the new challenges posed by the changing employment scenario. Through its industrial and information technology policies, a rapid increase in large-scale investments in different sectors was also envisaged. This appeals for the highest echelons of skill enhancement and preparation to be made accessible to the youth of Kerala for involvement in the makeover of Kerala's economy.

Concerning the process of migration, Kerala is a leading state in terms of migration. There are historical, economic, and social reasons for the large-scale international migration from Kerala (Kaimal & Paul, 2020). The economic sector of Kerala is lagging due to its high dependence on agriculture and agro-based industries. The industrial sector in Kerala is backward due to a lack of infrastructural facilities, a militant labor force, trade unionism, power shortages, and scarcity of land. This leads to high unemployment rates which often become a push factor for migration. The educational level of Kerala youth is also very high and the opportunities available for employment are very limited in Kerala. This often leads to migration to other places in search of employment.

As far as Kerala is concerned migration is a central force of economic growth. Thus migration proved a pivotal role in alleviating poverty in Kerala (Pattath, 2020). Concerning the migration of skilled professionals, the leading categories include: IT professionals, health professionals, engineers, etc. The Arab countries of the Middle East were the destination of 95 percent of the emigrants, with Saudi Arabia alone accounting for nearly 40 percent of the total. Other than Gulf migration, the prime destination of Kerala migrants is the United States, which amounts to 2.2 percent of the total migration. Migration leads cultural change in both the place of origin and destination (Zachariah, Mathew, & Rajan, 2003). There are two components to the migration decision: Cultural and economic. If the economic motive dominates, migrants that reflect the cultural mix of their origin country brings countries closer together.

Review of Literature

The emigration of laborers to the Gulf is considered to be the central aspect of the Kerala economy. As K.C. Zachariah, E.T. Mathew, and S. Irudaya Rajan in their study on "Impact of Migration on Kerala's Economy and

Society" (1999) rightly said that around 1.5 million Malayalees were living outside and they were sending approximately Rs. 4000 as remittances. The study also states that around three-quarters of a million emigrants returned – they depend on their savings and work experience and skills acquired while abroad. The study also analyzed the dependence of families on remittances for education, subsistence, and other economic needs and necessities. The study considered the economically backward Muslims from the districts of Thrissur-Malappuram in Kerala as the mainstay of emigration to the Gulf region while the educationally forward categories including Syrian Christians, Nairs, and Ezhavas, from the middle part of Kerala, form the center of internal migration (Zachariah, Mathew, & Rajan, 1999). But nowadays this trend is changing and currently religious differences are becoming less and less significant on the emigration scene in Kerala.

Migration is the single most important economic factor that influences every aspect of Kerala society. Its influence is not only limited to migrant households but has also permeated to every section of the Kerala populace. B A Prakash in an article stated that ever since the 1970s, the influx of Gulf remittances and its expenditure has created incomparable economic changes in the industrially backward Kerala economy (Prakash, 1998). The study clearly states that the migrant households' economic status and standard of living changed considerably due to migration. With the help of migration, they were successful in acquiring high incomes, more assets in the form of houses and property, and high consumption levels, etc. It is also observed that migration played an important role in the poverty reduction of Kerala. The success of the Kerala model of development is considered to be the effect of migration and remittances. But migration also pushed up the land prices, consumerism and inflation levels, prices of construction materials, charges of education, health, and transport services, etc. making it difficult for the fixed middle-income people to survive and maintain a standard of living (Prakash, 1998).

Considering the nature of the labor force migrating to the Gulf region, KC Zachariah, BA Prakash, and S Irudaya Rajan mention that mainly unskilled and semi-skilled workers were the backbone of migration and they were mainly engaged in construction, production, and transport activities. Only one-fifth of them were professional and technically qualified. The other chief categories of Kerala emigrants were mainly working in clerical, service activities, and sales. Among them, more than three-fourths of emigrants were employed in regular employment and getting monthly salaries (Zachariah, Prakash, & Rajan, 2002).

Skilled migration is not new to migration literature but its prevalence in the international scene has become noticeable in the present millennium. Concerning the concept of skilled migration, Yining Tan (2021) in the study on "Gendered skilled migration: American women in China" explained that skilled migration has become increasingly gendered. Positioning within the background of globalization and mobility, this article inspects skilled women emigrants from the US to China. Grounded in in-depth interviews piloted in the Pearl River Delta Region of China, this article targets to address these questions: What are the factors that influence skilled women migrants' agency in migration decision-making? How is agency reflected in skilled women's post-migration experience, including labor market and social relationships in the Chinese context? This research revealed a paradoxical dynamic in skilled migration which analyzes the gender-wise differences in decision-making even for skilled migrants. The study states that being highly skilled is not a guarantee for gender equality in sharing of domestic work and responsibilities. Secondly, despite high levels of education and skills, the options available for women migrants in the labor market were very limited and they have to depend on their spouses economically for meeting their needs after moving to China. Thirdly, though the women migrants were not all working in professional segments, they all acquired initiatives to accomplish their talent through home-schooling and volunteering for community-building events. Through these types of undertakings, the American women succeeded in using their existing skills or advanced innovative skills to handle the post-migration realities; yet, their actions were constrained by the structural forces, conventional gender norms, and socially constructed definitions of skills (Tan, 2021).

The migration of skilled workers is an emerging field of study and this is considered to be an important variable affecting the economic growth of the nation. The brain drains are considered to be a serious problem affecting not only developing countries but also developed countries, As Chandra Shah and Gerald Burke (2005) in their study on "Skilled migration: Australia" point out, migration patterns to and from Australia are becoming complex with migration programs increasingly targeted towards meeting the needs of the labor market and regional development. The paper deals with the impact of skilled labor supply as a result of migration both temporary and permanent from Australia in the last three years. The paper points towards the occupational mobility of permanent immigrants. The study looks at skill wastage and skill shortages and ways to minimize the former through appropriate programs including occupational licenses, updating occupation-specific skills, and giving up-to-date information on the labor market and its functioning (Shah & Burke, 2005).

Thus, the influence of migration on Kerala society is intense. It emerged to be the backbone of the so-called Kerala model of development. Migration has redefined the cultural and economic background of Kerala (Kaimal, 2019). Even though the migration of Keralites has been studied widely by different researchers, the migration of skilled workers in Kerala is not a widely enquired field of research.

Significance of the Study

Kerala is considered to be one of the major states which depend on remittances from foreign countries. There were places in Kerala that were known as Gulf pockets in which every household consist of one Gulf emigrant. The emigration trends in Kerala witnessed changes due to the emigration of skilled workers to the Gulf region. The migration of skilled workers was triggered by many factors including the growing educated unemployment rate in Kerala, the failure of the system to provide job opportunities to the needy, and also the growing consumerism and the increasing career aspirations of the educated youth. The slow growth of the manufacturing sector and high dependence on the service sector set forth all the necessary push factors for the emigration of skilled workers. Now Keralites view emigration as a way to attain a high standard of living. The emigration of nurses, IT professionals, and engineers was on the increase in modern Kerala society. As a result of emigration, many changes were witnessed in the lifestyle and their attitude towards Kerala and Keralites. The present study is very significant as it reveals the influence of emigration on the changing lifestyle among skilled workers. It also compares their perspective on facilities available in Kerala and the Gulf region. The increasing emigration of skilled workers and the resultant brain drain is considered to be a drawback of the Kerala model of development which created high indicators of social development without economic development. Thus, the study is very significant as it reveals the emigration of skilled professionals to the Gulf region.

Methodology

Theoretical Framework

The impression management by Irving Goffman and the social capital and rational choice approach by James Coleman provided the theoretical framework for the study. Impression management, otherwise known as "self-presentation", is considered to be the conscious or subconscious efforts by people to influence or change others' perception about a person, object, or event by modifying and controlling particular information in social interactions. The emigrant skilled professionals in their interactions, especially with their relatives and friends in the homeland, create an impression that they were special. In Coleman's view, social capital exists in the social structure of relationships with others. This social capital is achieved by them as a result of emigration that enables the professionals to choose the lifestyle they like.

Objectives

1. To identify the socio-economic background of the respondents.
2. To find out the changing nature of their lifestyle.
3. To compare the perspective of these emigrated professionals towards the facilities available in Kerala and the Gulf region.

Sampling and Method

The study is based on the mixed method in which qualitative and quantitative data were used. Data collection was conducted using a questionnaire and interview guide. The snowball sampling method was used to select the respondents. A sample size of 100 respondents was selected for the study. The data was collected from emigrant workers from the Gulf region.

Findings and Discussion

Skilled professionals are on an increase in the current millennium. The most direct effect of skilled emigration is a reduction in the number of educated workers who are pivotal in the productivity and economic growth of a developing nation. The findings of the study are divided into three sections based on the objectives. The first section deals with the socio-economic profile of the respondents. The second section deals with changing nature of lifestyle among respondents and the third section compares the perspective of these emigrated professionals towards the facilities available in Kerala and the Gulf region.

The socio-economic profile deals with different variables in the social and economic background of the respondents. The majority of the respondents (60 percent) were in the 20–40 age group (Table 4.2).

Table 4.2 Education of the respondents

Education	*Frequency*	*Percent*
B. Tech/M. Tech	35	35
BSc/MSc Nursing	24	24
MBA	16	16
MCA	13	13
Others	12	12
Total	100	100

The above table reveals the education status of the respondents. A total of 35 percent of the respondents were B.Tech/M.Tech graduates; 24 percent have a BSc/MSc Nursing degree; 16 percent were MBA holders; 13 percent have an MCA; and others (CA, M. Com, and MA/MSc.) constitute 12 percent. This means that most of the skilled professionals were highly qualified and technically skilled workers.

Most of them were married (85 percent) and have a family visa and 45 percent of their spouses were also working. A total of 34 percent were Christians, 31 percent were Hindus, and 35 percent were Muslims. Most of them came from extended families and their parents remained in their native places (Figure 4.1).

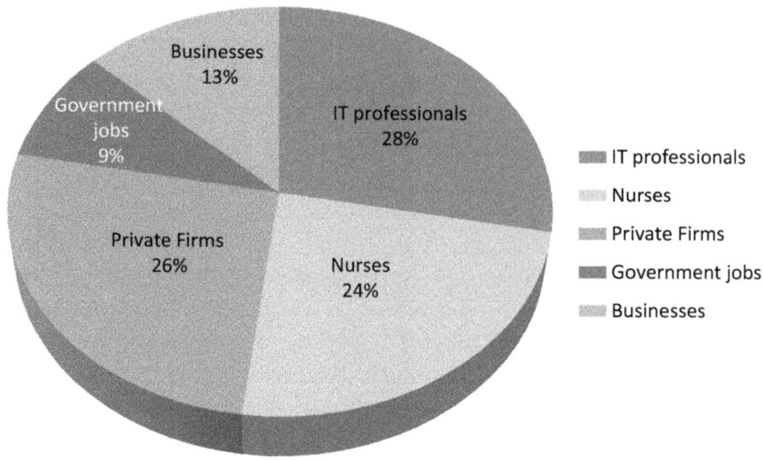

Figure 4.1 The occupation of the respondents

The above figure 4.1 reveals that 28 percent were IT professionals, 26 percent were working in Private Firms, 24 percent were nurses,13 percent engaged in business and only 9 percent were employed in government jobs.

The second section deals with the changing nature of their lifestyle. The study revealed that 73 percent of respondents' consumption patterns changed (Figure 4.2).

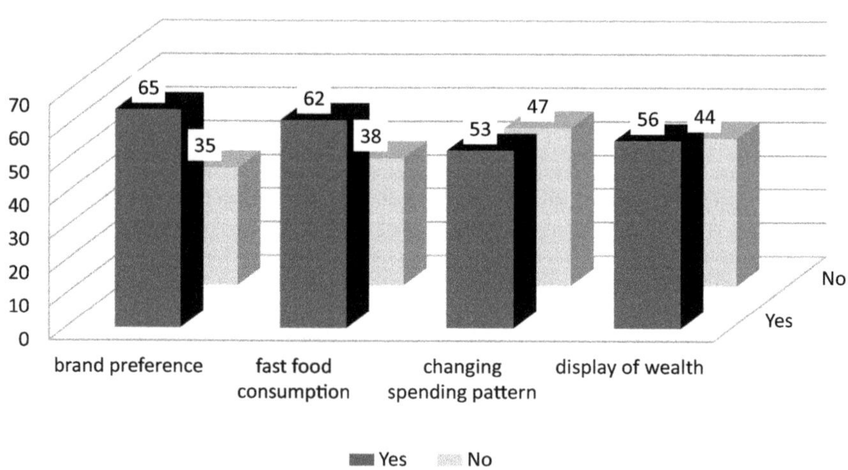

Figure 4.2 Consumption pattern

Firstly, this was seen in brand preference for consumption. After migration most of the respondents shifted to the consumption of branded goods (65 percent). They prefer branded clothes and electronic gadgets like the Apple iPhone. Secondly, with regard to the consumption of fast food – most (62 percent) of the respondents agreed that their fast-food consumption increased after migration. They like to try new food items and also buy and consume food frequently from outside. Thirdly, there were changes in spending patterns. The majority (53 percent) of respondents agree that their spending patterns changed drastically. They considered that they have no hesitation in spending money when they visit their native place. They spend lavishly among their relatives and friends and also purchase new clothes, sweets, ornaments, electronic gadgets, and toys for their relatives and friends. Many of the respondents even gave a lot of money to religious institutions and other NGOs. As Goffman says, this is considered to be an aspect of impression management. The migrated professionals want to impress their relatives by providing gifts and money to them. Through this, they gain respect and special consideration from their relatives and religious intuitions. This creates a feeling that they are special and superior to their relatives and friends. Fourthly, 56 percent agreed that they like to display their financial strength to others so they want to have an exhibition of their status in front of others (Table 4.3).

Table 4.3 Spending money on home

Spending money for Home in the native place	*Frequency*	*Percent*
Buy new house/apartment	32	32
Constructed new home	22	22
Renovated old family home	23	23
No	23	23
Total	100	100

Another important aspect of their changing lifestyle is that the majority (77 percent) spend money on their home. The study revealed that 32 percent bought/constructed a new home or apartment in their native place. A total of 22 percent constructed new homes in their share of land; 23 percent renovated their old family house based on new trends; and 23 percent were not interested in spending on a home in their native place.

Another important aspect of their changing lifestyle is that they became more quality conscious while purchasing products. A total of 83 percent preferred expensive items as they were good in quality and service facilities, whilst 56 percent agreed that their dress code changed after they migrated. Thus, migration has allowed them to change their lifestyle to a new orientation. This new lifestyle is more consumerist in orientation and includes the priority of seeking high quality and an expensive outlook. As James Coleman views it, the social capital achieved by them as a result of migration enables them to adapt to a lifestyle that displays their status and superiority in front of others.

Thus the topographies of the changing lifestyle among skilled professionals as a result of migration consist of the following aspects: (1) Changing consumption patterns, (2) spending money on home/assets, (3) preference for expensive products, (4) quality consciousness, and (5) display of status. The new lifestyle of the skilled professionals can be represented through the below model. Here the various aspects of the changing lifestyle are shown in various circles and these aspects were equally influencing their attitudes and preference (Figure 4.3).

The third section is based on qualitative data. Here comparison of the perspective of migrated skilled professionals regarding the facilities available in Kerala and the Gulf region is made. It was revealed from the study the migrated professionals were very much attached to their native place and they all felt nostalgia about Kerala. The main differences they feel include:

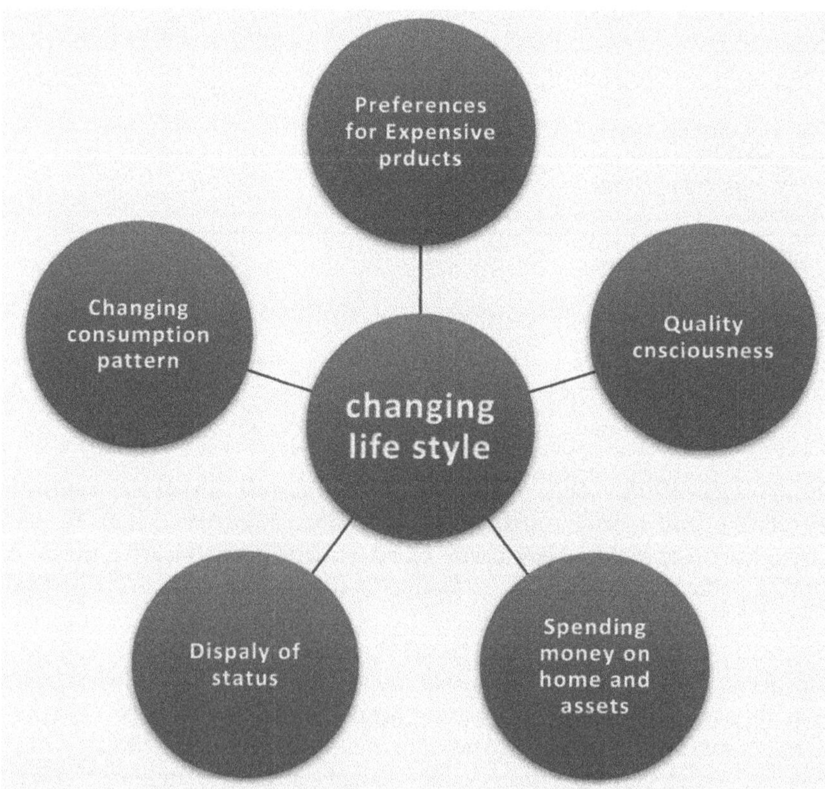

Figure 4.3 Changing lifestyle – topographies

Firstly, the Gulf region mostly consists of desert, and compared to it they consider Kerala as heaven which as there is a moderate climate and nature's greenery. Despite this, they prefer to stay in the Gulf because of the monetary gain and the opportunities available for the growth and development of their career. Secondly, they consider the quality of products available both in the Gulf and Kerala to be different. They feel the laws are very strict hence aberrance is not to be seen.

Thirdly, the medical facilities available in Kerala are cost-effective compared to the Gulf region. They viewed that in the Gulf region small clinics are more common than big hospitals. Such hospitals were not so affordable to common people. Fourthly, the shopping facilities and supermarkets available in the Gulf regions were excellent. Even though Kerala also has all these facilities available in its leading cities, the system is different. Fifthly, the most disgusting aspect they feel regarding Kerala is road traffic and the lack of good infrastructural facilities. The roads in Kerala have traffic blocks and jams which leads to a waste of time and money. But in the Gulf regions, roads, and infrastructural facilities are excellent as it allows free movement and travel facilities.

Conclusion

Thus, the migration of skilled professionals is not a new phenomenon. The present century witnessed the increasing migration of skilled professionals to different parts of the world. Based on the theory of the push and pull factors of migration, it is obvious that the migration of skilled professionals was also the result of many factors like better prospects, repaying financial burdens like educational loans, buying a new home, and raising their standard of living. The study revealed that the emigrated skilled professionals show homogeneity regarding socio-economic variables. They were having a good occupation due to high educational qualifications. Most of them were youngsters and possessed family visa. Their lifestyle also changed due to migration. Their consumption pattern changed and now they have become more consumerist which has altered the spending pattern of the masses. They become more brand conscious and quality conscious. Most of them like to invest money in their native place in the form of a home. The skilled professionals were satisfied with the facilities available in the Gulf region and considered that the enforcement of strict laws makes life more disciplined in the area. Though they were ready to adapt to the social conditions in the Gulf region, they feel nostalgia regarding Kerala and Kerala culture.

Areas for Future Research

The gendered skilled migration of Keralites and the migration of IT professionals and the emigration of health professionals are possible areas for future research.

References

Kaimal, L. S., & Paul, A. M. (2020). A sociological preview on the effects of migration on families left behind in homeland. *Asian Review of Social Sciences (ARSS)*, *9*(1), 9–13. https://www.trp.org.in/issues/a-sociological-preview-on-the-effects-of-migration-on-families-left-behind-in-homeland

Kaimal, L. S. (2019). *Consumerism and Consumption Pattern among IT professionals in Kerala* (Unpublished doctoral dissertation, 2019). Mahatma Gandhi University, Kottayam, Kerala. https://mgutheses.in/page/?q=T%203607&search=sociology&page=3&rad=all#22

Kozhanov, N., Young, K., Calabrese, J., Husari, R., &Mammadov, R. (2021, July 13). India's relations with West Asia: What patterns and what future? Retrieved July 14, 2021, from https://www.mei.edu/publications/indias-relations-west-asia-what-patterns-and-what-future

Kumar, N. (2014). Recent trend and pattern of Indian Emigration to Gulf Countries: A diaspora perspective. Retrieved July 14, 2021, from https://paa2014.princeton.edu/papers/141653

Pattath, B. (2020). Keeping up with Kerala's Joneses. In 1430303434 1039559276 S. I. Rajan (Ed.), *India Migration Report 2020: Kerala Model of Migration Surveys*. United Kingdom: Taylor & Francis. https://www.google.co.in/books/edition/India_Migration_Report_2020/G9oBEAAAQBAJ?hl=en&gbpv=1

Planning Board, K. S. (n.d.). KERALA looks ahead. Retrieved July 14, 2021, from http://keralalooksahead.com/skill_devlop/

Prakash, B. A. (1998, December 8). Gulf Migration and Its Economic Impact The Kerala Experience. Retrieved July 10, 2020, from http://www.keralaeconomy.com/admin/pdfs/two%20im.pdf

Shah, C., & Burke, G. (2005). *Skilled Migration*. Australia: Monash University.

Tan, Y. (2021, May 21). Gendered skilled migration: American women in China. *Asian Geographer*. https://doi.org/10.1080/10225706.2021.1930079

Zachariah, K. C., Prakash, B. A., &Rajan, S. I. (2002, March). Gulf migration study: Employment, wages and Working conditions of Kerala emigrants in the United Arab Emirates. Retrieved July 10, 2021, from https://www.researchgate.net/profile/Irudaya-Rajan-Nil-2/publication/5127033_Impact_of_Migration_On_Kerala's_Economy_and_Society/links/5db7dfd8299bf1a47bfa36e8/Impact-of-Migration-On-Kerala's-Economy-and-Society.pdf

Zachariah, K. C., Mathew, E. T., & Rajan, S. I. (1999, January 1). Impact of migration on Kerala's economy and society. Retrieved July 14, 2021, from https://www.researchgate.net/profile/Irudaya-Rajan-Nil-2/publication/5127033_Impact_of_Migration_On_Kerala's_Economy_and_Society/links/5db7dfd8299bf1a47bfa36e8/Impact-of-Migration-On-Kerala's-Economy-and-Society.pdf

Zachariah, K. C., Mathew, E. T., & Rajan, S. I. (2003). Dynamics of Migration in Kerala; dimensions, differentials, and consequences. Orient Logman Private Limited. https://doi.org/https://books.google.co.in/books?id=D497alRZPcoC&printsec=frontcover#v=onepage&q&f=false

5 Expatriate Organizations and Social Capital

The Case of Kerala Muslim Cultural Centre

Muhammed Shabeer T

Introduction

> The civilization of India, like a banyan tree, has shed its beneficent shade Away from its own birthplace … Indians can live and grow by spreading Abroad.
>
> (Rabindranath Tagore)

In the interconnected world, migration has become an inevitable reality and it finally forms a diasporic community. The origin of the word "diaspora" can be traced in the Greek word *die* and *sperin* which mean "dispersion" or "spread" or "scatter". The term "diaspora" means people living or settled permanently in other countries, but maintaining affection for their homeland. India became part and parcel of the globalized world by adopting new economic policies in 1991. In the globalized era, migration became a way of life for the educated youth and besides that there are innumerable reasons behind the individuals that impel them to leave their homeland, but they are looking for better life for themselves and their families. The Indian Diaspora may be considered the oldest diaspora in the world. It is also now the largest diaspora in the world, followed by Mexico, the Russian federations, and China; in 2015, 16 million people from India were living outside of their country of birth (United Nations, 2016).[1]

The United Nations defines migration as "persons outside their country of birth or citizenship 12 months or more". Migration is a process of finding a new way of livelihood. Basically people are migrating for a commercial purpose. India is occupying the top position of the origin of international migrants[2] together with the world's largest beneficiary of remittances.[3] Indian migration to the Persian Gulf countries is not a new phenomenon. The Gulf Cooperation countries host the largest expatriate of the Indian community. Indeed Diaspora is one of the great assets of a country. According to the Kerala Migration Survey 2018, there are over 2.1 million Keralites emigrants globally and 24 lakh Keralites working in Gulf Cooperation Council (GCC) countries and remittances received in Kerala accounted for approximately 85,000 crore.[4] The study will concentrate on

DOI: 10.4324/9781003369370-7

the role of expatriate organizations particularly KMCC. The KMCC works to ameliorate the social and political backwardness of downtrodden communities through its philanthropic orientation. In addition to this, this study seeks to initiate a discussion on the social responsibility of the expatriate community. This study is explorative and investigative in nature. Primary data was collected from the official website of Dubai KMCC, and a report of KMCC and secondary data was collected from books, newspaper articles, and the internet.

Roots of Migration from Kerala

The definition of the word migration can be "the movement of people from one place to another". The word migration is derived from the Latin word *migrare*, means to change one's residence. Migration is an important process that has contributed significantly to the process of political integration, urbanization, demographic distribution, industrialization, economic growth and development, cultural diffusion, and social integration. The movements of Keralites to different parts of the world are not an amazing one. People cross their boundaries for higher wages and better employment opportunities. According to the study by S Irudaya Rajan, Zachariah, and Mathew, the historical roots of Kerala migrants consist of four types and stages.[5]

- First, there was a migration wave towards the British states, as labor was needed for working in plantations,
- In the second stage, there was migration towards African countries mostly by school and college teachers.
- In the third stage during the 1960s, there was labor movement toward North America and Western Europe to overcome labor shortage of these continents.
- The fourth stage came when the avenues in the Persian Gulf opened up in the 1970s. The Malayalee community experienced some degree of migration in the Gulf countries. Many economic opportunities emerged with Gulf migration. Migration is one of the indivisible components of demography as well as the economy today. It is important to note that the prosperity of Kerala came via the Gulf.

Social Capital

The term "social capital" first appeared in academic circles in the United States in 1916 in a book published by Lyda Hanifan. The author discussed how to improve the conditions of schools with the help of neighbors. In recent years, the term has attracted popular attention with the publication of *Bowling Alone: The collapse and revival of American community* by Robert Putnam in 2000. Putnam argued that while Americans have become wealthier, their sense of community relationship has withered. People spend more time in office space than in social space which, in turn, reduced community sentiment and socializing with neighbors, friends, and even family.

Social capital exists in society and exists between actors in society. Robert Putnam stated "social capital is formed by features [social organisations] social life networks, norms and trust that enable participants to act together more effectively to pursue shared objectives."[6] Social capital is a kind of social asset that helps social relationships to grow and which ultimately would benefit individuals and groups of individuals. Social capital provides the participatory attitude of community and networks of people are at its heart – above all the idea of interconnection of society is at its core. It starts and ends with actors in society.

Social capital finds a new way of rebuilding society in a positive and productive way. In other words, we can say that it is a productive way of social engagement. Joining hands with societal networks is a sign of a matured way of socializing process. The byproduct of social capital is cooperation, togetherness, harmony, and tolerance in society.

Robert Putnam's social capital consists of "norms of reciprocity and networks of civil engagement" as well as trust, all of which "can improve the efficiency of society by facilitating coordinated actions."[7] Putnam theorizes that an active civil society is one in which people come into regular contract with others through mutual participation in activities of personal and communal interest. His social capital highlights that the high level of social capital had a high level of civic participation and a high level of welfare performance. In short, civic participation creates developmental activities in society.

Citizens have created an atmosphere of mutual co operations, vital social networks, equal political relations and the tradition of citizen participation.[8] This chapter will explore how an expatriate organization is shouldering the responsibility of philanthropic activities and also it is very interesting to note that it is working as a frontal organization of a political party. The Indian Union Muslim League (IUML), a political party, effectively used people's voluntary engagement in the creation of social capital.

Kerala Muslim Cultural Centre (KMCC)

The Indian Union Muslim League (IUML) is a political party in India. It is recognized by the Election Commission of India as a state political party in Kerala. It was founded on 10 March 1948 in Rajaji Hall,[9] Madras. Qaide Millath Mohammed Ismail Sahib was the first president of the IUML. The main motto of the IUML is the consolidation of Muslims and other weaker sections of society to make them worthy citizens of India through the motto of honorable existence. The Malabar zone of Kerala is deeply rooted with Muslim League affiliation. In the 1970s, the oil boom started in Gulf Co-operation Council (GCC) countries, which created more job opportunities and, in particular, the Malayalees or Keralites from the Malabar zone (northern Kerala) migrated to the Gulf countries for jobs. The community sentiments were at their very peak even during their migration to Gulf countries. In the 1980s, the Muslim League affiliated members came up with a notion to organize the platform for redressing their problems and coordinating their party's strength and boosting its spirit on Arab soil.

The KMCC (Kerala Muslim Cultural Centre) is a classic example of how an expatriate community is organized in culturally and politically different spaces and emerges as a powerful group in that particular area. The KMCC is the largest expatriate organization across the globe. It was established in 1985 as a frontal organization of the Indian Union Muslim League (IUML). The KMCC was born from the Chandrika Readers' Forum which was formed to popularize the Chandrika Malayalam daily among Malayalees of GCC (Gulf Cooperation Council) countries. Currently, there are more than 200 organizations of Malayalees in the GCC countries and the KMCC is the largest outfit among them.[10]

The avenues in the Persian Gulf opened up in the 1970s. The Malayalee community experienced some degree of migration in Gulf countries. Many economic opportunities emerged with Gulf migration. It is important to note that the prosperity of Kerala came via the Gulf. The expatriate community realized that forming an expatriate organization indeed is a means of prestige. In its nascent stage, the KMCC was primarily concerned with the social and economic welfare of Indians in the Gulf countries. The KMCC has extended its service and work sphere beyond the GCC countries and started a new chapter in the field of philanthropic activities in Kerala and across India, irrespective of the social background of its beneficiaries. The KMCC is a synonym of philanthropic activities. The KMCC should strive to protect the integrity of India and work for the progress of the Indian nation and the central objective of the organization is to engage in a high level of philanthropic activities. For instance, the C H Centre (named after C H Mohammed Koya, the former Chief Minister of Kerala from the Indian Union Muslim League) offers free dialysis for very needy patients, the construction of *Baithul Rahma* (House of Mercy) for the needy all over India, free legal consultation related to immigration, labor, and consular matters which is held every Friday at 8.30 pm in the Dubai KMCC office. Dubai KMCC is an authorized center for Indian passport and visa services. Dubai KMCC is a registered organization in Dubai under Social Regulatory and Licensing (community development authority), the Government of Dubai, and the Islamic Affairs and Charitable Activities Department. Through the MY SUPPORT program, Dubai KMCC provides monthly financial aid to retried Dubai KMCC members for a specific period. Besides all these, the KMCC all over the world helps to bring home to India the body of deceased Indians.

The various political parties in India have frontal expatriate organizations: The INC (Indian National Congress) has two different foundations:

(1) OICC (Overseas Indian Culture Centre) and (2) Priyadarshini Cultural Centre. The CPI-M (Communist Party of India (Marxist) has Navodaya as its expatriate organ, PDP (People's Democratic Party) has PCF and SDPI (Socialist Democratic Party of India) has Fraternity Forum, INL (Indian National League) has INCC (Indian National Cultural Centre) but above all the IUMLs (Indian Union Muslim League), yet KMCC remains the leading champion among expatriate organizations.

Role of the KMCC in Social Sphere

The KMCC is one of the reputed expatriate organizations and has deep roots in all GCC countries. The organization has already achieved a great name in serving humanity by introducing relief, promoting educational facilities, and helping every brother and sister. The KMCC has so far conducted several social and charity drives to help the poor and needy.

The CH Mohammed Koya Memorial Charitable Centre

The reason behind the thought to start CH Centre is that the poor rely on the Calicut Medical College for their healthcare needs. The adequate space for staying cannot even be imagined by the penniless and about their daily foods and medicines. The CH Centre came into existence to overcome the harsh situations of needy and impoverished people in 2001 with the blessings and prayers of Panakkad Sayyid Muhammad Ali Shihab Thangal.

CH Centre is registered under the Societies Act[11] (563/2011) and got the acceptance of relaxation from the Income Tax and got the registration under FCRA[12] (Foreign Contribution Regulation Act) on 718/2009. CH Centre again attracted recognition from Kerala State Government, the local self-governments from Malabar Zone which began to contribute a maximum of Rs 25,000 and its order issued on 1 April, 2006 and it increased in August 2011 by Rs 50,000 under the order of Ministry of Panchayath and Social Justice. The following are the activities carried out by the CH Centre.

The Shihab Thangal Dialysis Centre

On 5 March 2010, the Shihab Thangal Dialysis Centre was inaugurated by MA Yosuf Ali, Managing Director of Lulu Group, and the function was presided over by Panakkad Sayyid Hyder Ali Shihab Thangal, President of IUML Kerala State. The center has become a relief to helpless kidney patients who have no money for their dialysis. The center has expended 1.14 crore[13] to import German dialysis machines. The services of nephrologists, doctors, and technicians are also available in CH Centres. Monthly, the center has been spending Rs 238,400 on staff salaries and Rs 310,000 on operational expenses.

In 2010, the operation of the center started with two shifts. The plethora of dialysis patients occurred to start one more shift and, which opened on 17 January 2011, the capacity of dialysis increased patients from 18 to 27 patients. During 2010–2011, the 86 kidney patients have done 5558 dialysis[14] from the CH Centre. Now, weekly two or three dialyses are provided to about 68 patients. From the opening of the scheme till 31 December 2011, an aggregate of 11,046 dialysis programs have been conducted for patients; and more than one crore rupees were spent on this noble deed (for one dialysis it costs Rs 948).

The criterion to find out the beneficiaries for dialysis is a very genuine way. The local inspection and home visit are conducted by the CH Centre team. The CH Centre has also extended its helping hands towards the poor who approached the CH Centre for financial assistance. During 2008–2009, the CH Centre donated Rs 18,20,698 and in 2010–2011 it spent Rs 25,68,867[15] on helping those in need.

Food Distribution

The CH Centre began distributing food to patients and their bystanders in Calicut Medical College. On an experimental basis, food distribution was confined to dinner only. From 7 July 2011 onwards, the breakfast distribution also started. The food distribution program benefited more than 450 patients and bystanders in the Calicut medical college. From 2008 to 2011, the center distributed food to 2,83,057 needy people.

The kitchen of the CH Centre has been renovated by Indian Oil Corporations under the community kitchen scheme. It has helped the center to prepare food in an easy way and ensured the sufficient supply of gas cylinders.

Volunteer Wing

The volunteer wing is one of the strongest parts of the CH Centre. Presently 160 volunteers are serving the needy people around the causalities, wards, and near the medical college in Calicut. These volunteers are well trained to handle to donate blood, medicine collection, and conduct medical camps. Their services are highly impressive under emergency situations. The volunteer wing holds meetings every month to evaluate its progress and correct its errors.

CH Medicals

A medical store is run to distribute free medicine to needy patients. In 2011 the Dubai KMCC spent 24 lakh on 17,000 patients to distribute medicine. It also operates Neethi stores to distribute medicines with 10–40% price reductions. Medical stores give medicines with a value of Rs 45,000–50,000 to patients per day.

Ambulance Service

CH Centre has three ambulances and it has been donated by Qatar and Saudi KMCC. The ambulance runs for needy patients at free of cost and for others at a low rate. The CH Centre ambulance service poses challenges to other ambulance services that are imposing high charges. In 2008–2009, 2009–2010, and 2010–2011, the ambulance service has benefited 1200 patients, 1650 patients, and 2500 patients, respectively.

The CH Centre is a product of socially committed and matured organization of the Indian Union Muslim League and its expatriate organization of KMCC. The main slogan of CH Centre is service to humanity. CH Centre acts as a shelter for needy patients and humanity. The activities of CH Centre resonate with the generous hands that are ready to help and serve humanity. This portion included the activities of CH Centre at Calicut medical college. And the activities of CH Centres in Trivandrum, Manjeri, Thaliparmbu, Thallasherry, Allapuzha, Kannur, Thrissur, Tirur, and Palakkad were not included due to lack of data.

Baithul-Rahma

Baithul-Rahma is an Arabic word which literally means "House of Mercy". It is a housing scheme initiated by the Indian Union Muslim League Malappuram District Committee and under the active support of its frontal expatriate organization, the KMCC. *Baithul-Rahma* projects are dedicated to Panakkad Sayyid Muhammad Ali Shihab Thangal, who was the former president of the Indian Union Muslim League Kerala State Committee. *Baithul-Rahma* provides housing for poor people.

In 2011, the Malappuram District committee of IUML planned to construct houses only once in each Panchayats of Malappuram District and not exceeding its cost above Rs 3.5 lakh. However, the positive responses of the public and supporters got the popularity for this project and decided to expand all over Kerala with an increasing amount of Rs 7–8 lakh per house.

The *Baithul-Rahma* project has built and donated 1340 houses[16] to families and another 129 are under construction, till September 2016. The fund mobilization was undertaken through the KMCC committees across the globe and almost 100 crores were spent on this project, till September 2016. The KMCC has built and donated 60 houses for the victims of the Muzaffarnagar riot in Uttar Prasdesh.

Conclusion

"Migration seems to be the single most dynamic factor in the otherwise dreary growth and unemployment scenario of Kerala in the last quarter of the last century".[17] Migration to the Persian Gulf countries led to a revival of the economy of Kerala as well as the political pulse of IUML through its expatriate organization, the KMCC. The KMCC is a deep-rooted and a well-organized expatriate foundation among the Malayalee community especially in the GCC countries and across the globe. The KMCC was formed by the far-sighted vision of IUML leaders to achieve the mission of honorable existence and political and social developments for the minorities of Kerala and India. Even though it is a frontal expatriate organization of a political party, namely, the IUML, its compassionate and philanthropic services attracted wide praise from everyone, particularly the Keralites.

The KMCC completed its four-decade-long journey and continues its dedicated services in social and political spheres. It was possible for the KMCC to achieve the distinction of becoming the largest expatriate organization owing to the large-scale migration of Muslims from the Malabar area to the Gulf countries. They uphold the value of minority identity politics even in the entirely different political and cultural milieu of West Asia. The sympathetic political supporters of the IUML opened new avenues of social support through the CH Mohammed Koya Charitable Centre and the innovative mission of *baithul rahma* (house for mercy). KMCC has functioned as the expatriate organization of the IUML carrying out the social mission of a political party successfully. It may be a rare phenomenon that a political party donates houses for the needy in memory of its leader and this kind of typical sociopolitical project may not be noticed anywhere else in the world.

In the UAE, the Dubai KMCC is a registered body under the community development Authority of Dubai as a social club and it also gives cause for pride to the Indian community as the sole Indian official invitee to attend the Dubai police parade on the UAE's national day.[18] The model of KMCC may be something worth emulating by other political parties in India and elsewhere because it is an inclusive model. The KMCC is initiating and taking efforts to solve expatriate issues and igniting the spirit of all round development of humanity as well.

The recent deluge in Kerala directly affected over a sixth of the state's total population and created a huge financial burden for rebuilding Kerala. The Malayalee diaspora has shown extraordinary support during the natural disaster and counted as an important support system from around the world. According to the Kerala Migration Survey (KMS) 2018, there are over 2.1 million Malayalee emigrants globally and 1.3 million return migrants.[19] One could say that the Malayalee diaspora has a moral responsibility to be part of the rebuilding efforts of Kerala after the devastating floods. The diaspora community swiftly acted on the demands of the state at the time of the disaster and supplied all necessity goods including pharmaceutical drugs to Kerala and the diaspora community; in particular, the KMCC are among the largest contributors to the Kerala Chief Minister Disaster Relief Fund (CMDRF).

The efforts and action of organized social networks of diasporic communities are evident in recent happenings in Kerala. We could conclude that the diasporic community is one of the greatest assets of Kerala in productive social capital creation as well.

Notes

1 International migration draft thematic paper 3 by Irudaya Rajan S and Zacharia KC. May 2018.
2 International Organization for Migration (IOM), *World Migration Report 2020* (Geneva: IOM, 2019) 3.
3 World Bank, "Migration and Remittances Recent Developments and Outlook", *Migration and Development Brief* 31 (April 2019) 6.
4 Irudaya Rajan S, 2018, Diaspora and Disaster, The Hindu October 9.
5 International migration draft thematic paper 3 by Irudaya Rajan S and Zacharia KC. May 2018.
6 Robert Putnam; Bowling alone. The collapse and revival of American Community, Simon & Schuster, New York, 2000.
7 Ibid.
8 Martti Siisianen, Two concepts of social capital: Bourdieu vs Putnam, paper presented at the ISTR fourth International Conference on The Third sector: For What and Whom?, July 3–8, 2000, Trinity College Dublin, Ireland.
9 www.iuml.com
10 Ilias M H, 2015, Trans local Kerala politics in the Gulf, Anthony Gorman and Sossie Kasbarian (ed), Edinburgh, Edinburgh University Publisher, pp. 303–337,
11 The *Societies Registration Act, 1860* is a legislation in India which allows the registration of entities generally involved in the benefit of society.
12 To regulate the acceptance and utilization of foreign contribution or foreign hospitality by certain individuals or associations or companies and to prohibit acceptance and utilization of foreign contribution or foreign hospitality for any activities detrimental to the national interest and for matters connected therewith or incidental thereto
13 CH Centre Calicut report 2014.
14 Ibid.
15 Ibid.
16 Islamic voice September 15, 2016 /http://islamicvoice.com/baithu-rahama projects
17 Irudaya Rajan S and Zachariah K, Kerala Gulf connections 1998–2011, Economic and Social Impact Of Migration , Orient Blackswan pvt Ltd , 2013.
18 National Day (Arabic: اليوم الوطني *;Al Yawm Al Watani")* is celebrated on 2 December each year in the United Arab Emirates.
19 Irudaya Rajan S, 2018, Diaspora and Disaster, The Hindu October 9 from Newspaper.

Part II

Economic Implications of Gulf Migration

6 India–GCC Countries Connection

Trends, Prospective, and Opportunities

Bhupesh Gopal Chintamani

Introduction

India and the Middle East have good ties that are visible for progressive development all around the world. In 2018, India received more than half the percentage of remittance alone from the Gulf Cooperation Council (GCC) region (RBI, 2018). Recently a newly launched Pre-departure Training Program (PDO) reported that it saw 50000 emigrants in India by the Ministry of External Affairs (MEA). In the year 2021, India repatriated its four million emigrants from 101 countries whose employment and income were badly impacted due to the Covid-19 conditional lockdown carried by such countries. In the top five, most of the repatriation was rolled out by the GCC countries, namely the United Arab Emirates (UAE), Saudi Arabia, Qatar, and Oman, in the list of the Vande Bharat Mission (MEA, 2021). This record addressed the issue of the Indian labor force participation in the GCC countries including blue-collar and white-collar workers, their issues of rehabilitation, and the resettlement of return migrants. Today, MEA expects that it is going to train 5 lakh Indians under the PDO schemes in the year 2022. Nowadays, GCC countries are the most common countries for Indians to migrate to as per the emigration data recorded by the MEA.

This chapter is an attempt to analyze the role of the GCC in the Indian economy, both from the perspective of emigration and remittances, in a detailed manner. From the perspective of emigration, MEA data is used to strengthen the historical incidence between the India–GCC connections in terms of future opportunities. Therefore, the present chapter has been organized into four different sections in association with the research objectives assigned for the study. The second section examines the India–GCC connection and present situation from the literature. The third section deals with the methodological adaptation of the study. The fourth section scrutinizes the trends and prospective of Indian migrant connections with the GCC countries. Finally, the fifth section provides a conclusion of the chapter.

DOI: 10.4324/9781003369370-9

Indian Emigrants

India is the world's largest exporter of labor as well as the top recipient of remittances. Since the "oil boom" of the 1970s, Indian migration to the Gulf has acted as a major source of revenue for the country as well as the backbone of the economies of high-migration states such as Kerala through remittance transfers. During this period, Indian migrant laborers have made significant contributions to the Gulf states' economic progress. The India-Gulf area is the world's second-largest migratory corridor. An estimated 8.5 million of the roughly 31 million non-resident Indians (NRIs) work in the Gulf. Indians account for more than 30% of the expatriate workforce in the Gulf states, where the proportion of non-nationals in the labor force is among the highest in the world. According to data from the Protectorate General of Emigrants (PoE), Uttar Pradesh (UP) and Bihar are currently sending more migrant laborers overseas, primarily to the Gulf nations, than Kerala and Tamil Nadu, reversing trends seen in previous decades. According to the PoE, the top desired destinations for these migrants are Saudi Arabia, the United Arab Emirates (UAE), and Kuwait, even though job opportunities have been reduced in recent years due to a drop in oil prices. Contrary to popular belief, statistics reveal that Kerala and other southern states are no longer mainly looking for Gulf employment nor looking for blue-collar workers. Kerala and Tamil Nadu have been surpassed by UP and Bihar. You can see the figures: 30% of our immigrants leave UP, 15% leave Bihar, Tamil Nadu, and West Bengal, while Kerala accounts for just 6%.

Emigration has improved and played a major role in household spending and non-spending choices (Chintamani, 2017; Guha, 2014; Sasikumar and Hussain, 2007; Sil, 2011, etc.). The economic impact of remittances on the overall wellbeing of Kerala has driven the study to inquire about the position of other states in the country in terms of emigration and remittances today (RBI, 2018). According to Taylor (1999), the choice of emigration might be a decision taken by the individual members, but other household features like the number of members in the household, socio-economic conditions also play an essential role in the decision-making of the out-migrants. Extensive studies have been undertaken to understand the impact of remittances for the states of Kerala, Punjab, Goa, Gujarat, Andhra Pradesh, and Bihar by (Zachariah et al., 2002a; 2002b; Zachariah et al., 2003; Sasikumar and Hussain, 2007; Kapuria, 2018; Kaur, 2018; Parida et al., 2015; Guha, 2014; Mohanty et al., 2014; Dey, 2015; Rajan et al., 2015; Chintamani, 2017).

Methodology

The present study is purely based on secondary data tools which have used emigration data through the e-migrant portal for study purposes. The Emigration Check Required (ECR) countries-migrant data is available only for the period year 2007 to the year 2020. An analysis of the study also utilized the Reserve Bank of India (RBI) data set on remittance to compare the remittance and ECR-migrant relationship. In addition, the use of ECR-migrant data and remittances data (RBI), and their detailed relation, is also connected to underline the trends and prospective of India in the GCC countries. The uniqueness of the present study is that it deals with emigration data to show India's connection to the GCC countries because state-wise remittance data is not available for India, which is a major limitation of the emigration studies.

Result and Discussion

This section has been divided into three sub-sections that discuss the state-wise Indian migrant in the Gulf, to ten emigrant states with destination and finally to five emigrant states with the respective years.

Indian Immigrants in the Gulf

Most of the Indian immigrants in the Middle East are low-skilled, semi-skilled, and unskilled migrant workers who come under the ECR categories of an emigrant. Today, the overall state-wise distribution of Indian laborers in the Middle East countries reveals that Uttar Pradesh and Bihar are the leading states for emigration from India to the Gulf Cooperation Council (GCC) countries. This trend also persists in the idea that the less developed states of India are more inclined towards migration at a domestic as well as international level to protect their families. Further, the fruitful policy dialog and trade partnership between the foreign investor (companies) by such a state division also increase domestic workers' participation in cross-border migration.

Figure 6.1 indicates the top ten states' representation from India whose domestic workers immigrated to the Middle East in search of employment. These GCC countries gathered a huge number of laborers from all over the world and most of them are from developing countries like India, Pakistan, Nepal, Bangladesh, Bhutan, the Philippines, etc. But in terms of the absolute and relative number of workforce participation, India ranks number one for GCC countries. India provides a large number and mixed nature labor force to the Gulf including unskilled, semi-skilled, and skilled workers in total. Historically, Kerala witnessed close association with Middle East countries in terms of generating employment for the states for centuries (Prakash, 1998; Rajan and Zachariah, 2010, 2019). The 21st century portrays a different picture for the Indian states where the states of Uttar Pradesh and Bihar showed the maximum amount of employee participation in the Middle East. In the case of Kerala, it is a time of demographic saturation that records a decline in their share portion in the immigration to the Middle East but it still holds close to 25 lakh migrants from the state to the GCC alone. However, previous literature suggests that there are numerous reasons for the new states to progress in the process of international migration from India to the

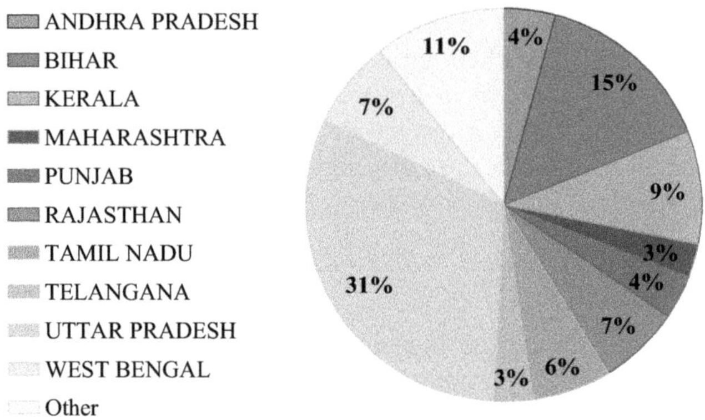

Figure 6.1 State-wise Indian immigrants in the GCC countries (2020) Source: Author's calculation using Ministry of External Affairs (MEA) data

Gulf. On the other hand, the upcoming states of Uttar Pradesh and Bihar indicate rising share portions in immigration to the Middle East. The reason is aligned with poverty, inequality, rising unemployment and underemployment, and the financial needs of the households across the states in the country (Adams,2004, Adam and Page, 2003 and 2004; Jadhav, 2003; Gupta, 2006; Zachariah and Rajan, 2007; Dey, 2015). In addition, the cost of living has increased everywhere but none of them suggest improvement in the income basket for the individuals within society which might have enhanced international migration for the recessive states for India.

Top Ten Emigrant States with Destination

Figure 6.2 suggests that Saudi Arabia is the most preferable destination among all the GCC countries. It is surprising to know that the individual state's scenario identified that a top-ranking state of Uttar Pradesh, Bihar, and West Bengal are following the destination trend of Kerala.[1] However, Uttar Pradesh and Bihar state exposed a large portion of total international migrants. Furthermore, the state of Andhra Pradesh mostly preferred to migrate to Kuwait followed by United Arab Emirates and Saudi Arabia, in the case, of Punjab, the United Arab Emirates (UAE) is the most preferred destination which is entirely different as compared to other states. Here, the reason could be that Punjabi holds the better amount of labor positions in the UAE and has a strong social network for migration to that destination. Thus, it is more practical as per the literature about how the Punjabi diaspora are committed and head towards their social network channel of migration. Therefore, it can be said that in the future the Punjabi migrant might grasp a strong position in the destination of the UAE within the Middle East.

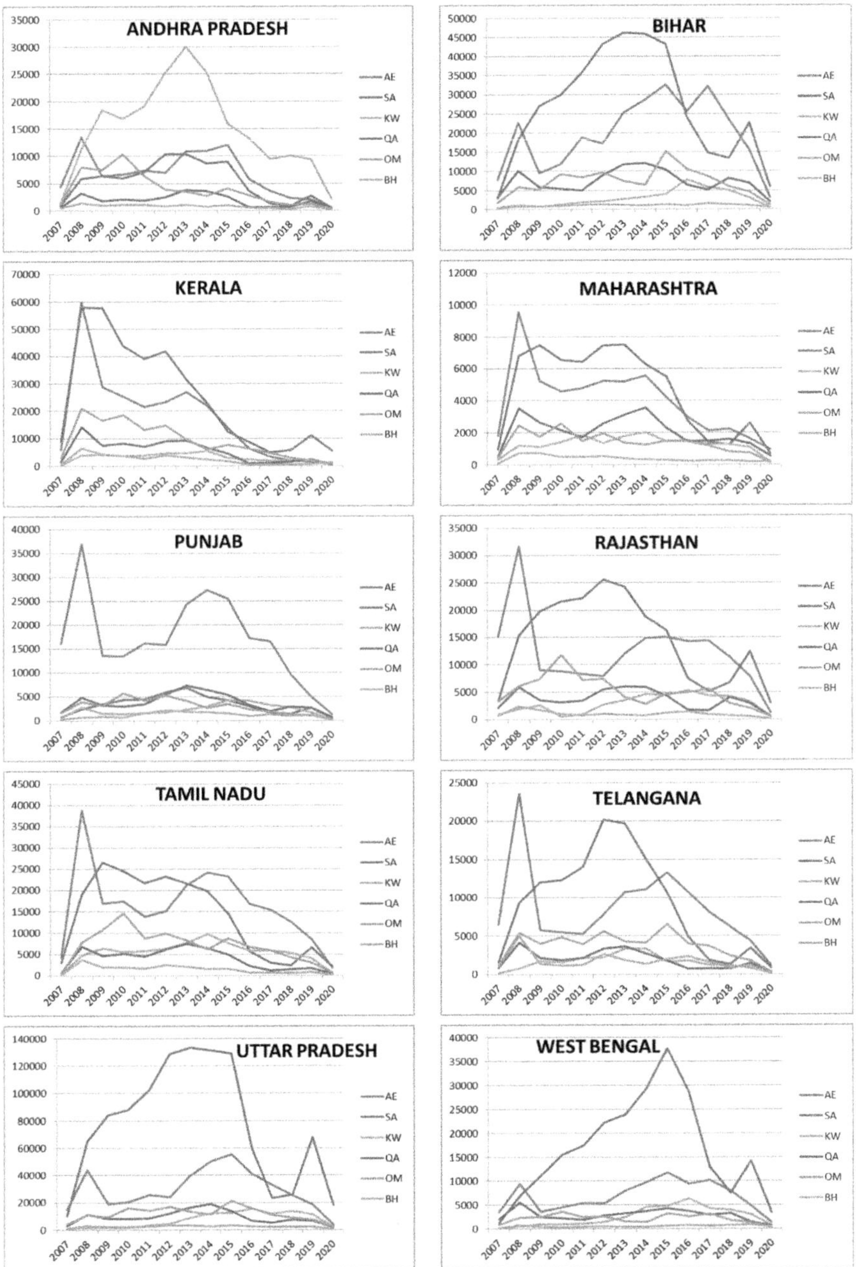

Figure 6.2 Top ten labor-sending states destination-wise representation Source: Author's calculation using Ministry of External Affairs (MEA) data

According to a review of the literature, the weak social-economic condition leads individuals to migrate from their household in search of a job to satisfy the basic needs of the family. In the case of international migrants for lower-skilled work in the Gulf region, we can observe a forceful or economic pull-factor for the migrants from all of the world. At the regional level rise of economic disparities unsatisfied the wants of the people that have pushed s lower-skilled workers in the Gulf nations to work. Eventually, this led individuals to move from their origin country and settle in various parts of the GCC corridors. The same has been witnessed from the top ten migrated states for the GCC countries (Nayyar 1994 and 2002).

The migrants settled down to such popular locations where they are bound to have social connections that highly enrich the number of migrants in such destinations. In many cases, it is an influential factor for being in the specific location for origin to destination county migrant. Thus, the estimated results of the emigration trend suggest that in the initial stage of migration there is diversification in the state-wise destination of migration, but the UAE and Saudi are the most preferred destinations followed by Oman and Kuwait overall. Bahrain is the least preferred destination of international migration from India for the top ten emigrant states. The analysis concludes that Uttar Pradesh and Bihar might follow an exact pattern of the level of migration of Kerala due to these states not only having similarities in the pattern but also having close with a range of ECR migrants. Another reason would be this Uttar Pradesh and Bihar are already facing economic and social challenges. Interestingly, in the case of the top 50 districts of ECR-migrant profile, Uttar Pradesh has a significant number – 21 districts – whereas seven districts of Bihar are ranked in the top 50 districts. Moreover, they have large migrant individuals into the county in a channel of internal migration, hence the substantial shift from domestic migrant to the international destination might attract in terms of economic payoff that suggest conducting state policy dialog (action plan) for the international migrant of Uttar Pradesh and Bihar.

The state of Maharashtra is at least level in terms of digits of the migrant in the total of ECR migrants. Of those who reside there, there might be a large number of migrants who do not require ECR status of migration because of their educational status. Most of the ECR migrants from the state of Maharashtra are from the Konkan region and districts of Ratnagiri and Sindhudurg (Tumbe, 2012). Telangana states also include the lower range of ECR migrants in the southern states of the country. From the state, Figure 1 also shows that Rajasthan, Telangana, represent mixed results for destinations, which means the migrants do not consistently following the same destination and it might be because these migrants are poor in terms of social-networking when emigrating.

Most important to know from Figure 2, that the years 2015–2016 onwards the trends of the Indian migrant from to the Gulf for all respective states has been a decline. The reason for this is that some Middle East countries are oil-producing, hence, there is a close connection not only between remittances and oil prices but there is also a positive correlation between oil prices per barrel and ECR outflow from India within such countries. Hence, we can see a decline of ECR migrants in Figure 2 due to lower Brent crude oil prices per barrel as compared to earlier years.[2] On the one hand, when oil prices per barrel are rising the emigrant (ECR) is seen to be inclined with the persistent oil prices per barrel. On the other hand, when oil prices per barrel are in decline the emigrant (ECR) flow also lowers, which possesses a positive association. This indicates whenever oil prices per barrel sharpen increases money income to the Gulf emigrants and that increases savings and remitter transfers to India.

Also, an increase of Brent crude oil prices per barrel increase oil import bill prices in the country but these remittances are helpful to rectify the trade balances which are due to the change in oil import prices. The slower piece of growth in the inflow recorded in 2018 is due to mandatory emigration clearances sought by Indian migrants (RBI, 2019).[3] Workers' remittances from abroad have worn to the global growth slowdown and continue supporting the balance of payments. Hence, it is expected after the economic situation returns to the normal level the number of ECR migrants from India to the GCC will increase, where Uttar Pradesh and Bihar are projected to rank in the top five for migration. Furthermore, both states may come under the top five remittance receiving states from the current rank of 7 and 13 of states recipient of remittances.[4]

Top Five Emigrant States with Years

Figure 6.3 specifies that the top five labor-sending states of India were Uttar Pradesh and Bihar, which recorded a substantial rise in the absolute outflow of emigrants from the states in total. On the other side, Kerala and Tamil Nadu recorded a substantial decline in their share of workers' outflow from the states to the GCC countries.

An absolute number of out-migrants data gives a detailed impression of the fluctuation that happens in the process of emigration and receiving remittances. These changing directions also show us the altered ranking for the states in the inward remittances positioning (RBI, 2018). It also revealed that during the years 2015 to 2018 the trends for out-migrant declined due to the decrease in the international oil price along with the weak economic situation in the world (WEF, 2018).

India and GCC Connections

India-Gulf Cooperation Council (GCC) countries constitute a strong and sizable amount of migration and remittances corridor in the world. A significant number of Indian migrants which is close to 31 percent out of the total Indian migrant in the world belongs to GCC countries (UNDESA, 2019) and that are mainly structured under the skilled, semi-skilled, and low-skilled occupation categories. In fact, these migrant workers reported too much sensory input in terms of the inward remittance to India. It is important to underline that the migrant workers help their origin households to protect the subsistence

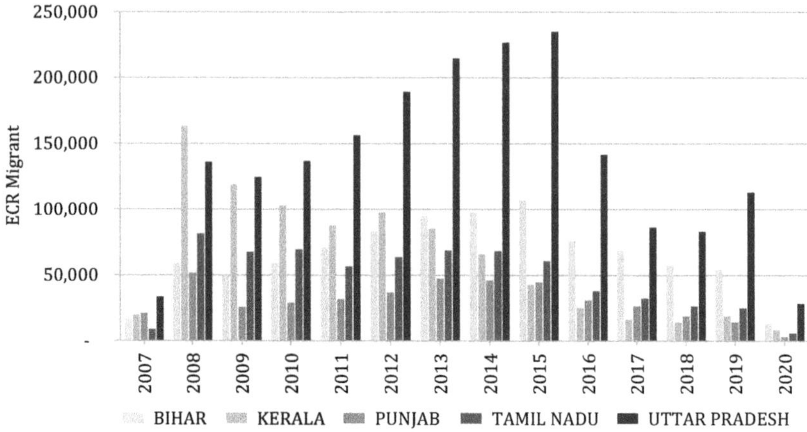

Figure 6.3 Top five labor-sending Indian states in the GCC countries (2020) Source: Author's calculation using Ministry of External Affairs (MEA) data

level of their households through a sharp rise in remittances which has been witnessed by India through inward remittance from GCC. On one side, it is surprising to notice that there is a change in the remittance ranking for the states. Maharashtra ranked first in receipt of remittances followed by Kerala, Tamil Nadu, Karnataka, etc., and revealed that no more Kerala became the number one. Also, the state of Uttar Pradesh and Bihar ranked seventh and twelfth in recent years (RBI, 2022) and it is all because Uttar Pradesh and Bihar had considerably sharpened their participation in emigration clearance to the Gulf (MEA).[5] Overall, Gulf Cooperation Council (GCC) countries steadily increased their share percentage in remittance from 24 percent during 2006-07 to more than 50 percent in 2016-17 for India and are depicted as the most important source of expatriate income to India (RBI, 2018). It is important to highlight here that covid-19 pandemic has devastated the India-GCC connection and observed that inward remittance has fallen up to 29 percent from 50 percent (in 2016-2017) from GCC to Gulf. It is understood that the unprecedented pandemic has badly impacted the outlook of India-GCC remittances and it will be back to its normal condition after a few years.

Conclusion

This chapter argued there is a structural shift of the Indian states in the ECR profile, like the role of Kerala in the India–GCC connection, not a new phenomenon; Uttar Pradesh and Bihar are soon to be leading states both in terms of ECR migration and inward remittances in the country from the GCC. Interestingly, in the case of the top 50 districts of ECR-migrant profiles, Uttar Pradesh includes a significant number – 21 districts – whereas seven districts of Bihar are ranked in the ranking. The analysis shows strongly that very soon Uttar Pradesh and Bihar will rank fourth and fifth in terms of inward remittances. The overall findings suggest that the GCC countries employ Indians overseas and attach close ties with the investment in India such as Saudi Arabia's investment in the Ratnagiri Refinery and Petrochemical Project. Therefore, understanding future opportunities for India in the GCC countries are more prominent in the coming years as addressed above.

Notes

1 For more details, check Annexure Table 6.A1.
2 ECR migrant data is used because overseas Indian including NRIs and PIOs total are not available under official records on regular annual basis at the MOIA department. Overseas Indian data is available only for a few years.
3 Reserve Bank of India (RBI), Annual Report 2018–2019, pp. 90.
4 Reserve Bank of India Bulletin November 2018.
5 E-migrant Portal https://emigrate.gov.in/

References

Adams Jr, R. H. (2004). *Remittances and Poverty in Guatemala*. Available at SSRN 625295.
Adams, R. H., & Page, J. (2003). *International Migration, Remittances, and Poverty in Developing Countries* (Vol. 3179). World Bank Publications.
Adams, R. H., & Page, J. (2005). Do International migration and remittances reduce poverty in development countries? *World Development*, *33*(10), 1645–1669.
Chintamani, B.G. (2017). *A Study on Remittances and Development Outcomes Evidence from India*. Global Research Forum on Diaspora and Transnationalism (GRFDT), *3*(9), 32.
Dey, S. (2015). Impact of remittances on poverty at origin: A study on rural households in India using covariate balancing propensity score matching. *Migration and Development*, 4(2), 185–199.
Gupta, P. (2006). Macroeconomic determinants of remittances: Evidence from India. *Economic and Political Weekly*, 2769–2775.
Guha, P. (2014). Migrants' Private Giving and Development in Central Gujarat, India. In: Rahman, M.M., Yong, T.T., Ullah, A.K.M.A. (eds) Migrant Remittances in South Asia. International Political Economy Series. Palgrave Macmillan, London. https://doi.org/10.1057/9781137350800_12.
Jadhav, N. (2003, October). Maximising developmental benefits of migrant remittances: The Indian experience. In Joint Conference of DFID-World Bank, London.
Kapuria, S. (2018). International migration from Punjab and challenges for governance. *Punjab University Research Journal of Art*, *XLV*(1), 1–19.
Kaur, A. P. (2018). International migration and impact of remittances on left behind wives: A case study of the doaba region of Punjab. In *Migration, Gender and Care Economy* (pp. 103–123). Routledge, India.

MEA (2021). Ministery of External Affairs (MEA) A State-wise list (as on 22 March 2021) of return migrant arrivals in India, Unstarred Question No. 4709, Lok Sabha, 23 March 2021 chrome-extension://efaidnbmnnnibpcajpcglclefindmkaj/http://164.100.24.220/loksabhaquestions/annex/175/AU4709.pdf

Mohanty, S. K., Dubey, M., &Parida, J. K. (2014). Economic well-being and spending ehavior of households in India: Does remittances matter?. *Migration and Development*, *3*(1), 38–53.

Nayyar, D. (1994). *Migration, Remittances and Capital Flows*. Delhi: Oxford University Press.

Nayyar (2002). Cross border movements of People. UNU World Institute for Development Economics Research (UNU/WIDER), Working Paper No. 194, August 2000 chrome-extension://efaidnbmnnnibpcajpcglclefindmkaj/https://www.wider.unu.edu/sites/default/files/wp194.pdf.

Parida, J. K., Mohanty, S. K., & Raman, K. R. (2015). Remittances, Household Expenditure, and Investment in Rural India: Evidence from NSS data. *Indian Economic Review*, 79–104

Prakash, B. A. (1998). Gulf migration and its economic impact: The Kerala experience. *Economic and Political Weekly*, 3209–3213.

Rajan, S. I., & Zachariah, K.C. (2010). Remittances to Kerala: Impact on the economy. Middle East Institute. https://www.mei.edu/publications/remittances-kerala-impact-economy Published February 2, 2010. Accessed December 7, 2017.

Rajan, S. I., & Zachariah, K. C. (2019). *Emigration and Remittances: New Evidences from the Kerala Migration Survey, 2018*. Center for Development Studies Working Paper No. 483.

Rajan, S.I., D' Sami, B., & Samuel Asir Raj, S (2015). *Tamil Nadu Migration Survey 2015*. Center for Development Studies Working Paper No. 472.

Reserve Bank of India (RBI). (2018). *Globalizing People: India's Inward Remittances*. RBI bulletin. Retrieved from https://rbidocs.rbi.org.in/rdocs/Bulletin/PDFs/1AR_14112018071B947 4B5D74DDC91FC8AA015C5A360.PDF

Sasikumar, S. K., & Hussain, Z. (2007). *Migration, Remittances, and Development: Lessons from India*. New Delhi: VV Giri National Labour Institute.

Sil, M. (2011). *International Remittances and Its Impact on Households and Village Development: A Comparative Study of Gujarat and Kerala States, India*.PhD Thesis,Tata Institute of Social Sciences (TISS), http://hdl.handle.net/10603/2718

Taylor, E. J. (1999). The new economics of labour migration and the role of remittances in the migration process. *International Migration*, *37*(1), 63–88.

Tumbe, C. (2012). Migration persistence across twentieth century India. *Migration and Development*, 1(1), 87–112.

WEF (2018, November). The global competitiveness report 2018. In World Economic Forum (Vol. 671).

Zachariah, K. C., & Irudaya Rajan, S. (2007) *Migration, Remittances and Employment: Short-term Trends and Long term Implications*. Centre for Development Studies Working Paper No. 395.

Zachariah, K. C., Prakash, B. A., & Irudaya Rajan, S. (2002a). *Gulf Migration Study: Employment, Wages and Working Conditions of Kerala Emigrants in the United Arab Emirates*. Center for Development Studies Working Paper No. 326.

Zachariah, K. C., Prakash, B. A, & Irudaya Rajan, S. (2002b). Working in Gulf: Employment, wages and working conditions. In K C Zachariah, K P Kannan and S Irudaya Rajan (eds). *Kerala's Gulf Connection: CDS Studies on International Labour Migration from Kerala State in India*. Thiruvananthapuram, Kerala: Centre for Development Studies.

Annexure 1

Table 6.A1 Top ten labor-sending states of India

State / year	*Andhra Pradesh*	*Bihar*	*Kerala*	*Maharashtra*	*Punjab*	*Rajasthan*	*Tamil Nadu*	*Telangana*	*Uttar Pradesh*	*West Bengal*
2007	9,388	16,198	19,706	4,216	21,011	25,487	8,777	11,326	33,370	7,630
2008	43,227	58,797	1,63,197	24,252	51,502	63,436	81,181	48,251	1,35,767	25,176
2009	41,592	49,370	1,18,777	18,900	25,647	43,954	67,335	27,055	1,24,341	20,710
2010	43,131	58,746	1,02,886	17,729	28,599	46,844	69,229	27,314	1,36,542	26,938
2011	43,052	70,932	87,404	16,721	31,537	42,745	56,237	28,880	1,56,023	28,474
2012	49,782	82,759	97,244	19,059	36,547	49,935	63,292	41,917	1,89,002	34,670
2013	59,789	94,609	84,970	19,383	46,977	50,617	68,407	43,629	2,14,712	39,419
2014	52,121	97,359	65,475	18,976	45,974	47,767	68,074	37,724	2,26,798	49,048
2015	44,644	1,06,719	42,755	15,217	44,381	45,925	60,455	36,096	2,34,958	62,343
2016	26,574	75,480	24,962	10,363	30,762	35,029	37,752	24,654	1,41,482	51,247
2017	17,138	68,322	16,337	7,687	26,449	31,914	32,083	17,240	86,173	33,955
2018	15,103	57,256	14,292	7,339	18,929	29,776	26,490	12,765	82,902	24,885
2019	17,697	53,573	19,070	7,543	14,012	28,830	24,785	13,023	1,12,849	25,539
2020	3,797	13,301	8,464	2,532	3,220	6,049	5,829	2,920	28,249	6,532

7 Gulf Migration, Remittances, and Development

The Indian Experience

Waseem Ahmad and Anisur Rahman

Introduction

India's commercial relations with the Arab world are historic. Energy and labor have been the two main drivers of India's economic connections with the Gulf Cooperation Council for the past four decades (GCC). India has been significantly reliant on regional energy supplies, and Indian expatriates have made up a sizable, if not dominant, portion of the regional labor market (Pant, 2017). There has been a symbiotic relationship, which has the scope to diversify and be even more productive. Diaspora communities have long been engaging in the development of their homelands. An AHCL report notes that the diaspora has a purchasing power estimated at around USD 300 billion. There is a greater need to reorganize Indian communities and civil societies living in the Gulf to actively participate in government initiatives, for which we should also frame effective work policies to counter the problems of Indian migrants to the Gulf. The Diaspora adopts various means to influence the governments of their homeland and host countries, the media, international state and non-state organizations, and their political allies. These include political lobbying, mass media campaigns, fund-raising demonstrations, the use of modern communication technology and participation in the elections. The labor migration from India to GCC can be traced back to the early oil discovery and exploration days. As soon as opportunities to earn better arose, Indians were the first among the groups of emigrants to flock to the Gulf countries and they were well placed to meet the growing demands. Thus, the migration of the Indian workforce to the Gulf region offers opportunities for providing gainful employment to the underemployed.

Changing Patterns and Trends of Migration

Every year a large number of Indians emigrate in pursuit of a better life. During the mid-1970s, the oil boom in West Asia, especially the Gulf countries, vastly changed the complexion of emigration. The steep hike in oil prices during 1973–1974 and thereafter led to a considerable increase in

DOI: 10.4324/9781003369370-10

Table 7.1 Labor-sending Indian states (top ten) during 2010–2017

State	*2010*	*2011*	*2012*	*2013*	*2014*	*2015*	*2016*	*2017*
Andhra Pradesh	43,131	43,052	49,782	59,789	52,121	44,644	26,574	11,138
Uttar Pradesh	13,6542	1,56,023	1,89,002	2,14,712	2,26,798	2,34,958	1,41,482	86,173
Kerala	1,02,886	87,404	97,244	84,970	65,475	42,755	24,962	16,337
Bihar	58,746	70,932	82,759	94,609	97,359	10,6719	75,480	68,295
Punjab	28,599	31,537	36,547	46,977	45,079	44,381	30,762	26,449
Rajasthan	46,844	42,745	49,935	50,617	47,767	45,925	35,029	31,914
West Bengal	26,938	28,474	34,670	39,419	49,048	62,343	51,247	33,955
Gujarat	8091	8403	6871	8418	7743	6795	4496	4194
Maharashtra	17,729	16,721	19,059	19,383	18,976	15,217	10,363	7687
Karnataka	16,955	15,582	17,819	17,670	14,953	11,867	6423	5144
Total	4,86,461	5,00,873	5,83,688	6,36,564	6,25,319	6,15,604	4,06,818	2,91,286

Source: Anisur Rahman and Naziya Naweed, Recent Trends in Indo-Gulf Relations, in India's *Foreign Policy Modi 2.0: Challenges and Opportunities*, ed. Sudhir Singh (New Delhi: Pentagon Press LLP, 2020).

the revenue of the oil-producing and exporting countries in West Asia. Initially, migration from India was dominated by Kerala, which sent 50% of the migrants. But now the situation has changed considerably. Today migration from other Indian states such as Uttar Pradesh, Bihar, Rajasthan, etc., has taken the lead as per the latest data available (Annual Report, Ministry of External Affairs, GOI). Within the GCC countries, the Kingdom of Saudi Arabia and the United Arab Emirates (UAE) are the major destinations of Indians that together accounted for more than 60 percent of the total deployment of Indian migrant workers in the region. It is interesting to note that development programs such as construction of roads, creation of amenities like schools, hospitals, houses, airports, office and commercial complexes, etc. were taken up in a big way in this region. This in fact led to create demands for not only highly skilled technical experts but also semi-skilled and unskilled workers. India was well placed to meet these emerging demands.[1]

It is noted that the labor outflow sustained for white-collar workers as well as for the high-skilled workers and registered an increase among unskilled workers in non-construction activities, so that the share of each of these categories in total out-migration rose. A large proportion of the out-migration was of workers employed in the service sector, so much so that the proportion employed in the manufacturing sector was small while that in the agricultural sector was negligible. Since emigration to the West Asian countries is temporary, it would appear to provide an example of international trade in services.[2] Today, the profile of demand for workforce has changed. There is now less need for unskilled and semi-skilled professionals and more for skilled and highly qualified professionals. India has prepared accordingly. There is no dearth of an eligible workforce in India (Kumar, 2014). The latest estimate by MOIA (full form) says there are about 30

Table 7.2 Composition of Indian workers in the Gulf countries 1991–2017

Countries	*1991*	*1999*	*2004*	*2008*	*2012*	*2017*
Bahrain	100,000	150,000	100,000	233,955	350,000	316,175
Kuwait	88,000	200,000	450,000	511,161	579,390	919,354
Oman	220,000	450,000	450,000	432,000	718,642	783,959
Qatar	75,000	100,000	100,000	239,000	500,000	697,500
Saudi Arabia	600,000	1,200,000	1,500,000	1,350,652	1,789,000	3,255,864
UAE	400,000	750,000	1,000,000	1,411,000	1,750,000	2,803,751
Others	22,000	150,000	NA	NA	NA	NA
Total	1,505,000	8,764,829	3,600,000	4,177,768	5,687,032	8,776,603

Source: Anisur Rahman Indian Labour Diaspora in the Gulf: An Overview in Indian Trade Diaspora in the Arabian Peninsula by Prakash C. Jain and Kundan Kumar, New Academic Publishers, New Delhi 2012, P 330; Annual Report Ministry of External Affairs https://www.mea.gov.in/Images/attach/lu6091.pdf. Ministry of Overseas Indian Affairs, Indians Abroad; https://pib.gov.in/newsite/PrintRelease.aspx?relid=116414.

million Indian emigrants in 130 countries.[3] Of these, almost six million are engaged in diverse jobs in these six GCC countries.[4]

Significance of Indian Workers to the Gulf

Indian communities constitute about one-third of the total expatriate population and about 12 percent of the total GCC population. The largest number of Indians lives in Saudi Arabia, followed by the UAE, Oman, and Kuwait. The Indian workers are preferred by Gulf States due to their sincerity and hard work. It is evident that they contribute in every sector of the Gulf economy.

Inflow of Remittances to India and Their Benefits

India receives more remittances from abroad than any other country. There are more than 31 million people in the Indian Diaspora spread all over the world (latest data, MEA, GOI). A total of 110 countries were identified where a significant number of Indians were living or working. Similarly, many countries such as China, Pakistan, Bangladesh, Sri Lanka, etc. have realized the significance of their diasporas. All these countries have their own policy for them. A diaspora contributes both to their host country and to their home country, primarily through the transfer of money they earn back to their home country, which is known as "remittance". The funds are used for developmental activities in these countries. In many developing countries, remittances are used for eradicating poverty and generating employment. These remittances are considered more stable than foreign direct investment (FDI). Remittances are rising at the global and national levels every year.

An important aspect of Indian labor migration to the Gulf has been its lion's share in the remittances sent home to India by the Indian Diaspora. Remittances were virtually negligible in the 1970s but rose to $2.8 billion in the 1980s. Since 2003, India has been the world's largest recipient, at least in absolute terms, of remittances, defined as the inflow of private transfers.

Table 7.3 Composition of the Indian Diaspora in the Gulf, 2017

Country	*No. of NRIs*	*PIOs*	*Indian Diaspora*
Saudi Arabia	3,253,901	1963	3,255,864
UAE	2,800,000	3751	2,803,751
Kuwait	917,970	1384	919,354
Oman	783,040	919	783,959
Bahrain	312,918	3257	316,175
Qatar	697,000	500	697,500
GCC	8,764,829	11,774	8,776,603

Source: Population of Overseas Indians (compiled in December 2017). https://www.mea.gov.in/images/pdf/NRIs-and-PIOs.pdf.

It is interesting to know that half of the remittances came from the Gulf alone.

The labor diaspora from India not only helps reduce unemployment but also earns foreign exchange. Remittances began in the mid-1970s. Initially, a large proportion of remittances came from developed countries, but these were gradually overtaken by those coming from the Gulf region.

In the middle of 1991, India faced a serious balance of payments crisis. Foreign exchange reserves had fallen to a level hardly adequate to meet essential imports for even a few weeks. The Indian migrants in the developed countries rapidly withdrew their dollar deposits from Indian banks. This warranted immediate action from India to avoid defaulting on its international obligations or a collapse of its economy for want of critical imports. The situation was averted for India by the slowly but gradually increasing remittances from Indian laborers in the Gulf (Kumar, 2014). Today India is at the top of the list of countries receiving remittances from its migrants abroad – close to ten percent of the worldwide remittances sent home by 258 million in 2017.[5]

India's Emigration Policy

According to the 1983 Emigration Act, one of the most important conditions for obtaining emigration clearance is the agreement/employment contract holding detailed terms and conditions of employment including wages. It must be signed by the foreign employer and the intending emigrant and produced before the competent authority in India for emigration clearance. In such cases the number of complaints on underpayment of wages or forcing the emigrants to renegotiate lower wages by foreign employers is low. Such emigration bypasses legal requirements like a valid visa and valid employment contract holding a Minimum Referral Wage (MRW) to be signed by the foreign employer and the intending emigrant before appearing for emigration clearance by the competent authority in India. As and when such complaints are received from emigrants, stringent action is initiated against the registered recruiting agents by way of suspension and cancellation of their license including forfeiture of their bank guarantee. Action is also initiated against unregistered agents, immediately on receipt of complaint, by referring such cases to the respective state governments or police authorities for investigation under Sections 10 and 24 of the Emigration Act 1983 and prosecution sanction is granted on priority under Section 27 of the Emigration Act 1983 on receipt of such request from state police authorities.

To ensure protection and welfare of our emigrants, India has incorporated better terms and conditions of employment in memoranda of understanding (MoUs) on employment of workers with the major labor-receiving countries – the five Gulf countries including Qatar, the UAE, Kuwait, Oman, and Bahrain. India has also signed an agreement on domestic sector workers with

Saudi Arabia. Under the above MoUs, periodical joint working group (JWG) meetings are held to sort out the issues of Indian workers in Gulf countries.

However, there is no statutory system of minimum wages in the labor market of most of the Gulf countries. It is regulated by the market conditions and depends on the agreement between the foreign employers and the emigrant. On the advice of the ministry, the Indian missions in the ECR countries including Gulf countries have put in place a system of minimum referral wages (MRWs) for all categories of workers by taking into account working conditions, cost of living, inflation, local employment market conditions, etc. in the host countries. Employment contracts are based on such MRWs or higher wages. The ministry also asks Indian missions to revise the MRW if or whenever required and such MRWs are published by the Indian missions every year.

After the 1990–1991 Gulf war the number of low-skilled workers in the Gulf declined due to the Indian government's tight monitoring of the ECR passports. However, the flow soon resumed to pre-Gulf war levels. This facilitated the proliferation of recruitment and placement agencies, sometimes colluding with prospective employers to prey upon and dupe illiterate job seekers.[6] Notwithstanding the recent initiative, the Indian government still does not have in place a comprehensive policy on labor migration or overseas employment on neither skilled migration to the west nor unskilled migration the Gulf.[7] Yet, the Indian policy paradigm for migrants in the Gulf nonetheless can be said to have shifted from protective-restrictive to welfare compensator, to developmental-restorative.[8] The 1983 Emigration Act, which replaced the 1922 Emigration Act, has been designed mainly to ensure protection of vulnerable categories of unskilled and semi-skilled workers, and women going abroad to work as home maids and domestic workers. The Act gives a regulatory and legal framework with respect to emigration of Indian workers for overseas employment on a contractual basis. Under the Act, "all recruiting agents" must register with the government before recruiting for overseas employment. Comprising many private-sector players, this includes nine state manpower export corporation established by the governments of Uttar Pradesh, Andhra Pradesh, Kerala, Punjab, Tamil Nadu, Karnataka, Himachal Pradesh, Haryana, and Delhi. At present, active private-sector recruiting agents are mainly located in Mumbai, Delhi, Chennai, and Kerala. Registered agents are held responsible for worker complaints regarding non-payment or delayed payment of wages, unilateral changes in the contract, arbitrary change of jobs, denial of employment, and inhumane working and living conditions, etc. A proposed amendment to the 1983 Emigration Act[9] is aimed at curbing the activities of illegal recruiting agents that operate clandestinely and protecting migrant workers.[10] The general policy of most countries including India has been to maximize the export of workers while minimizing the negative consequences of labor migration. There is no simple way to classify the numerous governmental policies and programmers pertaining to labor migration.

Regulations and the Welfare of Indians

This mainly includes the regulation of recruiting agents. The protector of emigrants is the custodian and authority of the entire emigration process. Foreign private employees must give power of attorney to their recruiting agents in India. In addition, a "demand letter" showing the personal categories required, conditions of work, salary, etc., must be submitted to the Indian embassy in the country concerned. When this letter is received by the recruiting agent, they obtain a recruitment sanction from the relevant regional protector of emigrants.

All the agreements the employer and the worker enter into are registered by the protector of emigrants and must conform to the labor laws in the country of immigration. The union government has framed legislation for setting up a central overseas workforce corporation to regulate the flow of Indian labor to foreign countries. Direct supervision of the recruitment of emigrant labor was found necessary because of the many malpractices indulged in by unscrupulous recruiting and travel agents, the plight of Indian laborers in the host countries, and, what is more disconcerting, the tarnished image of Indian workers. The proposed workforce corporation will not be the first official agency to regulate the outflow of labor; there are seven emigration officers in various regions.

The recruitment of paramedical personnel for the Gulf countries had been a money-spinning racket in the hands of unscrupulous private agencies hitherto but is now regulated with the entry of some of the state-run public sector corporation in the business. The Indian government has established a "May I Help You" counter in New Delhi, which provides information and guidance to overseas workers and receives complaints on non-payment of wages in host countries and complaints against agents in India.[11] The Emigration Act 1983 authorizes the protector to reject an application for recruitment on grounds that the terms of employment are discriminatory or the job offends human dignity or is unlawful by our laws or on other grounds.[12] To ensure no foul play, the recruiting agencies in India are required to execute a contract specifying the terms and conditions of employment made between the worker and their prospective employer. The Ministry of Labor has also issued guidelines which stipulate that the employers or their agents in India must offer salaries and prerequisites to Indian recruits on par with workers of other nationalities engaged in similar work. The labor ministry is aided in this by the Indian mission in the host countries. The missions must stay informed about the different countries recruiting Indian labor.[13] On hearing claims of "inhumane working conditions" the labor ministry has prepared a draft model agreement. Foreign employers must provide according to the model agreements free trip passage, free furnished accommodation commensurate with the category of work, free medical care, and free transportation. The employment contract holds, in addition, provisions for overtime wages, hours of work, terminal benefits, and compensation for accidents.[14] There are laws and selective restrictions on the emigration of women; the intent of this law is to discourage exploitation of young female domestic servants, a problem that has been reported in many host countries.

The Indian government also has introduced a landmark Overseas Citizenship of India (OCI) initiative, which affords partial dual citizenship benefits. Another measure, which primarily caters to Indian workers in the Gulf – who send large remittances back home but can never hope to become naturalized citizens of the countries where they work because of restrictive regimes – grants Indian citizens abroad the right to vote in Indian elections.[15] These two major policy measures aim to empower migrant workers to participate in India's socio-economic and political development rather than merely looking to India for protection and welfare. The measures are complemented by the introduction of Parvasi Bhartiya Samman awards to 15 overseas Indians each year to recognize achievements of the Indian Diaspora and their contribution to strengthening of India's relations with other countries, promoting the honor and prestige of India, and fostering the interests of overseas Indians.[16]

A *Times of India* report said that Qatar Airways was one of the most popular airlines for Indians who live abroad (Sinha, 2017). Due to the recent Qatari crises, there were about 650,000 Indians who are affected as rightly the concern was expressed by media and the Ministry of External Affairs. What came as an astonishing revelation to the masses was that the figures outnumbered native Qataris by almost 2:1. From this one could ascertain the fact that owing to the huge presence of Indians in the Gulf countries, the diaspora can play a vital role in Indian–Arab relations. When foreign minister Sushma Swaraj expressed her concern regarding the Indians who could have got stuck in Qatar, she strived to maintain diplomatic balance, especially at a time when PM Modi was exploring new avenues to strengthen economic as well as security ties with the Arab world.

India's Soft Power Approach

India's soft power policies emanate from its moral and political philosophy shaped by thinkers like Tagore, Gandhi, and Nehru. Tagore, who won the Nobel Prize in Literature 1913, advocated universalism – the concept of *Vasudhaiva Kutumbakam* or global family. The ideas of *Satyagraha* (seeking truth) and *Ahisma* (non-violence) espoused by Gandhi received worldwide attention and compelled the British to quit India. The legacy of Gandhi was carried forward by Nehru in crafting early independent India's foreign policy. Similarly, as we know, a diaspora adopts various means to influence the government of the homeland and host countries, the media, international state and non-state organizations, and their political allies. These include political lobbying, mass media campaigns, fundraising demonstrations, use of modern communication technology, participation in the election, and several others.[17]

COVID-19 and Its Implications for Emigrants

The COVID-19 pandemic is a global health crisis that put the entire world economy at a halt. How this pandemic is affecting the migrant economy cannot be ignored or sidelined. The pandemic continues to have a widespread impact on workforce globally, migrant workers are among those suffering the most due to this ongoing crisis. In India too, the Gulf region, which seemed so open to us Indians, may well be shutting its doors on us due to the pandemic. It will impact lives, remittances, and economies. The presence, role, and well-being of the nearly eight million strong Indian workforce, which includes the greatest professionals, blue-collar employees, and ambitious enterprises, is critical in this matrix of cooperation. They have been instrumental in their host countries' economic development, and they are well-liked and recognized for their contributions and disciplined approach, and they are favored above other expats. They send about $40 billion home every year, and this money usually stays in the nation for extended periods of time, contributing over 10% of India's foreign exchange reserves (Trigunayat, 2020).

Now the COVID-19 pandemic produces unprecedented effects on the migrant economy. In addition to virus, the impact has gone beyond public health to social and economic issues, especially for migrant workers. Human rights groups and construction associations have rightly expressed their concerns that migrant workers are at greater risk. Migrant workers are among the hardest hit by the COVID-19 pandemic, says the ILO Director-General, Guy Ryder. There are crowded living conditions, harsh containment measures, limited access to healthcare and basic services, poor working conditions, and exploitative labor systems. The millions of migrant workers are forced to return home as a result of losing their jobs in the host countries. They are going to face unemployment and poverty in their home countries. Migrant workers have found themselves stranded in host countries without access to social protection and little money for food or accommodation.

Conclusion

There is a need to further strengthen our relations with West Asia, especially with the Gulf countries. The West Asian countries fully realize the economic and diplomatic potential of India. They are willing to expand their ties with India in strategic fields. Working together would enable them to meet the challenges of globalization. India can be instrumental in promoting stability in the region, which also helps its own energy and security requirements, and workforce employment. It would be in India's own interests too to further develop economic, diplomatic, and cultural relations with these countries. Emphasis should be given to diversify relations beyond trade and energy and focus on human resources, our great strength. We must develop a sound bilateral labor policy that addresses the issues concerning Indians working in the region and policies need to be put in place to protect stranded migrant workers and to ensure the reintegration of those who return to their home countries.

Notes

1 Govt of India, Ministry of Overseas Indian Affairs, Annual Report 2004–2005.
2 Deepak Nayyar, Migration, *Remittances and Capital Flows: The Indian Experience* (Delhi: Oxford University Press, 1994), 30.
3 MOIA, 2012.
4 Pravasi Bharatiya July 2012.
5 Statistics taken from United Nations International Migration Report, 2017.
6 *Overseas Indian*, Vol. 1, Nos. 1-4 (2006), a monthly publication of the Ministry of Overseas Indian Affairs, Government of India, New Delhi.
7 Binod Khadria, ed., *India migration report 2009*, *International migration Diaspora studies project*, Jawahar Lal Nehru University, New Delhi.
8 Binod Khadria, "*Skilled labour migration from developing countries*: Study on India," *International migration papers*, Vol. 49, International Labour Office, Geneva (2002).
9 *The Hindustan Times*, 22 May 2006.
10 *Proceedings of the conference of the Indian ambassador of Gulf countries*, Doha, Qatar, 20–21 March 2006 Ministry of Overseas Indian Affairs, Government of India, unpublished memo.
11 Arnold Fred and N.M. Shah (eds.), *Asian Labour migration: pipeline to the Middle East*, 1986.
12 *Hindustan Times* (New Delhi), 1 January 1984.
13 Nitish Chakravorty, "West Asia lure: protecting the migrant labour" *Hindu* 13 November 1978, 65.
14 Nair P R Gopinathan's "India" in Gunatilleke G.(eds.) *Migration of Asian workers to the Arab world*, 1989.
15 The Indian government had announced this step at the fourth Parvasi Bhartiya Divas at Hyderabad in January 2006, and reaffirmed it5s commitment recently at in Delhi at the eighth PBD in January 2010.
16 *Annual Report 2008–2009, Ministry of Overseas Indian Affairs*, Government of India, New Delhi (2009).
17 Chimaya R Gharekhan (19 April 2018) 'The Soft Power of India' *The Hindu.*

Reference

Annual Report 2008–09, Ministry of Overseas Indian Affairs. (2009). New Delhi: Government of India

Binod, Khadria, ed., *India Migration Report 2009*, *International Migration Diaspora Studies Project.* New Delhi: Jawahar Lal Nehru University.

Gharekhan, C.R. (April 19, 2018). The soft power of India. *The Hindu*

Kumar, N. (2014). Recent trend and Pattern of Indian Emigration to Gulf Countries: A Diaspora. Retrieved from https://paa2014.princeton.edu/papers/141653

Nair, P. R. (1989). Gopinathan's "India". In Gunatilleke, G. (eds.) *Migration of Asian Workers to the Arab World*, Washington D.C..

Pant, G. (2017, March 16). Redefining the drivers of India-G.C.C. Economic relations. Retrieved from https://www.mei.edu/publications/redefining-drivers-india-gcc-economic-relations

PravasiBharatiya | July 2012

Trigunayat, A. A. (2020, April 20). GCC and the Indian Diaspora in the context of Covid-19. Vivekananda International Foundation. Retrieved from https://www.vifindia.org/print/7374

Zachariah, K. P. K., & IrudayaRajan, S. (Eds). (n.d.) *Kerala Gulf Connection; CDS Studies of International Labour Migration from Kerala State in India* (pp 13–45). Thiruvananthapuram: Centre for Development Studies.

8 Family Tax, Indian Expatriates, and the Saudi Economy

Muhammad Azhar[1]

Introduction

Since July 2017, Saudi Arabia has imposed a new tax called the 'family tax' or 'dependent tax' on the dependents of the expatriate workers in Saudi Arabia. Expatriate workers have to pay Saudi riyal (SR) 1200 per annum per dependent. This tax would increase every year by SR 1200 till 2020 when it would reach SR 4800 per annum per dependent, thus increasing the strictness of family tax manifold. It seems that the Saudi policy of imposition of the family tax had two objectives before it. The first objective has been to create an alternative source of finance other than oil and mobilize revenues for the Government expenditure. The second objective has been to discourage and make it increasingly costlier for the expatriates to stay in Saudi Arabia. In the Saudi policymakers' view it could also result in more employment opportunities for Saudi nationals. It must be mentioned that expatriates constitute more than one-third of the total Saudi population (Saudi Arab Monetary Authority (SAMA), 2018). It is estimated that the number of Indian expatriate workers in Saudi Arabia exceeds 3.2 million. Saudi Arabia has the largest concentration of Indian passport holders staying in any country outside India (Azhar, 2017). The dependents of these workers number in lakhs. There is no doubt that the imposition of family tax in Saudi Arabia would make the stay of these dependents difficult. The outflow of dependents of expatriates from India as well as other manpower-exporting countries began in large numbers immediately after the Saudi decision to impose family tax (Basheer, 2017). Meanwhile those remaining may be contemplating or preparing for sending back their dependents. In the end, only dependents of public sector expatriate employees could remain as they are exempt from this tax. The fee also does not apply to domestic helpers such as drivers and cleaners. It only applies to expatriates working in commercial entities (Robinson, 2017). However, the exemption granted to the domestic helpers is least beneficial as Saudi Arabia permits the family visa to only those people who earn a monthly salary of SR 5000 (Rao, 2017). This, converted to Indian rupees at the rate of SR 1 = INR 18.58, comes to approximately 93,000 rupees per month. It would be extremely difficult

DOI: 10.4324/9781003369370-11

to trace such highly paid domestic helpers. The family tax is to be utilized as an instrument to mobilize the financial resources to compensate for the declining oil revenues. It was estimated that at the time of the imposition of family tax, the number of dependents of expatriate workers in Saudi Arabia was also very significant. According to the Public Authority for Statistics, there were 11 million expatriates working in the Saudi private sector, with 2.5 million of their dependents staying with them in Saudi Arabia (*Khaleej Times*, 2017). Thus, there is no doubt that the imposition of family tax in Saudi Arabia along with its strictness has made the stay of these dependents increasingly costlier. This has forced a significant proportion of expatriates to opt for other alternatives mainly sending and setting their dependents back to their countries of origin. The outflow of dependents of expatriates in Saudi Arabia has already occurred in large numbers (Ghoshal, 2017). Those remaining have been reported to be contemplating or preparing to send back their dependents to their countries of origin, as they consider it uneconomical to keep their families in Saudi Arabia and quickly decide to relocate their family members (Al-Maeena, 2017-A). And hence an exodus of dependents of expatriate workers is certain to take place except those working in the public sector in Saudi Arabia. However, for how long expatriate employees of the Saudi public sector remain exempt from the tax is a question which would certainly haunt them. And therefore, the family tax as an alternative source of mobilization of revenues could dry up within a few years (Al-Maeena, 2018-A). As far as the generation of employment for Saudi nationals is concerned, these could be determined by the forces of the labor market, as it cannot be made to behave in a diametrically opposite way just by penalizing expatriate workers. It requires significant structural changes in the Saudi economy as well as society. Saudi Arabia will have to reform all those labor laws that have resulted in creating severe distortions in the Saudi labor market (El-Katiri, 2016). And therefore, the objectives of family tax are very difficult to be achieved. Further, the exodus of dependents of expatriates would also have negative impact on Saudi businesses and in turn on the Saudi economy. Which in turn would bring down the income and employment further in Saudi Arabia (Al-Maeena, 2017-A). This chapter studies the various kinds of impacts of family tax on Indian expatriate workers in Saudi Arabia as well as on the economy of Saudi Arabia.

Tax Regime in Saudi Arabia

In Saudi Arabia there is no individual income tax system. Long back in the 1950s Saudi Arabia introduced personal income tax both for nationals and non-nationals. However, this was found difficult to be implemented. The new tax law was very soon revised to exclude nationals from its purview. It remained only for non-nationals (Oxford Business Group, 2016). However, during the massive inflow of oil revenues in the early 1970s, income tax on non-nationals was also done away. It was done to attract foreign manpower to build the Saudi economy. Later on during the 1980s, with the collapse of oil price and consequent decline in oil revenues, the Saudi Government tried again to reintroduce income tax for foreigners. However, it could not be implemented due to intense opposition from expatriates and the fear of the exodus of expatriate workers from the country (Oxford Business Group, 2016).

It is worth mentioning that only non-Saudi investors are subject to income tax in Saudi Arabia. Saudi investors have to pay Zakat, an Islamic obligation. Meanwhile, citizens of other Gulf Cooperation Council (GCC) countries are also considered as Saudi citizens for the purpose of taxation and they are also liable for Zakat. All companies owned by non-Saudis are subject to income tax, whereas, companies owned by Saudis have to pay Zakat. However, in case a company is owned by both Saudi and non-Saudi nationals, the portion of taxable income attributable to non-Saudi is liable to income tax. But the part of the Saudi share goes into the assessment of Zakat (Oxford Business Group, 2015). Since 2017, the tax laws have been amended. Even Saudi investor and companies operating in oil and hydrocarbon and natural gas sectors have been brought under the ambit of income tax (Ey-Global, 2017). Further, the continuous decline in oil revenues inflow has forced Saudi Arabia to bring in new types of taxes including the family tax and value-added tax. Further, at one point of time, Saudi Arabia was considering to impose income tax also on non-nationals. However, this proposal could not be approved (Kerr, 2016). The very talk of such kind of proposal reflects the thinking of Saudi policymakers. And there may be efforts in future to implement income tax for non-nationals. It should also be noted that there have been no taxes from local, state, or provincial government in Saudi Arabia on income other than the regular income tax or Zakat discussed above (International Monetary Fund, 2015).

The absence of personal taxes accompanied by heavy subsidies on utilities, energy and food items, etc., for both national and non-national population in Saudi Arabia had been important factors in the determination of the real wages in Saudi Arabia (Ahmad, 2014). This worked as incentive, allurement, and attraction for expatriate workers including Indian expatriate workers to work in Saudi Arabia. The main objective of such workers has been to earn money, save it, and send it back to India or their country of origin (Azhar, 2015). But a large number of expatriate workers in Saudi Arabia opted to take their family members as they qualified for it and also they could afford it. It should be noted that the Saudi Government fixed a minimum salary of SR 5000 per month for expatriates to become eligible to bring their family members to stay with them in Saudi Arabia (Rao, 2017). It is further reported that nearly 86 percent of expatriate workers in Saudi Arabia had a monthly salary of less than SR 2000 (Saudi-Expatriates, 2017). However, the welfare nature of the Saudi State made it a popular destination for expatriate workers from India and other countries. The Saudi General Authority for Statistics estimated that there were about ten million expatriates in the Kingdom with 2.5 million dependents, adding to about one-third of the total Saudi population (Global Authority for Statistics, 2017).

The Family Tax

The continued depression in global oil prices has significantly reduced the oil revenue inflow in Saudi Arabia. The persistence of low oil prices for such a long period of time has made the Saudi financial position alarming (SAMA, 2017). This has forced the Saudi Government to scout for other alternative sources in the mobilization for financial resources (International Monetary Fund (IMF), 2016). Expatriates seem to be an easy and soft target in the strategy to mobilize additional financial resources. Further, the Government of Saudi Arabia as well as other neighboring countries have been portraying expatriate workers as responsible for the existing unemployment among nationals. Somehow, the impression is being given that the departure of expatriates would solve the unemployment of nationals (Al-Ghamdi, 2017-A). The imposition of family tax or dependent tax in Saudi Arabia has been a corollary to the above approach.

The Government of Saudi Arabia imposed family tax or expatriate dependent fee from July 2017 (Basheer, 2017). It requires an expatriate worker to pay SR 1200 per annum per dependent of the expatriate family. The tax has to be paid in advance. Table 8.1 provides the detailed family tax structure in Saudi Arabia. An expatriate worker with wife and two children has to pay SR 3600 per annum as family tax. This comes to about INR 69,000. The family tax proposes to increase the rate of taxation by SR 100 per year per dependent. Thus by 2020, the family tax would increase to SR 4800 for each member of the expatriate family. At the present rate of exchange, this would be about INR 92,000. Thus by 2020, an expatriate family with a wife and two children would have to pay

Table 8.1 Family tax structure in Saudi Arabia (Saudi riyal per annum)

Description of the family	*2017*	*2018*	*2019*	*2020*
Wife only	1,200	2,400	3,600	4,800
Wife + 1 child	2,400	4,800	7,200	9,600
Wife + 2 children	3,600	7,200	10,800	14,400
Wife + 3 children	4,800	9,600	14,400	15,200
Wife + 4 children	6,000	12,000	18,000	24,000
Wife + 4 children + 1 parent	7,200	14,400	21,600	28,800
Wife + 4 children + both parents	8,400	16,800	25,200	33,600

Source: Estimation based on family tax rates provided in various newspapers published from Saudi Arabia.

SR 14,400 per annum as family tax. At the present rate of exchange, this comes to about two lakhs and 76000 rupees per annum. Various scenarios of family tax on different sizes of expatriate family in Saudi Arabia are depicted in Table 8.1.

The Saudi Government has been arguing that each member of the expatriate community in Saudi Arabia costs the Government about SR 1500 per month in terms of subsidies on water, electricity, petrol and gas, and other essentials (Al-bawaba, 2017). The fee has to be paid to the Department of Passport at the time of renewal of the residential permit which is called *Iqama*. The family tax was estimated to generate SR 65.0 billion by 2020 (Al-bawaba, 2017). The introduction of taxes as a reform in Saudi fiscal policy to mobilize revenues especially due to declining oil prices has been the priority agenda of the Saudi Government. There have been pressures and recommendations to find ways to increase the non-oil fiscal revenues (International Monetary Fund (IMF), 2017). However, the introduction of family tax in Saudi Arabia has been unique as well as controversial. The positive and negative aspects of the family tax have been debated very hotly in Saudi Arabia. The arguments advanced in support of the family tax are as follows (Al-Ghamdi, 2017-B). First, the revenue collected from the dependent tax would affect the budget deficit to a certain extent. It should be noted that due to depressed oil prices, Saudi Arabia has been facing a substantial deficit in its budget year by year. Thus the imposition of family tax could be an effective strategy to control the budget deficit. It would also not impinge on natives as it is designed for expatriates only. The second argument is that this would recover a portion of the cost of subsidies that benefit expatriates. The Saudi Government has been claiming that it has to spend substantial money through various types of subsidies on expatriates. With a persistent low inflow of oil revenues, the subsidies are becoming an unaffordable burden on the economy. The family tax could partially correct this. The third argument is that the imposition of family tax would result in many expatriates leaving Saudi Arabia. Saudi nationals can replace these expatriates in the job market. Thus the family tax would be helpful in solving the problem of unemployment among Saudi nationals. The fourth argument concerns the cover-up business, which is called *Tasattur* in Arabic. *Tasattur* refers to the practice where a Saudi citizen permits an expatriate to run a business in his name against a fixed percentage of profit (*Saudi Gazette*, 2019). This results in an outflow of capital from Saudi Arabia. The Saudi Government has been trying to curb all forms of *Tasattur* across all the sectors of the Saudi economy. The family tax is supposed to reduce the *Tasattur* business and check the exaggerated outflow of capital from Saudi Arabia. The fifth argument in support of the tax is that it would result in reduced demand for public utilities such as electricity, water, and fuel. It must be mentioned that Saudi Arabia has been providing substantial subsidies on these utilities available to both its citizens and expatriates. Through the family tax, Saudi Arabia wants to redirect such expenditures on expatriates to its citizens.

Sixth, it would result in a reduction of the expatriate population in Saudi Arabia.

The arguments advanced against the imposition of family tax are as follows (Al-Ghamdi, 2017-B). First, the family tax is expected to create an exodus not only among the dependents of expatriates but expatriates themselves. Thus, the family tax as an instrument of revenue mobilization may get punctured earlier than expected. The revenue generation by family tax would become abysmally low as there would remain few dependents of expatriates worthy of being taxed. Second, the exodus of expatriates would result in reduced economic activity in Saudi Arabia. It would result in slowdown of the Saudi economy. The slowdown in the economy would negatively affect the Saudi private sector. Third, the imposition of the family tax would considerably reduce the purchasing power of expatriates. This would result in the substantial fall in their standard of living. This would result in reduction in their productivity and also decline in demand for many commodities. Fourth, the Saudis cannot automatically replace the job left by the outgoing expatriates. The functioning of the labor market is not so simple. Expatriates are employed mainly because of unavailability of the nationals for that kind of job for various reasons. Also the majority of expatriates, who keep their dependents with them, are employed in the technical and vocational fields. Thus Saudis can benefit only in small numbers in terms of employment opportunity, generated as a consequence of the imposition of the family tax. Fifth, many firms in Saudi Arabia have either closed down or on the verge of closure because of the exorbitant fee for employing the expatriates. The Labour Ministry under the naturalization program of the workforce, has been charging SR 400 per expatriate worker in 2018 from the firms in which expatriates outnumber the nationals. This would be increased to SR 800 per expatriate worker by 2020. Companies where nationals equal or outnumber expatriates are not totally exempted. They were also charged with SR 300 per expatriate worker in 2018 which would increase to SR 700 by 2020 (Al-Misbahi, 2017). The imposition of yet another tax in the form of a dependent tax has complicated the situation further. With the closure of some firms, some Saudi nationals are also bound to lose their jobs. Sixth, the outflow of the dependent of the expatriates has affected the demand for various commodities. The companies engaged in production/business of such commodities are facing substantial decline in their revenues and profits. A passionate comparison of merits and demerits finds that the gains of the imposition of family tax would not outweigh the loss in the long run. In the short run also it would result in complications to the Saudi economy (Robinson, 2017).

Reforms in Subsidies in Saudi Arabia

While deciding to impose the family tax, the argument was advanced that the Saudi Government has to spend SR 1500 per month per expatriate in the form of subsidies on petrol and gas, electricity, water, and other essentials. However, in recent years the Saudi Government, forced by the declining oil revenue inflow, has opted for significant reforms in subsidies. It is trying to gradually minimize the subsidies in order to reduce pressure on the economy. The first target has been the fuel, i.e. petrol and gas (Kerr, 2015). It should be noted that oil and gas prices in the Kingdom have been minimal as compared to any country in the world. Table 8.2 provides data about the fuel prices in the recent past.

From the data in the table, it can be found that Saudi Arabia has been pursuing gradual but steady reforms in fuel pricing. In December 2015, the Saudi Government announced that it would be reforming prices of water, electricity, natural gas, and petroleum products over the next five years. And it raised the prices of different types of fuel with immediate effect (APICORP, 2016). From the table, it is found that the price of Octane 91 fuel increased to SR 0.75 per liter from SR 0.45, a hike of 60 percent. The price of Octane 95 fuel increased to SR 0.90 per liter from SR 0.60, a hike of 50 percent. The prices of diesel for transport as well as diesel for industries and utilities were also increased, as did the prices of kerosene. The reform continues so that the fuel price is brought to the market level, reducing the extravagant fuel consumption and downsizing the subsidies on fuel (Morenhout, 2018). The resolve of Saudi Arabia to reform the pricing of fuel was demonstrated again when the fuel prices were again increased starting 1 January 2018 (Halligan, 2018). From the table, it is observed that the price of Octane 91 was raised by 82 percent while the prices of Octane 95 were hiked by 126 percent. The price of diesel for industries and utilities was increased by eight percent only. On the other hand, the price of diesel for transport and kerosene was not hiked and remained the same. Thus, a

Table 8.2 Fuel prices in Saudi Arabia (SR per liter)

Fuel	*December 2015*	*January 2016*	*January 2018*	*Growth % (December 2015–January 2018)*
Octane 91	0.45	0.75	1.37	204.4
Octane 95	0.60	0.90	2.04	240.0
Diesel for industries and utilities	0.26	0.33	0.378	45.4
Diesel for transport	0.26	0.47	0.47	81.0
Kerosene	0.54	0.64	0.64	18.5

Source: (1) Roznama Rashtriya Sahara, New Delhi, 2 December 2017, p. 12.
(2) Saudi Arabia Sets out strategy to reform subsidies and domestic energy usage, *Saudi Arabia* 2016, Oxford Business Group, www.oxfordbusinessgroup.com (Accessed on 30 October 2017).
(3) Energy Price Reform in the GCC: Long Road Ahead, APRICORP Energy Research, Vol.1 No.4.

gradual increment in fuel prices in Saudi Arabia has taken place. However, compared to international standards it is still at a low level. A comparative study of global oil prices mentions that on 4 November 2019, the gasoline price prevailed at $ 0.55 per liter in Saudi Arabia, whereas, the per liter gasoline price in Pakistan, the USA, and India ruled at $ 0.73, $ 0.78, and $ 1.07, respectively (Gasoline, 2019). Further, Saudi Arabia in its reform drive was reported to be aiming to reduce electricity and water subsidies by SR 200 billion ($ 53 billion) and reduce non-oil subsidies by 20 percent by 2020 (Rawuf, 2016). In this endeavor the electricity prices in Saudi Arabia were raised after a long period of about a decade and a half. Although small consumers were left untouched, the rise in tariff varied between 19 percent to 45 percent for various categories of consumers (*Arab News*, 2016). The water consumption in Saudi Arabia has been one of the highest in the world. This was due to a very low price of water as compared to its cost of production. It was estimated that water was supplied in Saudi Arabia at five percent or less of the cost of production (Global Water Intelligence, 2017). The Saudi Government decided to hike the water prices by 50 percent from 16 December 2015. It was argued that the hike would limit the high consumption of water and result in preserving water resources without any negative impact on the citizenry (*Arab News*, 2015). However, due to a public outcry against the water price rise, a replacement of the then water and electricity minister occurred. The new minister assured working on a water tariff acceptable to citizens aggrieved over rising costs. The Saudi authorities decided to pursue a more gradual approach to its strategy by raising water tariffs to a more cost-reflective level (*Arabian Business*, 2016). Thus, the level of subsidization of important commodities and services is being drastically cut down and intended to be brought to nil.

The data about the fuel subsidies in Saudi Arabia has been provided in Table 8.3. The data is for 2013–2015. The table gives information about oil, natural gas, and electricity subsidies provided by Saudi Arabia. It finds that the fuel subsidies in Saudi Arabia were lowered from $ 61.6 billion in 2013 to $ 48.6 billion in 2015, thus declining by about 22 percent.

Further, the Saudi Government decided to remove subsidies on seven services which include port services, passport fee, car driving license fee, car transfer, traffic violations, removal of residence permits (*Iqama*) for

Table 8.3 Fuel subsidies in Saudi Arabia (US dollar billion)

	2013	*2014*	*2015*
Oil	41,459.6	41,320.9	29,479.9
Electricity	12,100.2	11,528.8	12,469.7
Natural gas	8,099.2	6,926.5	6,695.0
Total	**61,659.0**	**59,776.2**	**48,644.6**

Source: International Energy Agency.

domestic workers, and tariff (custom) protection for 192 commodities. The Saudi Government also decided to raise visa fees and approved the imposition of fees on municipal services (Taha, 2016). The subsidy reforms in Saudi Arabia have been estimated to be in a right and successful direction. A survey revealed that the subsidy cuts were positively influencing the Saudi economy (Wald, 2018). This means that the prices of all the commodities and services would be determined by the market forces of demand and supply. And there would be no government interference to artificially keep these prices down. However, Saudi Arabia has introduced a new welfare system designed to help low- and middle-income Saudi families deal with the rising prices. It is paid as a monthly installment. The maximum payment has been at SR 938 ($ 250) and the minimum has been at SR 300 ($80) per family. The payments were through bank transfers. This benefited approximately three million Saudi families consisting of around 10.6 million beneficiaries. This makes up about half of the Saudi national population (*Arab News*, 2017). Thus, a large part of Saudi national population is being insulated and protected from the rising prices, whereas the expatriate population without any such cover are left to fend for themselves and bear with the increases. And at least for expatriates, down the line after four decades since the 1970s, the second decade of the 21st century Saudi Arabia does not remain similarly remunerative. And the argument that the Saudi Government has to spend a large amount of expenditure on expatriates and their dependents stands to be corrected in the era of reforms.

Impact on Indian Expatriate Workers

The combined impact of various taxes i.e. the family tax, value-added tax, beverage tax etc. has been detrimental to the real wages of all expatriates in Saudi Arabia. Further, the wages of expatriate workers are already cut or frozen with the continuous low oil revenues. It has already been discussed that the steep hike in prices of petroleum products, increase in electricity charges, water charges, natural gas utilities, many services and imposition of value-added tax has exposed the fallacy of the argument of subsidy expenditure of SR 1500 per month per expatriate/worker advanced for legitimizing the family tax. The ongoing reforms and cut in subsidies have considerably reduced the Saudi subsidy burden and per capita subsidy expenditure in Saudi Arabia. With the national population being compensated, it is the expatriates who have no cushion against the price rises. The reforms have resulted in price rises and substantial hikes in Saudi inflation rates (Al-Fozan, 2019). The information about inflation in Saudi Arabia is provided in Table 8.4.

From the table given above, it is found that compared to the base year 2007, the Saudi Consumer Price Index has risen by about 39 percent by 2018. In the context of cut and freezes in expatriate wages, the impact on the real wages of expatriates can be easily visualized. The problem got further

Table 8.4 Consumer Price Index in Saudi Arabia

Year	*Price statistics*
2007	100.0
2008	106.1
2009	110.5
2010	114.7
2011	119.8
2012	122.4
2013	126.7
2014	130.1
2015	132.6
2016	137.6
2017	136.5
2018	138.8

Source: (1) Consumer Price Index, General Authority for Statistics, www.stats.gov.sa (Accessed on 17 September 2019).
(2) Inflation rate, Saudi Arab Monetary Authority, www.sama.gov.sa (Accessed on 23 April 23 2019).

accentuated with the proposal of imposing fees on expatriate remittances (Al-Qahtani, 2018), although, the Shoura Council did not approve it. But it was to be in addition to 5 percent value-added tax on money transfer fee (*Saudi Gazette*, 2018). Further, it was also reported that Saudi Arabia was considering an imposition of income tax on foreign residents. It must be mentioned that Saudi's income tax-free status was an important factor in attracting expatriate workers (Kerr, 2016). Although it is yet to be finalized its consideration is also alarming. Confronted with these factors, it has become very difficult for almost all middle-income Indian expatriates as well as expatriates of all labor-exporting countries to maintain their families in Saudi Arabia (Karim, 2018). This has forced the major chunk of Indians as well as other expatriate workers in Saudi Arabia to send back their family members and dependents to India or their countries of origin (*The Times of India*, 2018). The process of return of dependents of expatriates including Indians started immediately after the imposition of the family tax. And it gradually acquired gigantic proportions in a very short period (Carey, 2018).

Impact on the Saudi Economy

The ultimate impact of the family tax has been the return of dependents of expatriate workers in large numbers. The Saudi plan to mobilize SR 65.0 billion from the family tax by 2020 cannot be realized with the declining number of dependents of expatriates. Rather, the magnitude of revenues from family tax would lower quickly (Robinson, 2017). Expatriates then would spend less within the Saudi economy and send more to their country of origin or India, as the case may be. This would result in increasing remittances inflow to labor-exporting countries. It was reported that the remittances to South Asian countries increased by an estimated 12.3 percent in 2018 as compared to 2017. In India, the remittances grew by over 14 percent in 2018 to $ 78.6 billion (KNOMAD, 2019). The return of a large number of expatriate families has affected negatively shops and small businesses. House rents fell and many grocery stores were reported to be closed (Al-Ghamdi, 2017c). The *Iqama* fee collection by Saudi Government would also be affected negatively by the dwindling expatriate dependents. Expatriates and their dependents while staying in Saudi Arabia have been paying phone bills to the Saudi Government. They have been paying house rents to Saudi landlords. They have been buying food from grocery shops owned by Saudis (Al-Maeena, 2018B).

The expatriates had been depositing their money in Saudi banks. They had been getting treatment at Saudi hospitals. The expatriates' children had been studying in schools owned by Saudis. The real estate market including offices, shops, and apartments has been affected negatively because of the departure of families of expatriates on a large scale. The departure of family members would also have a negative effect on the productivity of expatriate workers (Al-Maeena, 2017B). Further, as a result of their leaving, the Saudi market would lose the vast liquidity provided by millions of dependents who were spending this money inside Saudi Arabia to purchase goods and services. The consequent reduction in demand for goods and services would weaken the Saudi market (Dahlan, 2017). This in turn would reduce the non-oil GDP further. Although in the initial years the Government of Saudi Arabia may be able to mobilize an increased revenue collection, very soon it will die down. And the net impact of family tax would be negative for the Saudi economy as the revenue collected on account of family tax may not compensate for the eventual decline in the Saudi GDP.

Conclusion

- The family tax was imposed for the purpose of diversifying the sources of mobilization of revenues and enhancing the magnitude of revenues in the era of low oil prices and low oil revenue inflow.
- The logic for justifying the family tax was the per capita expenditure on dependents in form of subsidies by the Government of Saudi Arabia.
- However, the removal of subsidies in its reform drive and direct payments to compensate the Saudi nationals makes this argument invalid.
- The lower and cheap cost of maintenance of day to day life has been an important factor in the consideration of real wage determination for expatriate workers.
- However, with the removal of subsidies and imposition of various kinds of taxes including the value-added tax, the day-to-day life has become costlier, more so for expatriates.

- This has resulted in substantial decline in the real wages for expatriates in Saudi Arabia.
- The imposition of family tax in such circumstances has forced a significant number of dependents of Indian expatriates to return to India.
- In the short term, there could be some positive gains in terms of revenue collection for Saudi Arabia.
- But in the long term, it would only result in overall losses for the Saudi economy as a whole.
- The net result of the family tax would be beneficial for the labor-exporting economies like India.
- Therefore, it seems that the uneasy decision regarding the imposition of family tax was rushed without doing the proper homework.

Note

1 Professor, Department of West Asian and North African Studies, A.M.U., Aligarh-202002 (India).

References

Ahmad, Hammad S. (2014), "The labour market in Saudi Arabia: Foreign workers, unemployment and minimum wage", *ENQUIRIES*, *6*(06), www.inquiriesjournal.com (Accessed on 18.09.2018).

Al-Bawaba (2017, July 06), "Is the Expat Tax Bad for Saudi Arabia's Economy?", www.albawaba.com (Accessed on 30.11.2018).

Al-Fozan, Dr. Abdullah (2019, September 08), "How energy price reforms in Saudi Arabia impact inflation", *Saudi Gazette*, http://saudi gazette.com.sa (Accessed on 19.09.2019).

Al-Ghamdi, Abdullah (2017a, May 10), "Get rid of expats by 2020, public sector told", *Saudi Gazette*, http://saudigazette.com.sa (Accessed on 20.08.2017).

Al-Ghamdi, Dr. Ali (2017b, July 26), "What we gain and lose from expat dependent fee", *Saudi Gazette*, http://saudigazette.com.sa (Accessed on 03.11.2018).

Al-Ghamdi, Saeed Alfarha (2017c, August 23), "Expat tax and its impact on market economy", *Saudi Gazette*, http://saudigazette.com.sa (Accessed on 22.02.2018).

Al-Maeena, Tarique A. (2017a, December 27), "The dependent fee may have a negative economic impact", *Saudi Gazette*, http://saudigazette.com.sa (Accessed on 27.12.2018).

Al-Maeena, Tarique A. (2017b, October 07), "Expatriate fee in Saudi Arabia comes at a cost", *Gulf News*, http://gulfnews.com (Accessed on 31.12.2018).

Al-Maeena, Tarique A. (2018a, March 24), "Saudi Arabia's expat tax cocundrum", *Gulf News*, http://gulfnews.com (Accessed on 06.05.2019).

Al-Maeena, Tarique A. (2018b, July 11), "Revisiting the expat dependent tax", *Gulf News*, http://gulfnews.com (Accessed on 01.12.2018).

Al-Misbahi, Abdur Rahman (2017, February 02), "Cancel expat levy, ICCI tells ministry", *Saudi Gazette*, http://saudigazette.com.sa (Accessed on 30.12.2019).

Al-Qahtani, Faris (2018, September 05), "Shoura discusses expat remittances", *Saudi Gazette*, http://saudigazette.com.sa (Accessed on 26.09.2018).

Apricorp Energy Research (2016, January), "Energy price reform in the G.C.C: Long Road Ahead", *1*(4).
Arab News (2015, November 02), "Water Tariff to rise 50 percent next month", www.arabnews.com (Accessed on 28.04.2019).
Arab News (2016, June 23), "Only 26% users affected by hike in power tariff", www.arabnews.com (Accessed on 26.04.2019).
Arabian Business (2016, May 17), "New Saudi Minister to set affordable water tariff", www.arabianbusiness.com (Accessed on 28.04.2019).
Azhar Muhammad (2015), *Indian Diaspora in West Asia*, A.M.U., Aligarh.
Azhar Muhammad (2017), "Indians in Saudi Arabia", *Journal of West Asian Studies*, Vol.20, A.M.U., Aligarh.
Basheer, K.P.M (2017, July 07), "Tax forces Indian families to exit Saudi", *The Hindu*, www.thehindu.com (Accessed on 21.10.2017).
Carey, Glen (2018, July 10), "Why expatriate workers are leaving Saudi Arabia in droves", *The Economic Times*, http://economictimes. Indiatimes.com (Accessed on 26.09.2018).
Dahlan, Abdullah Sadiq (2017, July 18), "The impact of dependent tax on markets", *Saudi Gazette*, http://saudigazette.com.sa (Accessed on 31.10.2017).
El-Katiri, Laura (2016, July 06), "Saudi Arabia's labour market challenge", *Harvard Business Review*, http://hbr.org (Accessed on 06.05.2019).
Ey-Global (2017, October 11), "Saudi Arabia amends income tax laws", www.ey .com (Accessed on 21.02.2018).
Gasoline Prices (2019), www.globalpetrolprices.com (Accessed on 05.11.2019).
Ghoshal, Somak (2017, June 21), "How Saudi Arabia's "Family Tax" is forcing Indians to return home", *Huffpost India*, www.huffingpost.in (Accessed on 21.12.2017).
Global Authority for Statistics (2017), "Population in Saudi Arabia – Mid 2017", www.stats.gov.sa (Accessed on 02.03.2018).
Global Water Intelligence (2017, October 12), "IMF urges restraint on Saudi water tariff reform", www.globalwaterintel.com (Accessed on 28.09.2018).
Halligan, Neil (2018, January 01), "Saudi Arabia hikes the prices of petrol", *Arabian Business*, www.arabianbusiness.com (Accessed on 05.11.2019).
International Monetary Fund (IMF, 2015), "Tax policy reforms in the G.C.C. Countries: Now and How?", www.imf.org (Accessed on 13.04.2017).
IMF (2016), Diversifying government revenues in the G.C.C. next step, Annual Meeting of Ministers of Finance and Central Bank Governers, Riyadh.
IMF (2017), *The Economic Outlook and Policy Challenges in G.C.C.* Countries, Washington.
Karim, Naimul (2018, March 16), "Time to go?", *The Daily Star*, www.thedailystar .net (Accessed on 26.09.2018).
Kerr, Simeon (2015, November 12), "Saudi Arabia looks to reform energy subsidy programme", *The Financial Times*, www.ft.com (Accessed on 30.10.2017).
Kerr, Simeon (2016, June 08), "Saudi Arabia considers income tax for foreign residents", *The Financial Times*, www.ft.com (Accessed on 21.02.2018).
Khaleej Times (2017, July 07), "Expats in Saudi to pay 100 Riyals tax per family member", www.khaleejtimes.com (Accessed on 21.02.2018).
KNOMAD (2019, April), "Migration and Remittances", *Migration and Development*, Brief 31, World Bank Group.
Moerenhout, Top (2018), *Energy pricing in the Gulf*, IISD.

Oxford Business Group (2015), "Tax System and Tax Regulations Saudi Arabia," http://oxfordbusinessgroup.com (Accessed on 21.02.2018).
Oxford Business Group (2016), "Saudi Arabia to use taxes to boost state revenues, Saudi Arabia," http://oxfordbusinessgroup.com (Accessed on 22.01.2019).
Rao, Ch. Sushil (2017, June 21), "Indians brace for Saudi family tax", *The Economic Times*, http://econimictimes.indiatimes.com (Accessed on 09.02.2018)
Rawuf, Abdul (2016, November 22), "Saudi may reduce water power subsidies further under new national programme", *Arabian Business*, www.arabianbusiness.com (Accessed on 30.10.2017).
Robinson, Gary (2017, January 06), "New Saudi expat levy set to harm businesses and families: Riyadh Chamber", *International Investment*, www.internationalinvestment.net (Access on 12.01.2018).
Saudi Arab Monetary Authority (SAMA, 2017), "Fifty Third Annual Report, 1438H (2017)", www.sama.gov.sa (Accessed on 17.12.2018).
SAMA (2018), "Fifty Fourth Annual Report, 1439H (2018)", www.sama.gov.sa (Accessed on 07.05.2019).
Saudi Gazette (2018, November 08), "5% VAT on money transfer fee", http://saudigazette.com (Accessed on 28.02.2018).
Saudi Gazette (2019, February 18), "Anti-tasattur programme wins approval from top", http://saudigazette.com (Accessed on 20.04.2019).
SAUDI-EXPATRIATES (2017), "Foreign workers population in KSA", www.saudi-expatriates.com (Accessed on 21.10.2017).
Taha, Sharif M. (2016, September 18), "Saudi Arabia: Subsidies on seven services set to go", *Arab News*, www.arabnews.com (Accessed on 30.04.2019).
The New Arab (2017, December 22), "Half of the Saudi Arabia's population are receiving welfare payments", www.alarby.co.uk (Accessed on 29.08.2019).
The Times of India (2018, June 08), "Ghar Wapsi: Why Indian expats in Saudi Arabia are sending their families back home", http://timesof india.com (Accessed on 26.09.2018).
Wald, Ellen R. (2018, August 08), "Saudi Energy Subsidy cuts an early success", *Arab News*, www.arabnews.com (Accessed on 05.07.2019).

9 Are Remittance Inflows Good for Economic Growth? Evidence from India Using the Linear ARDL Approach

Shahid Bashir and Mohsin Majeed

Introduction

Over the past few decades, remittances have become an important driver of economic growth in many developing countries. Fundamentally, remittances are the payments or gifts made by an emigrant to family members or others back home (Jijin, Mishra, & Nithin, 2021). The growing amount of remittances to developing countries is gaining much interest in recent years because of its macroeconomic impacts on the countries receiving it. For many developing countries, remittances typically outweigh Foreign Direct Investment (FDI), portfolio inflows from financial markets and official development assistance (Chami et al., 2008). After FDI, remittances have become the second-largest source of international finance (Aggarwal, Demirguc-Kunt & Peria, 2011). Such mounting aggregate remittance inflows are expected to have a significant macroeconomic impact on the receiving countries. Thus, it becomes increasingly important for policymakers to understand the effects of remittance inflows on economic growth and devise appropriate policy strategies accordingly. Beyond the fact that remittance inflows reduce poverty, boost human capital and decrease inequalities, their actual macroeconomic effects are still not clear (Bajaras, 2009). Some studies have documented that remittance inflows have a detrimental impact on the recipient countries in terms of appreciation of exchange rate, increase in the inflation rate, and decrease in the labor supply (Acosta, Lartey & Mandelman, 2009). The present study is an attempt to investigate the remittance-growth nexus in India with a most recent sample. Indian economy stands out to be a perfect case for such investigation because India has experienced mounting remittance inflows in the past decade. Specifically, the present study primarily focuses on how the real GDP growth rate is affected by these remittance inflows in recent years. There is a lack of unanimity among the existing studies regarding the relationship between remittances and economic growth.

The empirical contributions of the present study to the existing body of literature are threefold. First, we are investigating the remittance-growth relationship with the most recent sample for India. Second, we augment the

DOI: 10.4324/9781003369370-12

unit root analysis by employing Zivot-Andrews unit root test, which considers structural breaks in the data as the existing studies have not taken structural breaks into consideration. Third, we have employed a ground breaking cointegration technique-Autoregressive Distributed Lag (ARDL) model propounded by Pesaran, Shin & Smith (2001) as a significant improvement over conventional cointegration techniques.

The structure of the paper is as follows. After the introduction, the section gives an overview of the scenario of inward remittances from the Gulf countries. The third section gives a synoptic view of the existing literature which reflects the present research landscape on the remittance-growth nexus. The fourth section provides a glimpse of the data and methodology used in the present study. The fifth section reports the results of our empirical exercise, and finally, the sixth section concludes the study.

Scenario of Inward Remittances from the Gulf Countries

The Gulf Cooperation Council (GCC) which includes countries like Bahrain, Kuwait, Oman, Qatar, Saudi Arabia, and the United Arab Emirates, constitute the immediate neighbors of India that are separated only by the Arabian Sea. The relationship between India and the Arab countries dates back to the Indus Valley Civilization. The Gulf countries together always had a tremendous economic importance for India. In recent times the GCC has emerged as the main trading partner of India.

India is the largest country of origin for international migrants and the GCC countries collectively host a majority of India's overseas workers. Indians make up more than 30 percent of the immigrant labor force in GCC (Calabrese, 2020). As far as the profile of migrants to the GCC countries is concerned, the nature of employment of most of the Indian migrant workers is contractual, and the majority of them (almost 70 percent) are either semiskilled or unskilled. Only 20 percent of the remaining migrants have "white-collar" jobs and about 10 percent are professionals (Bhandari & Malik, 2008). Of nearly 31 million nonresident Indians (NRIs), around 8.5 million are living in the GCC countries which makes India–GCC the world's second-largest migration corridor. India has been the world's top most remittances recipient nation followed by Mexico and China. The Gulf countries have always been a place of attraction for India workers mainly because of wage differential and sound job opportunities. Since the oil boom of the 1970s, Indian migration to the Gulf has been one of the most important sources of income particularly for the states like Kerala, Maharashtra, and Karnataka which collectively receive about 50.7 percent of the total remittances inflow to India (RBI, 2018). In 2020, despite the pandemic, India received $83 billion as remittances from the world and continued to be the largest remittances recipient nation. In 2020 there was only a small decline of 0.2 percent in remittances mainly as a result of the decline from the UAE which was offset by the increase in remittances from the USA. In

2021 India received $87 billion in remittances which are expected to reach 89.6 billion in 2022 as a large proportion of returned laborers from Arab countries await return (World Bank, 2021). During the last couple of years, the migration from India to the Gulf has witnessed a slack mainly due to the economic slowdown, fluctuations in crude prices, and changes in labor policy in these countries. In addition, Covid-19 has posed a new threat to the international mobility of labor. As per world bank reports, the remittances to low- and middle-income countries have decreased by 1.6 percent in 2020 because of the Covid-19 pandemic.

To give a glimpse of the distribution of inward remittances, we have used the data from the RBI Inward Remittances Survey 2016–2017. Figure 9.1 demonstrates that India received about 82 percent of the total remittances from just eight nations, viz., the United Arab Emirates, the United States, Saudi Arabia, Qatar, Kuwait, Oman, the United Kingdom, and Malaysia. It is also evident that the share of the GCC countries in the total inward remittances is more than 53 percent, excluding Bahrain. If we talk about the state-wise distribution of inward remittances, Figure 9.2 reveals that four states received almost 59 percent more of the total remittance inflows, viz, Kerala, Maharashtra, Karnataka, and Tamil Nadu with 19, 16.7, 15.0, and 8.0 percent share, respectively. The RBI survey also revealed that 59.2 percent remittance inflows are used for consumption purposes and 8.3 percent for investment purposes. This lends strong support to our finding that remittance inflows spur economic growth in both the short term and long term. The justification for this finding is that both consumption and investment are the key factors which boost the economy's aggregate demand and eventually push up economic growth.

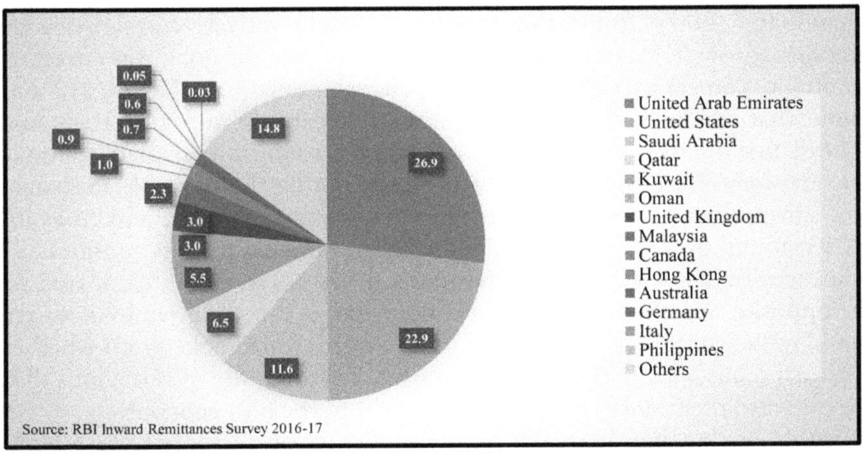

Figure 9.1 Country-wise share in inward remittances (%)

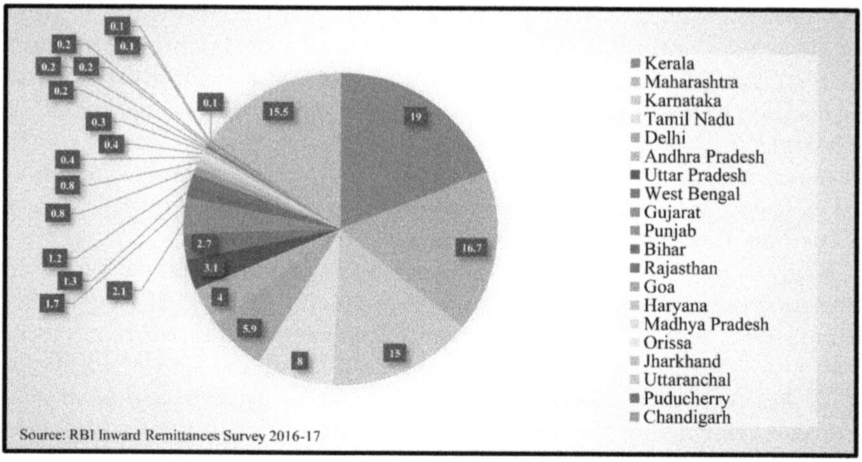

Figure 9.2 State-wise share in inward remittances (%)

Review of the Literature

The inward remittances of the workers play an important role in influencing many macroeconomic indicators of a country and GDP is an important one among them. A bulk of literature suggests that remittances have a positive and significant impact on raising economic growth. Ahmed, Zaman, and Shah (2011) concluded that remittances favorably affect economic growth in both the long run and short run by studying the remittance-growth nexus in Pakistan for the years 1976–2009 using a bounds-testing approach. Similarly, in another study conducted in the same country with a similar econometric technique for the period 1991 Q1 up to 2007 Q4, Shahbaz, Ahmad, and Chaudhary, (2009) found that remittances are positively correlated with economic growth. Hassan and Shakur (2017) studied the nonlinear effects of remittances on per capita GDP growth in Bangladesh during 1976–2012 and found that the inward remittances initially negatively impacted economic growth but became positive at a later stage forming a U-shaped relationship between the two variables. It is worth noting that a stable exchange rate can positively affect the remittances as Rahman, Foshee and Mustafa (2013) found in the US, changes in exchange rates exert more pronounced influences on the changes of remittances in the long run as compared to the opposite. Another side of this phenomenon is if inward remittances are found to be fruitful for an economy, it also needs to be looked into whether outward remittances have the same impact. Theoretically, it is obvious that the outward remittances must be detrimental to the host economy.

Saudi Arabia has been the most attractive place for workers from India, Pakistan, Bangladesh, and Afghanistan. A study in Saudi Arabia by

Alkhathlan (2013) for the period 1970–2010 using the ARDL approach found a negative relationship between outward remittances and economic growth in the long run. Now coming to the Indian economy, a rapid rise was seen in remittances especially after the economic reforms of the 1990s. India has become one of the top recipients of the remittances. In India too, the inward remittances play a prominent role in the country's growth path, e.g., Jayaraman, Choong, and Kumar (2012) adopted the augmented the Solow model and employed a bounds-testing procedure to find out the long-term relationship between remittances, FDI, foreign assistance, and economic growth in India for the period 1970–2009. The study finds that for four decades (1970–2009), remittance inflows, and the development of financial sector had a favorable impact on the economy's growth trajectory. These remittances do have a positive effect on the GDP of a country through many channels as macroeconomic variables are interwoven and do have an impact on one another. Besides, it has been found that remittances have a positive impact on certain macroeconomic variables which in turn help the economy to grow. Narang (2020) found that remittances in India from 1975 to 2017 caused the gross fixed capital formation and the household final consumption expenditure to increase, which plays an important role in determining the gross domestic product of the economy. In the present study, we have also incorporated external debt as an independent variable in the model, so it is important for us to highlight the effects of external debt on the economic growth of a county as well. There are contradicting studies as far as the impact of external debt is concerned. Sometimes it fuels economic growth, but that is not sustainable for too long. In most cases, the external debt has been found detrimental to the economic growth as found by Ohiomu, (2020) using ARDL in Nigeria. Similarly, Qayyum and Haider (2012) investigated the impact of foreign aid, external debt, and governance on economic growth for 60 developing countries for the period 1984–2010 using an extended version of the neo-classical model of Solow and Swan. The results revealed that governance and foreign aid stimulate the output, but the external debt reduces the output growth. Presbitero, (2005) found support for the negative linear relationship between external debt and economic growth, and between debt service and investment with strong effects in low-income countries than the overall sample of 152 developing countries over the period 1977–2002. In some studies, the external debt has been found helpful but to a certain level only, e.g. Gómez-Puig and Sosvilla-Rivero (2017) found that an increase in debt has a negative impact on economic growth after a certain threshold level in all the European countries except for Belgium for 1961–2015. The study results also show that a decrease in debt does not have any significant impact on the economic performance of euro-area countries.

Data and Methodology

The present study utilizes the data from 1975–2019 for the Indian economy. The availability of the data primarily drives the selection of the sample period. Our empirical exercise uses data of four macroeconomic variables – real GDP growth rate (GDP), remittances (REM), external debt (ED), and inflation (CPI). The data have been retrieved from the World Development Indicators database of the World Bank. Table 9.1 gives an overview of the description of these variables.

Table 9.1 Variable description

Variable	*Description*
Real GDP growth rate (GDP)	Annual percentage growth of GDP at market prices based on constant local currency units (proxy for economic growth).
Remittance inflows (REM)	Personal remittances received as a percentage of GDP. It comprises personal transfers and compensation of employees.
External debt (ED)	Total external debt stocks as a percentage of gross national income.
CPI	Annual percentage change in Consumer Price Index (proxy for inflation).

We started our econometric analysis by checking the stationarity properties of the variables. We used Augmented Dickey Fuller (ADF) and Phillips-Perron (PP) tests. Since these conventional unit root tests do not account for the possibility of structural breaks in the data and Perron (1989) pointed out that the power to reject a unit root hypothesis decreases when the stationary alternative is true and a structural break is ignored, we augment our unit root analysis with the use of the Zivot-Andrews (1992) unit root test. This test endogenizes one structural break in the data.

To test the relationship between remittance inflows and economic growth, we have employed wwwwwAutoregressive and Distributed Lag (ARDL) bounds-testing procedure by Pesaran, Shin and Smith (2001). The ARDL model is a significant improvement over the earlier cointegration techniques in terms of its potential merits. The beauty of this model is that it can be used irrespective of knowing the order of integration of the variables – i.e. if the variables are I(0), I(1), or have mixed order of integration but none of the variables should be I(2) (Pesaran, Shin, & Smith, 2001). This technique is also suitable under small sample scenarios and provides consistent estimates. One more important merit of this technique is that if the lag length is correctly chosen, the problem of endogeneity is automatically corrected (Pesaran, Shin, & Smith, 2001).

The ARDL representation of our empirical model is as follows:

$$\Delta GDP_t = \partial_0 + \delta_1 \sum_{i=1}^{p} \Delta GDP_{t-i} + \delta_2 \sum_{i=0}^{q} \Delta REM_{t-i}$$

$$+ \delta_3 \sum_{i=0}^{q} \Delta ED_{t-i} + \delta_4 \sum_{i=0}^{q} \Delta CPI_{t-i}$$

$$+ \left(\psi_1 GDP_{t-1} + \psi_2 REM_{t-1} + \psi_3 ED_{t-1} + \psi_4 CPI_{t-1} \right)$$

$$+ \varepsilon_t (1)$$

Where $\delta_1, \delta_2, \delta_3$ and δ_4 are the short-run coefficients, ψ_1 ,ψ_2,ψ_3 and ψ_4 are the long-run coefficients and ε_t is an *iid* error term.

The presence of a long-run relationship (cointegration) is tested using standard Wald test/F-statistic in which the null hypothesis of no cointegration ($H_0 : \psi_1 = \psi_2 = \psi_3 = \psi_4 = 0$) is tested against the alternative of cointegration ($H_1 : \psi_1 \neq \psi_2 \neq \psi_3 \neq \psi_4 \neq 0$). To arrive at a conclusion, the calculated F-statistic is compared with the upper bound [I(1)] and lower bound [I(0)] critical values. If the calculated F-statistic is greater than the upper bound critical value, there is cointegration among the variables while as if the calculated F-statistic is lesser than the lower bound critical value, there is no cointegration. If the F-statistic falls in between the upper and lower bound critical value, the result is inconclusive. The appropriate lag length is chosen by Akaike Information Criterion (AIC) or Schwarz Bayesian Criterion (SBC). Once the optimal lag length is chosen and cointegration is present, we estimate the following ARDL(*p*, *q*) model:

$$\Delta GDP_t = \partial_0 + \delta_1 \sum_{i=1}^{p} \Delta GDP_{t-i} + \delta_2 \sum_{i=0}^{q} \Delta REM_{t-i}$$

$$+ \delta_3 \sum_{i=0}^{q} \Delta ED_{t-i} + \delta_4 \sum_{i=0}^{q} \Delta CPI_{t-i}$$

$$+ \left(\psi_1 GDP_{t-1} + \psi_2 REM_{t-1} + \psi_3 ED_{t-1} + \psi_4 CPI_{t-1} \right) + \varepsilon_t (2)$$

While the short-term relationship can be estimated using the ARDL-ECM model:

$$\Delta GDP_t = \partial_0 + \delta_1 \sum_{i=1}^{p} \Delta GDP_{t-i} + \delta_2 \sum_{i=0}^{q} \Delta REM_{t-i}$$

$$+ \delta_3 \sum_{i=0}^{q} \Delta ED_{t-i} + \delta_4 \sum_{i=0}^{q} \Delta CPI_{t-i}$$

$$+ \varphi ECT_{t-1} + \varepsilon_t (3)$$

where ECT is the error correction term and φ symbolizes the speed of adjustment to restore long-run equilibrium after a shock hits the system in the short run. For diagnostic checking, we employed the Jarque-Bera test for normality, Lagrangian Multiplier (LM) test for serial correlation, Breusch–Pagan–Godfrey (BPG) test for heteroscedasticity, and Ramsey RESET test for model specification. We also used CUSUM and CUSUMSQ to test the stability of the estimated model.

Empirical Results

Descriptive Statistics

Table 9.2 gives an overview of the descriptive statistics and correlation coefficients of the variables. It is evident from panel A of Table 9.2 that remittance inflows as a percentage of GDP have an average level of 2.11 percent and reached the maximum value of 4.17 percent in 2008. External

Table 9.2 Descriptive statistics and correlation analysis

	GDP	*REM*	*ED*	*CPI*
Panel A: Descriptive statistics				
Mean	5.834	2.112	19.889	7.362
Median	6.119	2.249	19.491	7.659
Maximum	9.627	4.168	33.157	13.870
Minimum	-5.238	0.436	11.096	-7.633
Std. Dev.	2.590	1.087	5.425	3.771
Skewness	-1.826	0.087	0.536	-1.168
Kurtosis	8.612	1.590	2.977	6.745
Jarque-Bera	84.07	3.781	2.159	36.536*
p-value	0.000	0.150	0.339	0.000
N	45	45	45	45
Panel B: Correlation matrix				
GDP	1	–	–	–
REM	0.230	1	–	–
ED	-0.037	0.113	1	–
CPI	0.106	-0.022	0.253	1

* denotes the significance at 1 percent level

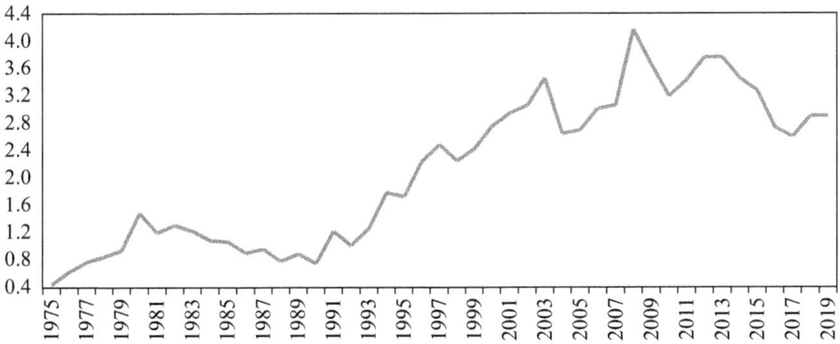

Figure 9.3 Trend of remittance inflows over time (% of GDP)

debt as a percentage of Gross National Income (GNI) has an average level of 19.89 percent and reached a maximum in 1993 (33.16 percent). If we look at the Jarque-Bera statistic, REM and ED are normally distributed but GDP and CPI are not. The correlation matrix in panel B of Table 9.2 indicates that a positive correlation exists between real GDP growth rate and remittance inflows which is consistent with the theoretical underpinnings. However, it should be kept in mind that correlation does not necessarily imply causation.

Figure 9.3 gives an overview of the trend of remittance inflows into the Indian economy during the sample period. It is evident that remittance inflows as a percentage of GDP exhibit a continuously increasing trend from 1991 onwards. The figure also reveals that there is a continuous decline in the remittance inflows from 1980 to 1990. Remittance inflows to India declined marginally from 4.16 percent in 2008 to 3.42 percent in 2011. These remittances declined due to the global financial crises of 2007–2008. Therefore, it can be inferred that global financial crises had a limited impact on remittance inflows in India. The possible reasons could be falling asset prices in India, rising interest rate differentials, and depreciation of the local currency.

Unit Root Analysis

As a first step of our econometric exercise, we check the stationarity properties of the variables using ADF and PP tests. This step is important because the ARDL bounds-testing procedure requires that none of the variables is I(2). Table 9.3 reports the results of ADF and PP tests. The results suggest that GDP and CPI variables are stationary at level while REM and ED become stationary after the first differences. Therefore, it can be concluded

Table 9.3 ADF and PP unit root test results

Panel A: ADF test					
		Level			
		GDP	*REM*	*ED*	*CPI*
Without constant	*t-Statistic*	-6.965*	-1.497	-2.571	-4.667*
	p-Value	0.000	0.525	0.106	0.000
Without constant and trend	*t-Statistic*	-8.040*	-1.953	-2.417	-4.619*
	p-Value	0.000	0.609	0.365	0.003
Without constant and trend	*t-Statistic*	-1.097	0.293	0.051	-1.750***
	p-Value	0.242	0.766	0.693	0.076
		First differences			
Without constant	*t-Statistic*	-11.290*	-7.332*	-2.792***	-6.674*
	p-Value	0.000	0.000	0.068	0.000
Without constant and trend	*t-Statistic*	-11.146*	-7.319*	-4.949*	-6.581
	p-Value	0.000	0.000	0.001	0.000*
Without constant and trend	*t-Statistic*	-11.430*	-7.218*	-2.802*	-6.757*
	p-Value	0.000	0.000	0.006	0.000
Panel B: PP test					
Without constant	*t-Statistic*	-6.952*	-1.497	-1.719	-4.725*
	p-Value	0.000	0.525	0.414	0.000
Without constant and trend	*t-Statistic*	-10.633*	-1.910	-1.579	-4.663*
	p-Value	0.000	0.632	0.785	0.002
Without constant and trend	*t-Statistic*	-2.022**	0.293	-0.131	-1.390
	p-Value	0.042	0.766	0.632	0.150
		First differences			
Without constant	t-Statistic	-37.891*	-7.341*	-4.889*	-12.467*
	p-Value	0.000	0.000	0.000	0.000
Without constant and trend	t-Statistic	-46.358*	-7.380*	-4.895*	-12.977*
	p-Value	0.000	0.000	0.001	0.000
Without constant and trend	t-Statistic	-36.841*	-7.218*	-5.074*	-12.549*
	p-Value	0.000	0.000	0.000	0.000

Optimal lag length based on SIC.
Probability is based on MacKinnon (1996) one-sided p-values.
-3.59, -2.93, and -2.60 are the critical values at 1 percent, 5 percent, and 10 percent level, respectively.
*, **, and *** denote the significance at 1 percent, 5 percent, and 10 percent level, respectively.

from these results that the maximum order of integration of the variables is 1 and the application of ARDL methodology becomes ideal in our case.

Since ADF and PP tests suffer from a major limitation of not accounting for structural breaks in the data, we applied the Zivot-Andrews test to overcome such limitations. The results are reported in Table 9.4. It is evident that GDP and CPI are stationary at levels with no structural break present but REM and CPI are non-stationary at level with structural breaks in 2008 and 1989, respectively. The structural break for REM in 2008 can be attributed to the global financial crisis of 2007–2008.

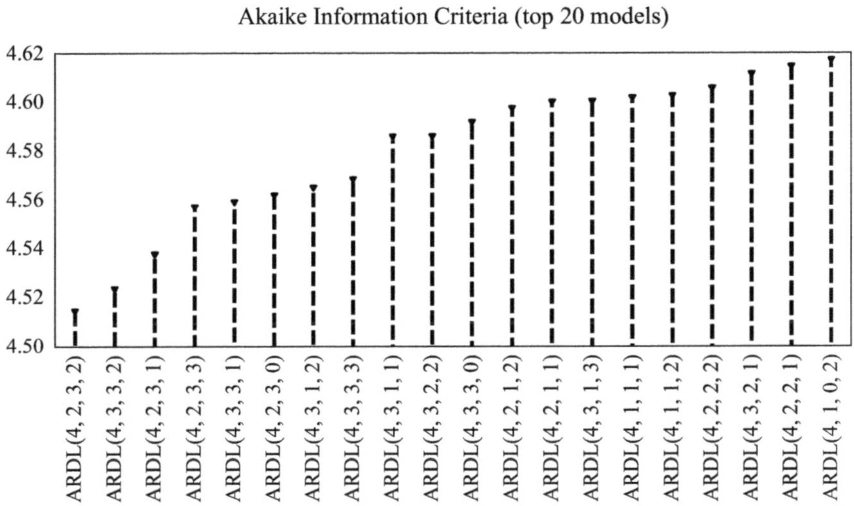

Figure 9.4 Model selection graph

Table 9.4 Zivot-Andrews unit root test results

Series	*Level*			*First difference*		
	t-Statistic (β)	*k*	*Break date*	*t-Statistic (β)*	*k*	*Break date*
GDP	-7.150*	3	1991	-5.408	4	2003
REM	-3.330	0	2008	-7.900*	0	1991
ED	-4.102	2	1989	-4.560**	1	1992
CPI	-5.646*	4	1999	-4.122	4	2006

Both the trend and intercept have been included. k is the lag length.
-5.57, -5.08, and -4.82 are the critical values at 1 percent, 5 percent, and 10 percent level, respectively.
*, **, and *** denote the significance at 1 percent, 5 percent and 10 percent level, respectively.

Cointegration Analysis

The results of ARDL bounds test are reported in Table 9.5. From the table it is clear that there exists a long-run equilibrium relationship between the underlying variables because the F-statistic is greater than the 1 percent upper bound asymptotic and finite sample critical value. The null hypothesis is that there is no long-run relationship among the variables.

Short-Run and Long-Run Dynamics

After the bounds test confirms the long-run relationship, we estimate the short-run and long-run coefficients presented in Tables 9.6 and 9.7,

Table 9.5 ARDL bounds test

				Critical values Asymptotic n=1000		Critical values Finite sample n=45	
Test statistic	*Value*	*k*	*Sig.*	*Lower bound I(0)*	*Upper bound I(1)*	*Lower bound I(0)*	*Upper bound I(1)*
F-statistic	6.865*	3					
			@ 1%	4.290	5.610	5.018	6.610
			@ 5%	3.230	4.350	3.548	4.803
			@ 10%	2.720	3.770	2.933	4.020

* denotes the significance at 1 percent level.

Table 9.6 Short-run coefficients (ARDL 4,2,3,2)

Regressor	*Coefficient*	*t-Statistic*	*p-value*
C	4.939634***	2.049129	0.0507
ΔGDP_t	-1.911307*	-4.911979	0.0000
ΔGDP_{t-1}	0.823620**	2.395841	0.0241
ΔGDP_{t-2}	0.507712***	1.984215	0.0579
ΔGDP_{t-3}	0.514203*	3.482485	0.0018
ΔREM_t	1.420757*	3.160818	0.0040
ΔREM_{t-1}	-0.969185	-0.833891	0.4119
ΔREM_{t-2}	-2.611406**	-2.164941	0.0398
ΔED_t	-0.168729***	-1.958281	0.0610
ΔED_{t-1}	-0.055540	-0.214548	0.8318
ΔED_{t-2}	0.313855	1.396869	0.1743
ΔED_{t-3}	-0.465168***	-1.977247	0.0587
ΔCPI_t	-0.018070	-0.102981	0.9188
ΔCPI_{t-1}	-0.084259	-0.554619	0.5839
ΔCPI_{t-2}	0.204162	1.393594	0.1752
ECT(-1)	-1.088997*	-8.485941	0.0000

Dependent variable is ΔGDP.
*, **, and *** denote the significance at 1 percent, 5 percent, and 10 percent level, respectively.
Optimal lag length is based on Akaike Information Criterion (AIC).

respectively. The appropriate lag length has been selected using the Akaike Information Criterion (AIC). It is evident that the long-run coefficients for REM and ED are statistically significant at 1 percent and 5 percent level, respectively. This implies a positive long-run relationship between remittance inflows and economic growth. With a 1 percent increase in

Table 9.7 Long-run coefficients (ARDL 4,2,3,2)

Regressor	*Coefficient*	*t-statistic*	*p-value*
REM	0.743343*	4.126870	0.0003
ED	-0.088279**	-2.236527	0.0341
CPI	-0.009454	-0.103732	0.9182

Dependent variable is GDP.
* and ** denote significance at 1 percent and 5 percent level, respectively.
Optimal lag length is based on Akaike Information Criterion (AIC).

the remittance inflows, the real GDP growth rate increases on an average by 0.74 percent. This finding is consistent with the findings of Ginliano and Ruiz-Arranz (2009) and Jayaraman, Choong, and Kumar (2012). Remittances form one of the main sources for the private savings of workers and their families that are spent in the home country. These savings are also mobilized for investment purposes by the families of workers at the home country and which drive the home economy. In this way, remittances fuel aggregate demand in the workers' home country and eventually spur economic growth. It can also be inferred that there is a significant negative relationship between external debt and economic growth and with a 1 percent increase in the external debt, real GDP growth decreases on an average by 0.09 percent. The external debt negatively affects economic growth due to the "debt-crowding-out effect" as debt raises interest rates, which discourages private investment. The coefficient for CPI is statistically insignificant which means that there is no relationship between inflation and economic growth in India. If we look at the short-run coefficients, the positive relationship between remittance inflows and economic growth in India also holds in the short run. No doubt the magnitude of the coefficient is twice the long-run coefficient. Similarly, the negative relationship between external debt and economic growth is valid also in the short run. The error correction coefficient is highly significant with the expected negative sign implying that disequilibrium is corrected in the subsequent year in full i.e., 100 percent.

Diagnostic Checking

From Table 9.8, it is clear that our estimated ARDL model qualifies all the diagnostic tests. The Jarque-Bera test reveals that the errors are normally distributed. LM test confirms the absence of serial correlation in errors. BPG and ARCH tests confirm that the model does not suffer from the problem of heteroscedasticity. Ramsey RESET test shows that our model is correctly specified.

Moreover, CUSUM and CUSUMSQ tests (Figure 9.5) reveal that the empirical model is stable because these test statistics lie within the 5 percent critical limits.

Table 9.8 Diagnostic checking

Test	*Test statistic*	*p-value*
Jarque-Bera χ2	1.870	0.392
Lagrangian multiplier test	0.111	0.979
Breusch–Pagan–Godfrey (BPG) test	0.870	0.595
ARCH	1.057	0.393
Ramsey RESET test	0.553	0.583

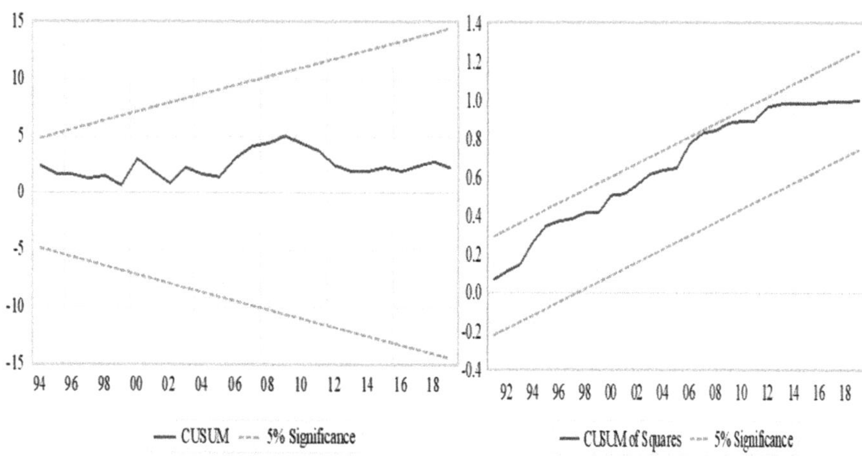

Figure 9.5 CUSUM and CUSUMSQ test

Conclusion and Policy Recommendations

The growing amount of remittances to developing countries is gaining much interest in recent years because of its macroeconomic impacts on the countries receiving it. After FDI, remittances have become the second-largest source of international finance. The share of remittances from the Gulf countries is more than 53 percent of the total inward remittances. This result is not surprising given the fact that the majority of the Indian migrants live in the GCC region. According to the figures provided by the Ministry of External Affairs, out of the total number of Indian migrants which exceeds 13.1 million, 23.6 percent are settled in the United Arab Emirates, 21.4 percent in Saudi Arabia and 9.8 percent in the United States. The remittance-growth nexus is a debatable issue in the macroeconomic literature. The existing literature has provided mixed evidence for both positive and negative relationships between these two variables. The mixed evidences could be attributed to the methodological and sample differences and country-specific characteristics. The present study investigates the remittance-growth nexus in India over the sample period 1975–2019. Our econometric exercise has employed a multivariate ARDL cointegration approach with external debt and CPI as additional relevant variables. It was found that remittance inflows spur economic growth in India. It was also found that external debt negatively affects the economic growth in the Indian economy. Since we have found that remittance inflows positively affect economic growth, policy implications indicate that India should adopt policy measures to encourage inward remittances. This can be done by offering a higher interest rate on NRI deposits to accelerate the growth of inward remittances. Moreover, the costs of foreign remittance transfers should be minimized.

Despite the promising results, the current study is certainly not free from limitations. It is a country-specific study; the findings should be interpreted with caution in terms of their generalizability. Another limitation could be the possibility of omitted variables bias in the estimation technique used because there could be other important macroeconomic variables which might significantly affect the remittance-growth nexus.

References

Acosta, P. A., Lartey, E. K. K., & Mandelman, F. S. (2009). Remittances and the Dutch Disease. *Journal of International Economics*, *79*(1), 102–116. https://doi.org/10.1016/j.jinteco.2009.06.007

Aggarwal, R., Demirguc-Kunt, A., & Peria, M. S. M. (2011). Do Remittances Promote Financial Development? *Journal of Development Economics*, *96*(2), 252–264. https://doi.org/10.1016/j.jdeveco.2010.10.005

Ahmed, J., Zaman, K., & Shah, I. A. (2011). An Empirical Analysis of Remittances-Growth Nexus in Pakistan Using Bounds Testing Approach. *Journal of Economics and International Finance*, *3*(3), 176–186.

Alkhathlan, K. A. (2013). The Nexus Between Remittance Outflows and Growth: A Study of Saudi Arabia. *Economic Modelling*, *33*, 695–700. https://doi.org/10.1016/j.econmod.2013.05.010.

Barajas, A., Chami, R., Fullenkamp, C., Gapen, M. T., & Montiel, P. (2009). *Do Workers' Remittances Promote Economic Growth? IMF Working Papers* (Vol. 09). https://doi.org/10.5089/9781451873009.001

Bhandari, L., & Malik, P. (2008). *India's Talent Migration*. Prepared for Manpower, Inc., New Delhi, November 8.

Calabrese, J. (2020, April 14). *India-Gulf Migration: A Testing Time*. https://www.mei.edu/publications/india-gulf-migration-testing-time.

Chami, R., Barajas, A., Cosimano, T., Fullenkamp, C., Gapen, M., & Montiel, P. (2008). *The Macroeconomic Consequences of Remittances. Occasional Paper*. International Monetary Fund, Washington, DC. https://doi.org/10.1016/j.jinteco.2018.01.010

Dickey, D. A., & Fuller, W. A. (1979). Distribution of the Estimators for Autoregressive Time Series with a Unit Root. *Journal of the American Statistical Association*, *74*(366), 427–341.

Giuliano, P., & Ruiz-Arranz, M. (2009). Remittances, Financial Development, and Growth. *Journal of Development Economics*, *90*(1), 144–152. https://doi.org/10.1016/j.jdeveco.2008.10.005

Gómez-Puig, M., & Sosvilla-Rivero, S. (2017). Heterogeneity in the Debt-Growth Nexus: Evidence from EMU Countries. *International Review of Economics and Finance*, *51*(March), 470–486. https://doi.org/10.1016/j.iref.2017.07.008

Hassan, G. M., & Shakur, S. (2017). Nonlinear Effects of Remittances on Per Capita GDP Growth in Bangladesh. *Economies*, *5*(3), 1–11. https://doi.org/10.3390/economies5030025

Jayaraman, T. K., Choong, C.-K., & Kumar, R. R. (2012). Role of Remittances in India's Economic Growth. *Global Business and Economics Review*, *14*(3), 159–177.

Jijin, P., Mishra, A. K., & Nithin, M. (2021). Macroeconomic Determinants of Remittances to India. *Economic Change and Restructuring*. https://doi.org/10.1007/s10644-021-09347-3

MacKinnon, J. G. (1996). Numerical Distribution Functions for Unit Root and Cointegration Tests. *Journal of Applied Economertics*, *11*, 601–618.

Narang, D. (2020). *Macroeconomic Outcomes of Remittances on the Indian Economy*. Delhi. https://doi.org/10.20944/preprints202005.0111.v1

Ohiomu, S. (2020). External Debt and Economic Growth Nexus : Empirical Evidence From Nigeria. *The American Economist*. https://doi.org/10.1177/0569434520914862

Perron, P. (1989). The Great Crash, the Oil Price Shock, and the Unit Root Hypothesis. *Econometrica*, *57*(6), 1361–1401. https://doi.org/10.2307/1913712

Pesaran, M. H., Shin, Y., & Smith, R. J. (2001). Bounds Testing Approaches to the Analysis of Level Relationships. *Journal of Applied Econometrics*, *16*(3), 289–326. https://doi.org/10.1002/jae.616

Phillips, P. C. B., & Perron, P. (1988). Testing for a Unit Root in Time Series Regression. *Biometrika*, *75*(2), 335–346. https://doi.org/10.1093/biomet/75.2.335

Presbitero, A. F. (2005). *The Debt-Growth Nexus: A Dynamic Panel Data Estimation*. Marche Polytechnic University, Ancona, Italy.

Qayyum, U., & Haider, A. (2012). Foreign Aid, External Debt and Economic Growth Nexus in Low-Income Countries : The Role of Institutional Quality. *The Pakistan Development Review*, *51*(4), 97–115.

Rahman, M., Foshee, A., & Mustafa, M. (2013). Remitances-Exchange Rate Nexus: The U.S.- Mexico Case. *The Journal of Developing Areas*, *47*(1), 63–74.

RBI. (2018). *India's Inward Remittances Survey 2016–17*.

Shahbaz, M., Ahmad, K., & Chaudhary, A.. (2009). Economic Growth and Its Determinants in Pakistan. *The Pakistan Development Review*, *47*(4), 471–486. http://www.jstor.org/stable/41261235

World Bank. (2021). *Migration and development-Brief 34*, World Bank, Washington.

Zivot, E., & Andrews, D. W. (1992). Further Evidence on the Great Crash, the Oil-Price Shock, and the Unit-Root Hypothesis. *Journal of Business and Economic Statistics*, *10*(3), 251–270. https://doi.org/10.1080/07350015.1992.10509904

10 The COVID-19 Crisis and Migration

Impact on the Kerala Economy

Muhammed Fazal

Introduction

COVID-19 put the whole world to a standstill as a paradigm for the negative externality of globalization. That is why COVID-19 is "the worst global crisis since the Second World War" (International Labour Organization, 2020). Any disaster, be it a pandemic or crisis, will easily and directly have ill repercussions for the common people or the poor for a long time, though the rich can overcome the situation after getting back on track. The Kerala economy is heavily backed up by remittances from its emigrants, especially in the Gulf Cooperation Council (GCC) countries. Though Kerala faced the Ockie cyclone, Nipah virus, and floods of 2018 and 2019, its economy remained resilient due to remittances. The COVID-19 crisis and lockdowns had effects both worldwide and on the state as it is a consumer state with conspicuous consumption. The Kerala economy will be affected unprecedently as the services industry, which is the most contributing sector, is most to be wounded for a long time with slower recovery than other sectors. This crisis poured oil on migration with the proximity of mass return foreign countries, especially those in the GCC with a considerable lack of remittances. In addition, the guest laborers are in the line of mass return.

The main concerns for return migration, as usual, will be the lack of remittances for the economy, and unemployment. Besides remittances, the GCC countries' migrants are rich in social gain as they are highly packed with social capital and absorption of various attitudes and cultures. Taking stock of both economic and social gains, the return migrants can be resettled well.

Migration and the Kerala Economy

Migration has become a 50-year-old Kerala tradition. Though the influx of emigration to the Gulf countries began in the 1970s due to a quadrantal hike in oil prices, its history traces back to the 1950s when 13 Keralites, illegally as was common then, left in a vessel for the Gulf and reached the Qatar shore after three months (Sanandakumar, 2015). Migration has helped the state frame the paradigm Kerala Model of Development in which the more

DOI: 10.4324/9781003369370-13

share of development which was from the primary sector directly turned to the tertiary sector, unlike any developed nation where it is in order via the secondary sector. In addition, it helped the creation of a peaceful and resilient state during communal tensions in the country. Without migration, Kerala would have been a literate, militant, explosive state. The majority are blue-collar job holders and low- or medium-income holders like salesmen, construction workers, drivers, etc. A total of 2.1 million Keralites live in various countries (Figure 10.1) with 90 percent in the Gulf, mainly in six countries – Saudi Arabia, the UAE, Qatar, Oman, Bahrain, and Kuwait – and the remaining are in other countries (Raja & Zachariah, 2019). Even with the lower-status job holders, most educated workers are Keralites with a minimum SSLC or plus two. About 20 million Indians live in 210 various countries. Ten million people of them are in the GCC region itself. Out of them, 2–2.5 million people hail from Kerala – that means one-fourth of Indian expatriates in GCC are Keralite (Ethiraj, 2020). Within the ten years of mass Gulf migration, the total number of emigrants reached about 2.3 lakh in the state. The year 2013 was one of saturation, the year in which the number of emigrants kept rising and started declining after that. Most of the emigrants leaving for the GCC region expect comfortable informal jobs which have been the backbone of Kerala for years; they used to return to the state and go to the same place or another in the region to get a job or seek a visiting visa. However, various reasons like the global and GCC crises have caused more people to return to the state.

Return Migration

Whenever migration started, return migration occurs accordingly. In Kerala's case, most migrants are in the informal sector with no sustainable

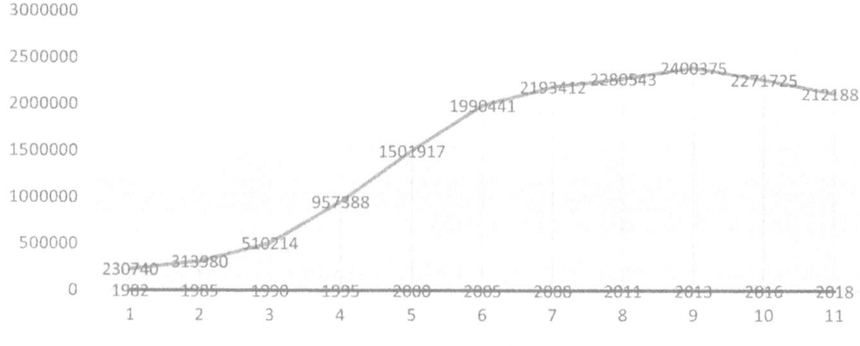

Figure 10.1 Trend of Kerala emigrants (1982–2018) Source: Calculation from Raja and Zachariah, 2019

Table 10.1 Return migrants – district-wise (1998–2018)

Districts	*1998*	*2003*	*2008*	*2013*	*2018*
Thiruvananthapuram	118878	103059	215280	218945	93662
Kollam	74106	69314	124066	127978	165504
Pathanamthitta	54537	83502	60554	36285	54506
Alappuzha	34572	43109	51024	70104	99929
Kottayam	18164	28368	26448	33898	41775
Idukki	5017	3766	3213	3242	6137
Ernakulam	45028	74435	68860	69545	23929
Thrissur	116788	86029	174655	103803	94279
Palakkad	39238	55008	85318	12383	57664
Malappuram	123750	141537	219736	299857	309881
Kozhikkode	60910	109101	72405	107491	151417
Wayanad	3327	3852	1930	12581	12046
Kannur	28263	45394	26416	109145	94457
Kasaragod	166677	47468	27222	47212	89610
Kerala	739245	893942	1157127	1252471	1294796

Source: Rajan and Zachariah (2019).

job security. The Kerala economy also benefitted mostly from the remittance from these unsecured contexts (Table 10.1).

As the majority of the migrants are temporal, the share of those who are laid off or lost jobs will increase every year which was 29.4 percent in 2018. The behavior or attitude of the migrants is that all will have endurance and disciple to cope with any adverse – natural and man-made – situations. That is why the number of returnees in that category will be a lot lower as the least shared category is that of overburden with 0.3 percent (Raja & Zachariah, 2019). The details of the reasons for the return migration of 2018 have been given in Figure 10.2.

Impact of COVID-19 on Migration

The COVID-19 crisis has become a ramification for the emigrants as they are at their wit's end both at home and in the GCC region. It has paved the way for GCC countries to localize and stabilize their economies due to multiple reasons. Many of them are forced to return. In the home country too, their return will be chaotic if proper rehabilitation isn't provided. They will be unemployed as they used to work in the informal sector as most of them are blue- collar job holders. Moreover, the remittance which helped about four to five persons in their households directly and many others indirectly will also affect the state economy in an unprecedented way. In addition, Kerala is in forefront of human development as the remittances play a lion's share. So, the crisis will affect charity and volunteering activities and many educational and other institutions for which remittance is the major backbone.

Education in Kerala is also a paradigm by which not much difference between social classes is seen. About eight percent of the total remittance is

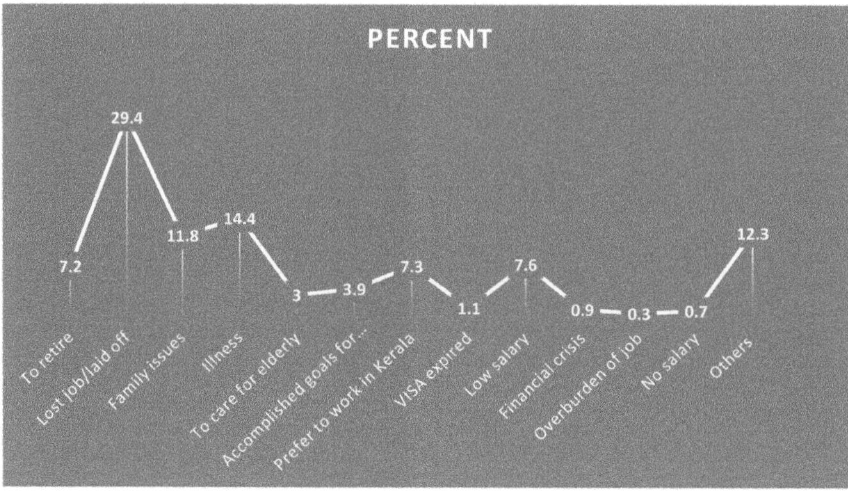

Figure 10.2 Reasons for return migration Source: KMS, 2018

wexclusively for the education of their children. By the return, it will also be affected.

The state is to be in a conundrum as manifold social and economic crises are prone unless proper rehabilitation occurs. The guest laborers who replaced migrants for the emigrants started to get higher and stabilized wages due to the remittance which is also a major issue the state is going to face.

About two lakh to three lakh people are expected to return leaving the GCC region, which counts about ten percent of the total migrant population by September (Varma, 2020). More than 4.27 lakh people have registered for return in NORKA Roots. More than 60,000 lost their jobs as per the present update which might increase due to the real crisis in the GCC countries. Visas of many people have been canceled or expired and many are uncertain about their way back to the region (Ethiraj, 2020).

Impact on Remittance

Kerala is a remittance economy as the amount of remittance comparing with Kerala Net State Domestic Product is much higher as it was about 36.5 percent in 2004. Annually, the chipping in remittance is about 40 percent of total bank deposits in the state. Every year the amount of total remittance kept increasing with high marginal increase except after 2008 and 2013 which showed the global financial crisis and the large return of migrants back to the state respectively.

Table 10.2 Remittances as share of NSDP, 1998–2018 (in Cr)

Indicators	*1998*	*2003*	*2008*	*2011*	*2014*	*2018*
Remittances	13652	18465	43288	49695	71142	85092
NSDP	53552	83783	140889	159144	196077	440515
Remittances as percent of NSDP	25.5	22.0	30.7	31.2	36.3	19.3

Source: KMS (2018).

The remittance from abroad was a major forward mover for Kerala. It helped Kerala economy mostly by enabling people to be financially capable of government aspirations that helped the state to advance in human development though the Per Capita Income is not so high and most of the people are middle incomed. The remittance contributes to economy similar to more than 20 percent of NSDP every year with 36.3 percent in 2014 and minimum 19.3 percent in 2018 (Table 10.2). This is the main factor in ameliorating the living standard of the state.

Though Kerala faced the Ockie cyclone, Nipah virus, floods of 2018 and 2019, Kerala economy proved to be resilient as remittance from abroad was an influencing factor as it didn't halt. But, as the environmental calamities are on the clouds every coming year in various forms in the State, the economy could be affected worse if the remittance is in dull swinging. In 2018, the state received about Rs. 80,000 which was about 25 percent of the state income. The state expected about Rs. 1 lakh crore as remittance by dint of remigration of many who lost their houses during Kerala floods in 2018. But, due to the current crisis, in 2020, the remittance will see a downfall of more than 20 percent as World Bank predicts or 15 percent with lack of 10,000–15,000 crore as Prof. Irudaya Rajan forecasts (Karun 2020).

Impact on Return Migration

Though the attempt for localization of the GCC economy was in vain many times, the COVID-19 crisis switched into a suitable way for them which are to be exploited in its way. As International Monetary Fund predicts, Middle East is bound to face an economic depression which is higher in last 40 years. The present situation has been poured oil with economic crisis, oil price war and COVID-19 impact on employment and economy for the GCC. To mitigate these crises, The GCC countries need to tap into their sovereign wealth funds and tighten their budgets by cutting fiscal spending. Hence, restricting the Gulf financing means sending thousands of foreign workers back to their home. This will affect many non-oil producing developing and underdeveloped countries which rely much on Gulf remittance: Egypt which received more than $25 billion in 2019; Lebanon which shares remittances similar to 12.7 percent of its GDP; Syria, Jordan, Morocco, etc.

are the major ones to get stitched. Kerala is more than all other nations in its banking upon remittances.

Due to the COVID-19 crisis, if many Gulf emigrants return back to the State and many Guest laborers return back to their respective states, it will create a humongous lacuna in the local labor sector. It is due to the unwillingness of local people to do home-based work and most of them may not be ready to do many blue-collar jobs in their homeland for keeping dignity.

The COVID-19 crisis caused unemployment for thousands of people in various GCC countries. Many such countries decided to lay off foreigners from government jobs in which hundreds of Keralites were involved. In the near future, the same rule is going to be implemented in the private sector too which will result in a hike in the unemployed. Kuwait also decided to nationalize its Kuwaiti population, replacing all foreign expats and advancing the use of automation and technology. As the current national Kuwait population consists of only less than 30 percent, it is busy implementing to rectify its "demographic imbalance". In the new rules to be implemented, it would lay off all foreign employees from the public sector, which consists of 26 percent expats, within one year by starting the elimination process within three months of the enactment of the legislation. If a Kuwaiti national isn't available for a job, only an expat can be replaced with a contract of a year with renewal if he or she is needed further. Like Oman, the law will be applied to all the private sector. All but all the emigrants look after five people on average including one guest laborer due to replacement migration. Therefore, if three lakh people (counting a maximum) return as part of the COVID-19 crisis, it will directly affect 1.5 million people and many more indirectly.

Three major influxes of (mass) return migration were experienced till now. The first one was due to the Iraq-Kuwait war in 1990–1991 from both countries. It was a Guinness record for mega evacuation by flight. 1.76 lakh Indians, more than half of them were Keralites (about ten lakh), were rescued by Air India carrying itself all the expenses required which was later refunded by the Government of India. The second one was during the global financial crisis of 2008 in which the World Bank predicted the return of five lakh Keralites but only about 50,000 people returned as Irudaya Rajan S predicted due to only the UAE being the most affected. The third one is happening presently due to the COVID-19 crisis.

Negligence from Home

Though the emigrants have done their utmost for the state, both the state and central governments, be it any alliance or party, gave negligence as the cause. The migration phenomenon is one which turned the state in a positive way, as the words of Irudaya Rajan S convey:

> at any point in time, the Gulf countries provided jobs to nearly ten percent of Kerala's working population. Without the Gulf migration, high levels of unemployment and poverty would have made Kerala a hotbed of terrorism, communalism and social tensions.
>
> (Sanandakumar, 2015)

All the effort done for them was window dressing as it is clear that there is no perfect database including all the details of each and every emigrant. Now NORKA Roots has started registration. If NORKA Roots-like measures were used long before for the proper estimation of full details, it would be more useful for the government in various matters including better policies. Now, everything is done based on the available data from the Kerala Migration Surveys from various years done by Irudaya Rajan and K Zachchariyah based on large surveys. In addition, the website of NORKA roots also shows a data of 40,00,000 as Keralites outside India which include return migrants too, 13,73,552 as Keralites outside the state ("Home – NORKA", 2020). Seeing the data, it is sure that it is manipulated to be a prediction, not the proper one. In many critical times, there are many non-profit organizations like the Kerala Muslim Cultural Centre, which is a relentless helping hand for all the Keralites in all possible ways – financially and socially – and more than a government can do and even in the cases where the home government was lethargic. The government was better to support such organizations financially as well to render more security.

Emigration to the USA started in the 1960s due to visa relaxation was only by the educated and the rich from Kerala. There is a general difference between the emigrants to the GCC and other developed countries. The remittances are highly chipped in from the GCC countries, unlike elsewhere. The Gulf emigrants went alone with no family and work to send money home while the other migrants migrated with family, either settled there or did not focus on remittances to their home country.

Migration: An Unsustainable Pillar for the Kerala Economy

Kerala is a remittance economy. The remittance to the state is increasing positively year by year without any effect due to return migration, financial crisis, or any global crisis. The arrival of remittances to the state increased year by year as there was once a 134.4 percent increase in 2008 compared with 2003 (Table 10.3). But, due to the impact of global crises, though the cumulative growth has increased, there was only a 14 percent increase in 2011 which rose to 43.2 to reach Rs. 71142 crore from Rs. 49,695 crore.

The same pattern is visible while comparing the remittance per households in Kerala. An average 16.3 percent of households in the state received remittances in 2018 (Rajan & Zachariah, 2019). All the 14 districts vary in their share of households in remittance (see Figure 10.3) as Malappuram

Table 10.3 Trend in total remittances (1998–2018)

Year	*Remittances (Cr)*	*Percent Increase*	*Remittances Per HH*
1998	13652	–	21,469
2003	18465	35.3	24,444
2008	43288	134.4	57,215
2011	49695	14.8	63,315
2013	71142	43.2	86,843
2018	85092	19.6	96,185

Source: Rajan and Zachariah (2019).

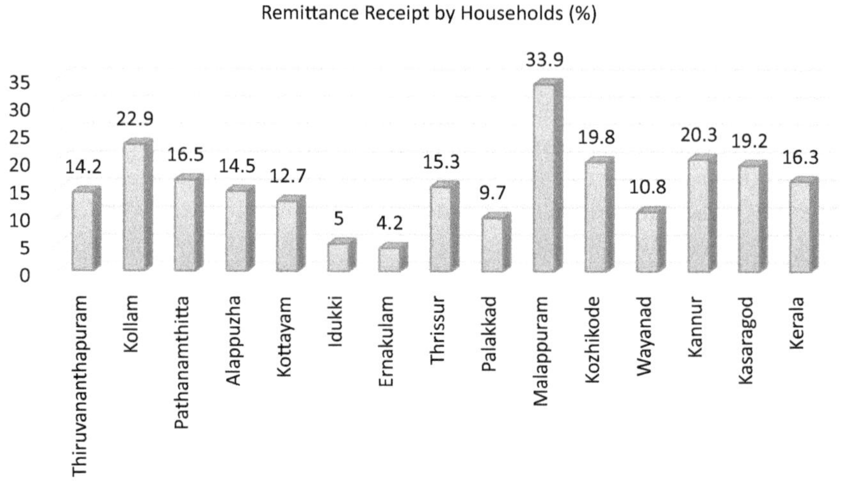

Figure 10.3 Percent of Households that received remittances in 2018 Source: Rajan and Zachariah, 2019

district is the highest with 33.9 percent and Ernakulam the lowest with 4.2 percent.

As the majority of emigrants are from lower or middle backgrounds, the major share of remittance for their homely purposes is 37.6 percent. Most of the households lived prosperously with the remittance. About 38 percent of people were using it for their daily living expenses by which the culture of conspicuous consumption started in the state (Rajan & Zachariah, 2019).

Remittance helped the state to be at the forefront of the human development index, hence ranking them on par with developed countries. It helped it to be a flourishing state socially and economically though not environmentally so that there is not much difference between the rural and urban parts in the human development dimensions. Remittance is the major support for better infrastructure, housing, and a fast-paced urbanized culture even in rural areas. The GCC country emigrants and their remittance were the major conduits for various charity and volunteering activities in the state. The Kerala economy stood financially unaffected during the natural calamities in every year from 2016.

The flow of remittance to the state for more than 50 years made everyone feel like a sustainable pillar for the economy of Kerala. This assumption is true for the policymakers too as there is no much needed rehabilitation program or better alternative for the emigrants and the return migrants. This argument got more briskness whenever the remittance was blissful during the risky situations and state calamities.

Migration and remittance are not a sustained bliss for the Kerala economy with COVID-19 crisis being a proof subsequently. There are differences between previous global and GCC-based crises and the COVID-19 crisis. All the previous crises were only financially related being global or GCC-specified but ways were there to recover without laying off foreigners in bulk. Any other non-financial crises like social or cultural issues or natural calamities were not affecting the emigrants at all. Any health issues like epidemics did not occur globally or in all GCC countries. The present COVID-19 crisis is basically a globally health-related case that created more fear and panic to the whole of mankind and affected the whole world economy as well as sheer lack of demand, production, and income in all sectors as the world came to a standstill confining people to their homes due to self, home, or institutional quarantines, lockdowns, and curfews. And the GCC countries have taken COVID-19 cases as a simple pathway to localize their economy and population. In addition, the economic boom in the GCC region will last for almost 15 years only, not more (Barbuscia & Sab, 2020). Besides the aforementioned two aspects, the exclusive aspect for Kerala is that it has ignored the agrarian economy, moving into cash crops before it became developed. Due to the Gulf boom and liberalization policies, the state jumped from agrarian sector to service sector without going to the secondary sector. If Kerala was an agrarian state with being a remittance economy, then it would be more advanced. For a sustainable economy, Kerala needs to return to the agrarian aspect well.

Though remittances are not sustainable, the state government could come up with many initiatives to protect the return migrants to make the remittances be sent forever. The government should facilitate self-employment of small enterprises for them. For that, courses and training classes should be arranged pragmatically for skills development and leadership trait teaching. Then they can find their way out either in Kerala or outside Kerala or India. In addition, their experience, skills gained abroad and multilingual expertise can be used for their betterment. Any expatriate of more than two to three years will be an expert in spoken Hindi, Urdu, and Arabic with little expertise in English. This multilingual oral expertise can be useful for jobs in other states too. If the government takes stock of this multilingualism of return migrants as a qualification, it might beget more productive and advanced developments for the state. In addition, the government should bring the agriculture tradition back to the state through various programs by making the state fully self-reliant and self-efficient in agricultural production.

Social Remittance Augurs Well for the Returnees

The migration is blessed with a continuous flow of social remittance too along with economic remittance (Levitt, 1999) for Kerala. The flow of circulating social remittances voluntarily or involuntarily is strong and continuous as they live in transnational social space (Levitt, 1999). Social remittances are ideas, practices, mindsets, world views, values and attitudes, norms of behavior, and social capital which are exchanged between the native and the host country and hold much influence on both (Mohamoud and Fréchaut, 2006). Knowledge, experience, and expertise are the main ingredients of social capital in the social remittance. Everywhere, the economic remittances are supposed to be in a unidirectional flow, with the migrants leaving their home countries while the social remittance is bidirectional (Goldring, 2004; Levitt and Lamba, 2011). Permanent return migration is the most influential transfer of social remittance (Markley, 2011). The Gulf emigrants are upskilled after leaving the low-skilled GCC countries' jobs. They used to live in diverse social and mental situations with disciple for years. They are experienced in many things and handle every situation with tactics. In addition, for Keralites who are monolingual usually will turn multilingual due to migration. Many emigrants possess linguistic social capital with English, Arabic, Hindi, and Urdu. As a result of the impacts of social remittances, lifestyle, food culture, new words, and lingual constructs, etc. there has been a high influence on the state.

So, social remittances can be utilized for the sake of the state and its prosperity. The majority of the emigrants are blue-collar job holders. Many left there as entrepreneurs or businessmen. Many laymen have turned businessmen or entrepreneurs in their life as expatriates. Many have returned permanently to being entrepreneurs or businessmen in the state. Many do the usual common blue-collar jobs after returning. So, if governments come up with many enterprises or opportunities exclusively for them, it can be made fruitful and an alternative for the remittance forgone. Preparing the proper database of the returnees scrutinizing their capabilities and extent of social capital is the need of the hour though it's a very hard task. Measures and methods should be prepared for them in the form of training, workshops, and other development programs. Though many of them just need to be shown their own strengths and gain confidence, many other people will need proper training. Giving them according to their strength and weakness, they can be employed in the state itself, other states, or other countries utilizing both human and social capital of the return migrants.

Guest Laborers and Challenges for the Kerala Economy

Guest laborer (*Athithi Thozhilaali*) is the term first used by Dr Thomas Isaac, the Finance Minister of Kerala, in his budget speech in February 2018 to refer to interstate migrant workers to the State. The term came into light after the government efforts to handle them during the COVID-19 crisis in the state. About 3.5–4 million guest laborers are working in all 14 districts of Kerala which counts about ten percent of the Kerala population (Peter & Narendran, 2017). In 2013, it was about 2.5 million as per the study of Narayana, Venkiteswaran, and Joseph (2013). There are about 2.1 million Kerala emigrants and about one million interstate migrants. Therefore, Non-Resident Keralites (NRKs) are also about 3.5 million who are also included with return migrants due to the possibility of cyclical migration. Migration of guest laborers is actually replacement migration as their population is almost on par with the population of NRKs. They work in various categories with high wages or salaries. Many of them are daily wage earners with high amounts similar to or a little lower than their counterparts in the GCC region. They all enjoy better wages, sustained work opportunities, and relatively better treatment in the State. Out of them seven lakh people are factory laborers.

Migrant workers from Tamil Nadu were the first to attract Kerala during the 1970s–1990s and ended being less in number due to the positive approach of their respective governments towards them. Later, people from ten states came to replace Kerala emigrants – West Bengal, Assam, Odisha, Uttar Pradesh, Bihar, etc. (Kumar, 2014).

The COVID-19 crisis also affected them due to lockdown, lack of remittances, income decrease of the people, etc. About five lakh guest laborers are expected to leave the state due to the crisis (Rajan SI). If 50–70 percent don't come back, then the Kerala economy will suffer. And if they return, then there is also the problem of giving higher wages as they were used to before the economic crisis in the state. In addition, the returnees have a lower chance to come back in the near future if everything is moving smoothly as Odisha and Bengal are waiting to reap the benefits in the coming months along with the new labor laws of Bihar, UP, etc. which claim localization of the work too.

Conclusion

In fact, COVID-19 has affected the whole world with drastic changes in lifestyles and breaking all the unbroken traditions. Due to the COVID-19 crisis, the Kerala economy will suffer regarding migration with a lack of thousands of jobs and lack of remittances that will result in affecting the aspects of state which were untouched or little affected with previous crises and calamities. The state had the feeling of sustainability in the prosperity of the Kerala economy with remittances. That feeling will be a mirage due to the current crisis. Though all the governments ignored the case of migrants for years, it didn't affect the Kerala economy as people got remittances from their hard work. Any globalized crisis is prone to affect Kerala a lot as it owes its openness to the world. From now on, it is the duty of the state to consider their cause and handle it properly along with considering revival measures for the economy. They are ought to provide suitable rehabilitation facilities pragmatically. In all the policy decisions, at least ten percent of considerations should be kept made as per their proportional representation. As the IMF report suggested the end of the GCC economic boom within 15 years, Kerala needs rehabilitation for returnees and the going-to-be returnees. Through adequate methods and measures as discussed above, Kerala can sustain its prosperity – economically and socially – either employing them in the state itself or outside after giving adequate skill development training and leadership programs.

The mass return of emigrants will create many problems socially and economically for the state unless they are rehabilitated well. Many of the returnees come back with nothing after two to three decades of expatriation. The possible alternative ways are interstate migration as happened during the 1970s and 1980s; migration to East Asian countries like Malaysia, Singapore, etc.; and creating new possibilities in Kerala itself. Scope could be made in the manufacturing and construction sectors, service sectors like tourism, and the primary sector as well.

The social remittance of the migrants is an investment for themselves. Therefore, mainly the social capital – knowledge, experience, and expertise – is auguring well for the return migrants and the Kerala economy as well if it is utilized in a proper way, giving them adequate awareness and understanding of their confidence and strength, and opportunities and possibilities in or outside the state.

References

Barbuscia, D., & Sab, Y. (2020). Gulf's financial wealth could be over in 15 years: IMF. *Reuters*. Retrieved from https://www.reuters.com/article/us-gulf-economy-imf/gulfs-financial-wealth-could-be-over-in-15-years-imf-idUSKBN2002HZ

Ethiraj, G. (2020). Is Kerala ready for a wave of counter migrants?. Indiaspend. Retrieved from https://www.indiaspend.com/is-kerala-ready-for-a-wave-of-counter-migrants/

Goldring, L. (2004). Re-thinking remittances: Social and political dimensions of individual and collective remittances. *Development and Change*, *35*(4), 799–840.

Home – NORKA. (2020). Retrieved 24 May 2020, from https://www.norkaroots.org

International Labour Organisation. (2020). *ILO Monitor: COVID-19 and the world of work*. Second edition – Updated Estimates and Analysis. Geneva. Retrieved from https://www.ilo.org/wcmsp5/groups/public/---dgreports/---dcomm/documents/briefingnote/wcms_740877.pdf

Karun, S. (2020). Covid-19: Remittances to Kerala expected to decline. *The Times of India*. Retrieved from https://timesofindia.indiatimes.com/business/india-business/covid-19-remittances-to-kerala-expected-to-decline/articleshow/75607214.cms

Kumar, N. (2014). Interstate unskilled migrants of Kerala, South India: The push and pull factors of long distance migration within a country. In Conference on Internal Migration and Urbanization. Dhaka: KNOMAD. Retrieved from https://www.knomad.org/sites/default/files/2018-01/Mr.%20Ajith%20Kumar%20INTER-STATE%20UNSKILLED%20MIGRANT

Levitt, P. (1999). Social remittances: Migration driven, local level forms of cultural diffusion, in. *International Migration Review*, 32(4), 926–948 .

Levitt, P., & Lamba-Nieves, D. (2011). Social remittances revisited. *Journal of Ethnic and Migration Studies*, *37*(1), 1–22, Retrieved from https://doi.org/10.1080/1369183X.2011.521361

Markley, E. (2011). Social remittances and social capital: Values and practices of transnational social space. *Qual Life*, 22(4), 365–378. Retrieved from https://pdfs.semanticscholar.org/70ee/d5c6b54e9fb1fed9f9129078a31bff311c8e.pdf

Mohamoud, A. A., & Frechaut, M. (2006). *Social Remittances of the African Diasporas in Europe*. Retrieved from https://rm.coe.int/168070ac75

Narayana, D., Venkiteswaran, C., & Joseph, M. (2013). *Domestic Migrant Labour in Kerala*. Thiruvananthapuram: Gulati Institute of Finance and Taxation.

Peter, B., & Narendran, V. (2017). *God's Own Workforce: Unravelling Labour Migration to Kerala*. Centre for Migration and Inclusive Development. Retrieved from http://cmid.org.in/wp-content/uploads/2012/10/Gods-Own-Workforce-CMID-Web.pdf

Sanandakumar, S. (2015). A fifty year old phenomenon explained: Malayalee migration to Gulf builds the new Kerala. Retrieved from https://economictimes.indiatimes.com/news/politics-and-nation/a-fifty-year-old-phenomenon-explained-malayalee-migration-to-gulf-builds-the-new-kerala/articleshow/49201357.cms?from=mdr

Rajan, S. I., & Zachariah, K. C. (2019). *Emigration and Remittances: New Evidences from the Kerala Migration Survey 2018*. Working Paper No. 483. Thiruvananthapuram: Centre for Development Studies.

Varma, V. (2020). COVID-19: Any changes in migration pattern from Gulf will affect 80 lakh people in Kerala, says expert. *The Indian Express*. Retrieved from https://indianexpress.com/article/india/kerala/any-changes-in-migration-pattern-from-gulf-will-affect-80-lakh-people-in-kerala-expert-6364230/

Part III

Gulf Migration

The Regional Perspective

11 Migration from Punjab to the Gulf Countries

Punjabi Migrants and Social Change in Left-Behind Families

Atinder Pal Kaur

Introduction

The interaction between South Asian nations and the Gulf countries is a recent phenomenon. When the GCC (Gulf Cooperation Council) countries became oil-rich in 1973 and enormously wealthy overnight, a sudden demand for foreign laborers arose. To fulfill the need for foreign laborers, people from Morocco, Libya, Algeria, Egypt, Lebanon, Jordan, Yemen, Syria, and finally from Asian nations such as in South Asia, South East Asia, and East Asia joined the Gulf nations as labor-exporting regions (Rahman, 2015). In this process, India also becomes a labor-exporting country to the Gulf.

The Gulf states restricted permanent settlement with the imposition of the "Kafala system" and this system forbade migrant employers from marrying locals and imposed limitations on mobility, causing them to stay temporarily. With restrictions and transitory workers, male members of families become the lone migrant, leaving their families behind in their home country (Arnald and Shah, 1986). Thus, the migration that began from India to the Gulf was circular and transient.

The first migration documented is from the Kerala state of India, and people as unskilled laborers started migrating to the Gulf nations to chase their luck. Migration from Kerala is extensively documented in different studies (Gulati, 1983; Zachariah,1997; Zachariah et al., 2003), while migration of Punjabis to the Gulf receives scant attention. On the other hand, the migration of Punjabis to developed nations continues to pique the interest of academics, with different studies pointing to Sikh migration to America (La Brack, 2015), Britain (Taylor and Singh, 2013; 2015), Canada (Verma, 2003), Africa (Bachu, 1985) China, Malaysia, Thailand, France (Jacobsen and Myrvold, 2011), and other areas of the world.

With this background, the present study is an attempt to shed light and provide an overview of Punjabi migration from the historical to the present-day scenario, with a specific focus on Gulf migration. Thus, the chapter structure is in two parts: (a) the first part of the paper will focus on Punjabi migration to the Gulf nations from a historical to present (b) the second part

DOI: 10.4324/9781003369370-15

of the paper will discuss changes in the left-behind families from economic to social terms due to Gulf migration.

In a theoretical sense, the study is based on ethnography and narrativity. The empirical data for this study was collected from the Doaba region of Punjab with qualitative methods. The primary survey was conducted in 200 households and 221 migrants were recorded. The data was collected in two stages to gain insight into Punjabi's migration. In the first stage, data was collected from families staying behind after the male migration i.e., including 200 households. The second stage data was gathered from ten key informative interviews (KII) to learn about village migration history to the Gulf nations and migration patterns in the villages. Data were obtained from ten return migrants to learn about their migration route and their migration experiences. An additional 25 migrants who paid holiday visits during data collection were also interviewed. Information was gathered regarding their choice of Gulf nations, the cause for such movement, and network relations used for migration.

Migration History of the Punjabi from the Colonial to the Present

The Colonial Period: The history of continuous migration from Punjab dates more than 125 years and primarily began under India's colonial authority when the British captured Punjab in 1849 (Nanda and Veron, 2015). After that, Punjabis began to migrate to other world areas as indentured laborers, mainly in British colonies and as army men (Singh 2008). The era of 1870 is often regarded as the beginning of Punjabi Sikh settlement in the Far East (South East Asia) when army personnel from Amritsar and Firozpur were recruited for police and paramilitary duties The Sikh settlements appeared in Malaya and Hong Kong in 1880s, where Sikhs worked as policemen (Sandhu, 1969). Sikhs began migrating to East Africa in the 1890s (Barrier, 2007); between 1903 and 1908, Punjabis entered North America and passed into the United States. The first migrants to America were primarily from the districts of Punjab's Doaba area (La Brack, 2015; Tinker, 1977).

The initial migrants were uneducated and semiliterate laborers from agricultural and military background. These migrants were mainly from the Malwa and Doaba regions of Punjab (Dusenbery and Tatla 2009). Migration to England by Punjabis showed initial signs in 1920 (Ballard and Ballard, 1977) and World War II was also a reason for migration by Punjabis to western nations. The major factor of this migration was a shortage of laborers in construction sites (Dusenbery and Tatla, 2009). Tatla (2004) documented that Malwa and Majha Sikhs dominated emigration in the 1880s, whereas Doaba peasants dominated towards the late 1910s.

The Postcolonial Phase: The post-1947 period is marked by a significant exodus of Sikhs from the Doaba region of Punjab. Their concentration was in three Western countries (the UK, Canada, and the USA). Emigration from the Malwa area began to dominate in the late 1960s. Sikhs immigrated to different European nations, mainly from the 1960s to the 1990s. Migrants traveled to Norway, Denmark, Finland, and Poland from Punjab.

These Punjabis worked as laborers in restaurants and started businesses. In certain areas, Punjabis twice migrated from South African nations, primarily Uganda, to European countries. In this scenario marital alliances and better job prospects caused them to permanently abode in European countries (Jacobsen and Myrvold, 2011). The presence of Punjabis in France is a relatively new phenomenon, in the late 1970s and early 1980s when a few Sikhs came as illegal immigrants first to Germany and Belgium, then to France (Moliner, 2011). After the Cold War ended in 1989, untouched land and sea routes opened up for Punjabi migrants, with many landing in Greece, Italy, and Spain (Zachariah and Rajan, 2007). In the contemporary period of globalization, the migration of skilled workers has been taking place to Australia and Canada, from almost the entire Punjab (Rajan and Percot, 2011).

Part I: Migration from Punjab to the Gulf Countries

The migration to the Gulf nations occurs in a later temporal frame, with the 1973 oil boom in the Gulf countries. The sudden growth of the construction industry as the Gulf countries, which became immensely wealthy overnight, embarked on a frenzy of building a new infrastructure of roads, ports, and airports, as well as schools, colleges, and administrative blocks as symbols of new wealth, accounted for the massive demand for laborers. Migrant labor was needed in construction projects and as well as trade and service industries, including domestic services. As a result, many Indian laborers began to migrate, mostly to the GCC countries. As a result, there was a change in the trend of migration from Punjab to the Gulf countries as unskilled laborers migrated, and it became an attractive destination for Punjabis (Zachariah, 1997).

Further, data from the primary survey evoked migration from Punjab to the Gulf in two phases. The first phase started in the late 1970s, and the second phase includes generational migration.

Phase I: During the first phase of migration, people were generally from farming families and had a basic level of education. These migrants were unskilled and gained skills after migration. After reaching the Gulf, these unskilled migrants worked as drivers, guards, carpenters, and masons. Survey results showed migration from Punjab to the Gulf nations dominated by other lower castes (OBC). Some visibility of Scheduled castes (Table 11.1) was observed.

In contrast, the Jat caste was fewer as they mainly migrated to developed countries (see colonial and postcolonial period, more information refers to studies by Taylor et al., 2013, 2014). The lack of job possibilities at the place of origin and large families with small land to produce remained the

Table 11.1 Basic information of migrants

Characteristics of migrants	*N= 221*
Age	
18–24	35
25–35	55
36–46	67
47–57	39
60+	25
Religion	
Sikh	153
Hindu	68
General	25
OBC	147
S.C	49
Marital status	
Married	182
Unmarried	39
Education	
Illiterates	75
5th pass	28
8th pass	20
Matriculation	50
12th pass	46
Graduate	2
Types of family	
Joint	54
Nuclear	167
Types of households	
Pucca	177
Semi Pucca	32
Kuccha	12
Years of migration	
1–5	50
6–10	45
11–15	35
16–20	18
21–25	20
26–30	15
31–35	20
36–40	12
40+	6
Channel of migration	
Agents	50
Friends	45
Neighbors	35
Relatives	34
Family members	57

(*Continued*)

Table 11.1 (Continued)

Characteristics of migrants	*N= 221*
Place of migration	
Dubai	63
Qatar	32
Abu Dhabi	42
Kuwait	27
Bahrain	15
Oman	22
Saudi Arabia	20
Occupation before migration	
Farmer	84
Truck drivers	14
Electrician	23
Carpenter	13
Masons	10
Mechanics	10
Agricultural laborer	35
Non-agricultural laborer	32
Occupation after migration	
Forman	10
Laborer	24
Truck drivers*	75
Carpenter	31
Electrician	21
Mechanics	10
Masons	43
Machine operator	5
Peon	1
Technicians	1

Source: Author calculation.

primary reasons for migration. They grabbed the available opportunity in front of their eyes. Following successful journeys to the Gulf, these people ensured a better lifestyle in the Gulf for their children, siblings, and neighbors after 30 years of migration.

The first migrant I came across in the village Rampur Jagir had 35 years of experience from the Gulf. In 1977, he was the third person from Rampur Jagir village, according to the Sarpanch. The first migration was that of labor migration, which was known as one of a "group visa", in which no single name was on the visa card. He paid Rs.5000 for migration and accompanied a party of 20 Punjabis. The majority of people migrated by taking out loans from money lenders or selling their gold for profit after they left.

After arriving in Dubai, Amreek worked as a laborer and learned the work of a carpenter, which was in high demand at the time. Later on, he learned to drive a truck and started his small truck business in Dubai. His son was in charge of his truck business in Dubai recently. When Amreek returned, he had not long ago retired from his position as a foreman.

He mentioned that "the Gulf companies had direct contact with agencies and conveyed their labor needs. The corporation determined residential locations; the experience may be pleasant or awful, but workers were required to stay because they did not own property in the area. As a result, individuals had to adapt because they needed money". He again mentioned that the truck driver or truck business was the most lucrative career in the Gulf.

During the late 1970s major migration from Punjab was that of labor. The overnight Gulf countries became rich due to a hike in oil prices and the creation of new wealth by various needed laborers. These needs for a workforce were met with labor migration from various parts of the world. The main feature of first-phase migrants was that the majority of them were farmers with basic education.

Phase II: Those migrants who traveled in the late twentieth century are included in the second stage of migration. The most distinguishing aspect of these migrants was that they were semi-skilled. Migrants in the second phase of migration were mainly literate and had one or two skills (driving, electrician, mason, etc.). Punjabis with less education were still able to move due to previously learned skills (carpenters, masons, service station workers, etc.) in their homeland. Some of them went on to become drivers. Some were able to relocate to the Gulf nations with the assistance of family, acquaintances, and relatives who had already settled there. The Gulf nations were the most appealing destination for migrants (special consideration was given to Dubai, Qatar, Abu Dhabi, and Saudi Arabia).

The second phase of migration was primarily seen in the migrant household's second generation. These were the families where those in their late twenties followed their father, siblings, relatives, and neighbors. People who migrated possessed two sorts of skills, such as truck drivers or electricians. They successfully obtained a driving license in the Gulf nations since they were knowledgeable about driving. Those who immigrated as electricians were already doing comparable jobs in their homeland. Migrants in such situations were individuals aware of the initial conditions of employment needs in the Gulf nations. As a result, these people picked their target nations based on their skills and benefits after migrating.

The movement of Scheduled castes to the Gulf nations became evident, with agricultural and non-agricultural employees from Kapurthala villages. Most Punjabi migrants were less educated, unskilled, or semi-skilled workers who worked in constructions, factories, labor, supervisors, carpenters, electricians, cleaners, and other fields.

Migration Process and Social Networks

The migration channel was essential to the migration process. Migrants use various ways to reach their destination countries. The two main migration channels are agents and social networking. Social networking is an essential in the context of Punjabis to the Gulf migration. The migration that occurred in the second phase depended on the social ties formed by their family members, friends, and relatives. They continue to be valuable information on destination countries and job possibilities.

The return migrant remained an important source of information regarding skill needs, employment possibilities, and places to stay. Another reason for relying on social networks is the cost of migration. The return migrants help in migration and become more reliable than agents. The migration process through agents remains costly and has to pay a high amount of approximately US$ 2000 (Oommen, 2016); however, the social network also helps to offset these expenses. The successful migration was found in which the father helps in his son's migration. After 40 years of migration, he made links with his factory contractor, which allowed him to start a truck business and opened a door for his son's migration.

Similarly, in another example, after ten years of Gulf migration, the first brother assisted his younger brother in his migration. The established link aided the new one in providing a pleasant stay after arriving at the destination, helping in finding a job, and providing a comfortable environment. Harminder mentioned as below

When you have a connection, you are less concerned about where you will stay, what you eat, and where you will begin your employment. It is easier to acclimatize to a foreign environment and also to grasp the norms and regulations of the country, which are the fundamental needs of the moment if you have a dependable person at your location of migration. Even having a companion can provide personal knowledge about where the visa procedure is reliable and straightforward.

During their vacation trips, return migrants stated that having a link in the Gulf is beneficial during the early days of migrating since you need a place to stay and know that you are not alone in a new area.

Remittances and Utilization

Remittances from the Gulf nations serve an essential role in alleviating poverty, providing economic stability, and raising families' socioeconomic status. Farming families migrated for various reasons, including a lack of cultivable land, large families, children's education, and the desire to save for the future. Meanwhile, in the Scheduled castes, migration is caused by a lack of non-farm employment possibilities, receiving lower wages for labor, and finally, profitable remittances returning after migration.

The most apparent difference in remittances received was between Rs. 10,000 and Rs. 100,000/-. Due to the employment of migrants, there is a gap in sending remittances. Typically, the truck driver remits more than a laborer.

Similarly, the marble cutter jobs had higher wages than an electrician. A significant share of remittances is generally spent on family needs, followed by children's education, health, debts, *shaguns* (money gifts), and finally, some savings. If migration continues to be successful, money is generally spent on constructing houses and purchasing land or gold after three to five years of successful journeys.

Part II: Social Change in Left-Behind Families

Male members of families that migrate contribute economic remittances, which are apparent in the Doaba villages through double-story marbled houses. Houses were often adorned both outside and inside with white marble and luxury goods. These buildings are typically white, with the name of the migrant and country name engraved in gold lettering on the outside wall of the dwellings. Other than this, water tanks in the shape of an airplane and footballs are on the house's roof. Sometimes, the home is in the style of a villa, which is also a display of riches.

Besides that, migrant residences had luxury things such as automobiles, air conditioners, LCDs, microwaves, and modular kitchens. Rooms were furnished with elegant beds, while drawing rooms were garnished with luxury sofa sets and dining tables.

Although not for agricultural interests, property was also acquired, in order to preserve a considerable holding and demonstrate affluence. Children also have technological devices such as mobile phones (the most recent iPhones), tablets, and laptop computers. These social remittances also move when migrants return home.

The education of children has become a priority. Surprisingly, daughters were obtaining higher education and working. Families still preferred sons, but gender prejudice has grown less evident. Children received their primary education in local private and convent schools. Parents favored English language schools.

At the micro level, women of left-behind families become more visible in their houses. Women's participation in family rituals and religious ceremonies, decision-making, weddings, and outdoor mobility has grown. There is a transition from the private to the public domain in women's lives, becoming heads of households. It also impacts the family's social fabric since there is a rise in nuclear families among migrant households.

At the macro level, migration boosted the availability of numerous facilities at the village level, such as a post office, Western Unions, banks, and schools. In addition, reconstruction of village roads and migrants assisted in charitable work in villages, such as the construction of memorial monuments, village entrance gates, and religious sites (*Gurdwara*). However, such developments exacerbate caste disparities and increase the divide between caste and familial relations. The *shareek* (extended kin) expressed dissatisfaction with migration from their relatives, claiming that it degraded them and gave them no significance in the *Parivar* (extended families). They offer lovely presents and give *shaguns* (money gifts) to relatives due to remittances, which became their norm. They flaunt off their money after building nice houses, while on the other hand, they have nothing to show off.

Even in the lower castes, migration has become a culture in the community, and their children wish to follow in their footsteps, but they had lack of economic resources. As a result, there are more family disputes, and parents often have to borrow money from moneylenders to send their children to the Gulf, which is in some situations, is not as fruitful as in others.

Conclusion

Jat Sikhs dominated migration from Punjab, and research concentrated on the flow of Punjabis to developed nations. During the colonial and post-colonial periods, migration was skewed toward learning about Jat Sikhs, with some priority given to Dalits, their place of migration, employment opportunities, and, finally, their links to Punjab. The rising emigration from Punjab to developed countries remains high, while migration from Punjab to the Gulf has been less noticeable.

Migration to the Gulf is mainly from the Doaba region, with most migrants belonging to the OBC and Scheduled castes. However, there is a rise in potential migrants, including young children who have completed compulsory schooling and are eager to follow in the footsteps of their village people and family members. The primary motivation for such movement was the availability of economic possibilities, which were already established by their networks, including family, kin, and neighbors. The migration channel is always close-knit with their family members and decreases the cost of travel.

The migrants and non-migrants give information, housing, financial assistance, and job stability, becoming a significant element in Gulf migration (King, 2012). Two more motivations that encourage Punjabis to migrate to the Gulf are the desire to preserve healthy finances and economic benefits. Community discussions include migrant vacation visits, showing off money, and recounting tales of their successful excursions in the Gulf nations spread out in villages, which also inspire others to move.

Furthermore, migrants often begin as target earners, aiming to make one trip and earn money for a specific reason. After migration, getting a firm idea of social mobility, there is a craving for consumer goods, and a way of life that is impossible to obtain through local work. So, the person who migrates once is likely to migrate again and increase their number of trips. It is so deeply rooted in community people's behavior and values attached to migration that it becomes community behavior (Massey et al., 1993).

For young men and women, especially in their community settings, migration becomes a rite of passage, and those who do not attempt to uplift their status through migration are considered lazy and undesirable (Reichert, 1981). Knowledge about foreign locales and jobs becomes widely disseminated, as do the values, feelings, and behavioral standards of the core culture throughout the region's society (Alarcon, 1992). Migration has also become a strategy for raising their quality of living, building houses, living a luxurious lifestyle, and offering a better education for their children. However, migration has generated competition among village residents, resulting in families bearing the expense of migration and increasing debt and loans. Gulf migration from Punjab has been influential in the case of the OBC caste, which includes marginal farmers who can save their remittances. In contrast, the Scheduled caste had to shoulder the expense of migration and experienced debt difficulties.

The left-behind families that previous researchers neglected become more visible, and women become de-facto heads of the household. As a result, women's role is growing in household decision-making, engagement in agriculture, and, finally, their mobility in the public realm.

References

Alarcon, R. (1992). Nortenizacion: Self-perpetuating migration from a Mexican town. In Jorge Bustamante, Clark Reynolds, & Raul Hinojosa (eds.), *U. S.-Mexico Relations: Labor Market Interdependence* (pp302–318) Stanford: Stanford University Press.

Arnold, F., & Shah, N. M. (1986). *Asian Labour Migration: Pipeline to the Middle East*. London: West View.

Bachu, P. (1985) *Twice Migrants: East African Sikh Settlers in Britain*. London. Tavistock Publication.

Ballard, R., & Ballard, C. (1977). The Sikhs: The development of South Asian settlements. In Britain in J. L. Watson (ed), *Between Two Cultures: Migrants and Minorities in Britain*. Oxford: Blackwell.

Barrier, N. G. (2007). Sikh emigrants and their homeland: The transmission of information resources and values in the early twentieth century. In A. K. Sahoo & B. Maharaj (eds), *Sociology of Diaspora vol (2)*. Jaipur: Rawat Publication.

Dusenbery, V. A., & Tatla, D. S. (2009). Introduction: NRIs are the New VIPs. *Sikh Diaspora Philanthropy in Punjab: Global Giving for Local Good* (pp 3–29). New Delhi: Oxford University Press.

Gulati, L. (1983). Male Migration to Middle East and the Impact on the Family: Some Evidence from Kerala. *Economic and Political Weekly*, 2217-2226.

Jacobsen Knut, A., & Kristina, M. (2011). *Sikhs in Europe: Migration, Identities and Representation*. Burlington: ASHGAIE.

Judge, P. S. (2003). Punjabi elderly men in multicultural Canada. In S. J. Varma & R. Seshan (eds), *Fractured Identity: The Indian diaspora in Canada* (pp 234–253). Jaipur. Rawat Publication.

Kaur, A. P. (2015). Male migration and its impact on emotional well-being of women. *IAHRW International Journal of Social Sciences Review*, *3*(1), 109–112.

Kaur, A. P. (2017). *Impact of International Migration on Women left behind: A Sociological Study of Kambojs in Punjab*. Unpublished thesis. Retrieved from http://shodhganga.inflibnet.ac.in:8080/jspui/handle/10603/209550.

Kaur, A. P. (2019a). International migration and impact of remittances on left behind wives: A case study of Doaba Region of Punjab. In Irduaya S. Rajan & N. Neetha (eds), *Migration, Gender and Care Economy* (pp. 103–123). New York: Routledge.

Kaur, A. P. (2019b). Migration and cultural challenges through gender lens: Punjabi transnationalism in Doaba Region (Punjab). *Research Monograph Series*, 5(4), 4–13.

Kaur, A. P. (2020). Impact of migration on gender roles: Study of left behind wives in rural Punjab. *Indian Journal of Health & Wellbeing, 11*(7–9), 407–411.

King, R. (2012). Geography and migration studies: Retrospect and prospect. *Population, Space and Place, 18*(2), 134–153.

La Brack, B. (2015). Punjabis in America. In Irudaya S. Rajan, V. J. Varghese, & A. K. Nanda (eds), *Migration, Mobility and Multiple Affiliations*. Delhi: Cambridge University Press.

Mangat, J. S. (1969). *A History of the Asians in East Africa, 1886–1945*. Oxford: Claren- don Press.

Massey, D, Arango, J., Hugo, G., Kouaouci, A., Pellegrino, A., & Taylor, J. E. (1993). Theories of international migration: A review and appraisal. *Population and Development Review*, 19(3),431–466.

Moliner C (2011). Sikh Migration to France. In I. S. Rajan & M. Percot (eds), *Dynamics of Indian Migration: Historical and Current Perspective*. New Delhi: Routledge.

Mooney, N. (2006). Aspiration, reunification and gender transnationalism in Jat Sikh marriages from India to Canada. *Global Network*, 6(4), 389–403.

Nanda, A. K., & Veron, J. (2011). In search of distant shores: Exploring contemporary emigration from Indian Punjab. In I. S. Rajan & M. Percot (eds), *Dynamics of Indian Migration: Historical and Current Perspectives* (pp 321–60). New Delhi: Routledge.

Nanda, A. K., & Veron, J. (2015). Dynamics of International Out-Migration from Punjab: Report on Punjab International Migration Survey. *Centre for Research in Rural and Industrial Development (CRRID), Chandigarh and Institut national d'études démographiques Paris.*

Oommen, Z. G. (2016). South Asian migration to the GCC countries: Emerging trends and challenges. In P. C Jain & G. Z. Oommen (eds), South Asian *Migration to Gulf Countries: History. Policies. Development* (pp. 17–45). New York: Routledge.

Rahman, M. M. (2015). Migrant indebtedness: Bangladeshis in the GCC countries. *International Migration, 53*(6), 205–219.

Rajan I. S. & Percot M (eds), *Dynamics of Indian Migration: Historical and Current Perspectives*. New Delhi: Routledge.

Reichert, J. S. (1981). The migrant syndrome: Seasonal US wage labor and rural development in central Mexico. *Human organization*, 56-66.

Sandhu, K. S. (1969). *Indians in Malaysia: Some Aspects of Their Immigration and Settlement: 1786–1957*. London: Cambridge University Press.

Singh, G., & Tatla, D. S. (2006). *Sikh in Britain: The Making of a Community*. Landon: Zed Books.

Singh, S. (2008). Punjabi diaspora in the Pacific Region. Paper presented at the Conference on India Diaspora: Migration and Development with the focus on the State of Punjab. Center for the Study in Rural and Industrial Development, Chandigarh, 14–15 January

Tatla, D. S. (2004). Rural Roots of the Sikh Diaspora. In I Talbot & S Thandi, (eds) *People on the Move: Punjabi Colonial and Post Colonial Migration*.(pp. 45–59) Karachi: Oxford University Press.

Taylor, S. (2013). Searching for ontological security: Changing meanings of home amongst a Punjabi diaspora. *Contributions to Indian Sociology*, 47(3), 395–422.

Taylor, S. (2014). The diasporic pursuit of home and identity: Dynamic Punjabi transnationalism. *The Sociological Review*, 62(2), 276–294.

Taylor, S. (2015). 'Home is never fully achieved... even when we are in it': Migration, belonging and social exclusion within Punjabi transnational mobility. *Mobilities*, *10*(2), 193–210.

Taylor, S., & Singh, M. (2013). Punjab's Doaban Migration-Development Nexus: Transnationalism and Caste domination. *Economic and Political Weekly*, 50–57.

Tinker, H. (1974). *A New System of Slavery: The Export of Indian Labour Overseas 1830–1920*. London/New York. 70.

Tinker, H. (1977).*The Banyan Tree: Overseas emigrants from India, Pakistan, and Bangladesh*. Oxford : Oxford Publication Press.

Verma, S.J. (2003) Punjabis in Canada: Finding the Roots of their Diversity. In S.J. Verma and R. Seshan (eds) *Fractured Identity: The Indian Diversity in Canada* (pp. 207-16). Jaipur: Rawat Publication.

Zachariah K. C. (1997). *Kerala's Demographic Transition Determinats and Consequences*. New Delhi: Sage Publication.

Zachariah, K. C., Mathew, E. T., & Rajan, I. S. (2003). *Dynamics of Migration in Kerala: Dimensions, Differentals and Consequences*. New Delhi: Orient Black Swan.

Zachariah, K. C., & Rajan, I. S. (2007). Migration, remittances and employment: Short-term trends and long-term implications. Working Paper 395. www.cds .edu. https://opendocs.ids.ac.uk/opendocs/bitstream/handle/20.500.12413/3100/wp395.pdf?sequence=1.

12 Mobility on the Margins

The Experience of Migration and Development in Kerala, India[1]

K Jafar

Introduction

The south Indian state Kerala is known for its unique pattern of development; the development process has been widely noticed for the state's intervention in social development. This was equally supported by the social reformation process initiated by religious and community organizations and political mobilization emerged in the state. Its recent development can be broadly identified as a process of mass education, international migration, and virtuous growth. Various local factors determine how different socio-economic groups and regions follow this larger model. The migration of workers and the inflow of their remittances have affected almost all spheres of Malayalee life and the regional development process. Studies have highlighted the positive effects of labor migration, especially its impact on upward socio-economic mobility of migrants and their families, the impact of male migration on families left behind, especially women and children, and the role of the diaspora in financing and mediating the everyday life of Keralites in different forms. Broadly, these narratives present Kerala's migration as a 'successful model' for local development and link the same with its record in social and human development indicators. This chapter revisits the larger model from the experience of the marginalized groups of being left out or participating in a limited fashion and explores some alternate narratives around Kerala's migration-led development model.

The chapter reviews the broad context and key features of Kerala's recent development experience and uses Malappuram district's experience, with the highest number of migrant households receiving foreign remittances in the state, to highlight how different regions and communities followed the macro patterns. The micro evidence presented in the latter part of the chapter is followed by a discussion on the absence and limited participation of marginalized communities in migration and concluded by remarks on the persistent nature of marginalization in Kerala.

DOI: 10.4324/9781003369370-16

Mass Education, Migration, and Development in Kerala

The recent literature identifies two distinct growth phases in Kerala's development process: The 'Kerala model of development' and 'virtuous growth' phases. These two growth phases are not independent but closely related. The high growth phase that emerged in the late 1980s can be seen as the result of specific strategies followed in the earlier phases. The state's experience during the 'Kerala model of development' and 'virtuous growth' offers new insights into the relationship between economic growth and human development. Broadly, the relationship can be identified into two chains; in the first case economic growth leads to human development whereas in the second case human development achievements contribute to economic growth (Ranis, Stewart, & Ramiez, 2011).

During the low growth, state involvement in the social sector created a rich human capital base in Kerala. However, the stagnant commodity-producing sectors could not employ this educated labor force, and this led to an increase in the rate of unemployment in the state, especially among the educated youth (Kannan, 1990; Kannan & Pushpangadan, 1988; Mathew, 1997; Prakash, 1988; Subrahmanian, 1990). Between 1983 and 1987–1988, the rate of educated unemployment in Kerala rose from 29.3 percent to 35.0 percent (Mathew, 1999: 113). In some cases, the educated youth were not willing to remain in the traditional agriculture and allied activity jobs; the educated workforce preferred 'white-collar' jobs (Mathew, 1999; Nair, 1999a, b). Many of them migrated out of the state and this process became very prominent when the West Asian countries were passing through the 'post-oil boom' development (Nambiar, 1995; Rajan & Kumar, 2010 & 2011; Zachariah, Mathew, & Rajan, 2003). The oil price hike in 1973 accelerated industrialization in West Asia and the same attracted a large number of foreign workers (Prakash, 1998). Among Indian migrants, the share of Keralites is more than 50 percent (Prakash, 1999:137–139). In the decade between 1981 and 1991, 555,000 persons migrated from Kerala to places outside India in addition to 189,000 who migrated to other states within the country (Zachariah, Mathew, & Rajan, 2002).

This led to a situation where the inflow of remittance income derived from the earlier international migration became a major part of the state income. For instance, remittance as a percentage of Net State Domestic Product (NSDP) increased from 0.57 in 1972–1973 to 10.2 percent in 1982–1983 and 19.19 percent in 1992–1993 (Kannan & Hari, 2002:207). The steady increase in the inflow of remittances led Kerala into a turnaround in growth and from 1987–1988 onwards the state economy moved from a slow growth phase into a high and steady growth phase. Many identified this turnaround as the beginning of a 'virtuous' growth driven by earlier investment in social development (CDS, 2005:44; Chakraborty, 2005; Kannan, 2005). While some scholars identify social development, remittances, and economic reforms as key factors behind this turn around others argue that these factors can probably act as necessary conditions for a turnaround in growth, but they cannot be sufficient conditions (Kannan, 2005; Mathew, 2005).

There are concerns over the sustainability, inclusiveness, and nature of this development model. For instance, the new growth phase need not follow the earlier strategy; the private nature of remittance income may change the investment priorities and possibilities of sustaining the earlier model of social development in Kerala. Once the state economy entered the high growth phase, there was a change in the pattern of public expenditure on education. In earlier years, Kerala's social sector expenditure had been higher than that of many other Indian states (Pradhan & Abraham, 2002). Recent experience, however, suggests that Kerala moved away from the earlier situation as real social expenditure declined (Aravindan & Menon, 2010). Expenditure on education at constant prices in Kerala has shown one of the lowest growth rates among all states; the annual growth rate of 3.2 percent recorded during the 1974–1975 to 1984–1985 period dipped to 1.1 percent during the subsequent period of 1985–1986 to 1991–1992 (George & Kumar, 1999). The percentage of public spending on education to total government expenditure, which was as high as 29.28 percent in 1982–1983 declined to 23.17 percent in 1992–1993 and 17.97 percent in 2005–2006 (Oommen, 2008). Even if the state is willing to continue to finance the large network of public services, the state's finance with high fiscal imbalance remains a challenge (Chakraborty, Chakraborty, Nath & Mitra, 2010).

On the other hand, the withdrawal of the state from prioritizing the social sector seems to have been offset by the fact that remittance income had greater involvement in education. Access to remittances influences the pattern of educational expenditure and thereby priorities (Sunny, Parida, & Azurudeen, 2020). The focus and priorities of private remittance income are different from those of the government in the earlier period. Private investment replaced government expenditure and shifted the focus from mass education to higher and professional levels. The declining trend in the enrolment in government schools and the corresponding growth of private un-aided schools reflects the significance of the private sector in the new growth phase.

The shift from public-funded mass education to private or remittance-driven private and professional education drives the new phase of development; the dynamic role of education continues but it need not follow the same circle. Instead, it may lead to a spiral flow of education, change in occupational patterns, and changes in the pattern of migration and remittances, and hence result in a different pattern of growth and development in the state (as depicted in Figure 12.1).

Within the state, the difference in the quality of human capital formation and the nature of migration shape the way different regions follow this macro model differently. For instance, Malappuram's experience with the largest number of workers migrating to West Asia and inflow of household

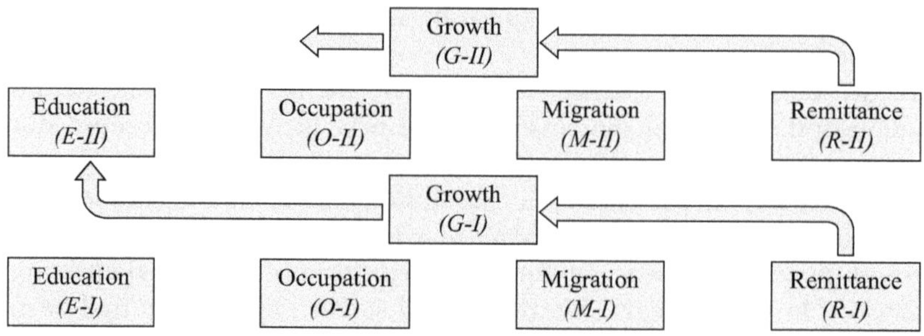

Figure 12.1 The dynamic role of education on Kerala's development: Emerging pattern. Source: Jafar (2018: 213).

remittances should be seen with its image as a 'backward' district (in terms of per capita income, rank in human development indices, and other measures). Along with this, its diverse geography and unique cultural composition offer many insights into how local factors affect this mass education and migration-led development process and the way it affects specific capabilities.

This chapter draws insights from three household surveys focusing on specific issues related to the Malappuram district's experience with this larger model. The first survey (2010) focused on 196 candidates who contested in three-gram panchayats representing the coastal, midland, and highland regions of the Malappuram district. The second survey (2011–2012) covers 752 households from the same gram panchayats and focused on the process of human development among migrant and non-migrant households. The third survey (2015–2016) covers 360 households from the same regions focused on formal and informal financial arrangements followed by migrant and non-migrant households.

The findings indicate how education and migration influence the pattern of development in Kerala. By improving the spending capacity of migrant households, it has influenced the state's educational system. The recent developments in Kerala's education such as the growth of private English medium schools and professional colleges are driven by the remittance income. The average per capita yearly educational expenditure for a student from migrant households (Rs.6192.74) is much higher than that for a student from non-migrant households (Rs.3023.17) as reported in 2011–2012. Naturally, more students from migrant households are enrolled in private un-aided English medium schools and self-financing colleges (Jafar, 2018:90).

These surveys also indicate that migration and access to remittances need not replace informal arrangements for contingency funds but widen the coverage of formal financial services among migrant households. On the social front, evidence indicates that migration influences the way women from migrant households participate in various public spaces (Jafar, 2018). Though it is well accepted, the available evidence to show the role of remittances in local politics is very limited. Almost all political parties have their active units functioning in almost all countries where Keralites are concentrated (Jafar, 2013). While identifying Malappuram district as a lower-end case of education-led development that Kerala experienced in recent decades, these varied effects reflect the differences across regions with diverse geographies, migration patterns, cultural compositions, and histories of development.

Kerala's Migration Model: Participation from the Margins

Kerala has a long history of migration; from the middle of the 19th century, the Malabar region had recruitment centers sending indentured labor. The migration of Cherumas by the middle of the 19th century can be seen as a way to seek freedom from a life 'of incessant toil and shameful exploitation by the landlords' (Joseph, 1988:40). Kerala had a negative net migration record till 1947; it attracted more migrants than those who left the state. Since independence, international migration follows two broad patterns: Migration of workers with skills and professional expertise, mainly to the USA, Canada, the UK, and Australia as permanent migrants (since the early 1950s), and migration of unskilled and semi-skilled workers to the oil-exporting countries of West Asia on temporary work contracts, following the oil price increase of 1973–1974 and 1979 (Rajan & Kumar, 2010:10–18). The migration of Keralites to the West Asian countries (Gulf migration) has some distinct features. The scale, concentration, duration, historical trade connection, specific policies followed in the host countries, nature, process, and impact on migrant families and local development make this different from Malayalee migration to other states of India and other countries.

Kerala experiences migration of educated workers to other parts of India; however, its role in transforming the larger pattern of development in the state is not evident as international migration. By and large, internal migrants have higher and professional education and are often associated with upward occupational mobility. In the case of international migration, many got pushed away by unemployment find migration as the survival strategy. Therefore, the impact of these two types of migration is poverty alleviation and local development. While considering the effect of remittance in reducing poverty and inequality, international remittances proved to be more poor-friendly than internal remittances. The bulk of remittances is received by wealthier families and therefore it does not lead to the redistribution of wealth to the lower strata of society. So, the promotion of internal migration (of highly educated from wealthy families) may reinforce the existing inequalities in Kerala. Instead, the state policy may look towards widening access to international migration to the poorest segments of the population and thereby enabling the redistribution of income through remittances (Pelletier, 2011).

We may look into the way certain socio-economic groups are left out of this larger model and try to see the implications of this exclusion. By sending the largest number of workers and receiving the highest amount of household remittances, the Malappuram district leads Gulf migration for several years. Given its lower rank in human development indicators, its migrants tend to gravitate around West Asian countries and certain types of jobs compared to professional migrants from other districts. Broadly, the share of migrant households was found to be highest among Muslims followed by Christians and Hindus. Muslim households account for the largest share of migrant households covered in all three rounds of the survey and the same reflects their majority in the sample and district population. Compared to this, migration from Christian households is limited but reported active participation among the professionally educated groups. Considering the complex nature of caste manifested and mediated among the Muslims and Christians, the table presents their combined share. The study does not focus on the caste or intra-community dynamics to see whether they have any influence on the pattern of migration reported during these surveys.

Within the Hindu households, migration remains limited among the backward and forward castes while households belonging to the SCs and STs seem to be excluded (Table 12.1). The details collected during the survey indicate that there are specific factors that enabled migration from marginalized communities. For instance, some of the Dalit migrants reported in the 2015 survey own land and asset which many do not have. Similarly, we came across cases where migration from the Dalit family was promoted/facilitated by another affluent migrant family, often with long years of association as employee and employer. The absence of such physical

Table 12.1 Migration pattern across social groups (share in %)

	2010		*2011–2012*		*2015–2016*	
	Migrant Hs (75)*	*Total Hs (196)*	*Migrant Hs* (354)*	*Total Hs (752)*	*Migrant Hs* (161)*	*Total Hs (360)*
Forward caste	6.67	7.65	1.41	2.79	3.73	3.06
OBCs	21.33	21.94	3.95	9.57	3.11	3.89
SCs	2.67	9.69	0.85	5.05	1.24	15.00
STs			0.00	1.06	0.62	13.06
Muslim/Christian	69.33	60.71	93.79	81.52	91.30	65.00
Total	**100**	**100**	**100**	**100**	**100**	**100**

Source: Primary surveys.
Migrant households: *At least one migrant or returned migrant

or social capital and social networks limits their access to migration or it hardly acts as the pathway out of vulnerability as it worked for many in the mainstream.

The pattern of land ownership, household income, education, especially the enrolment rates in higher and professional levels and other factors which enable mass migration from the state indicate poor endowments among the Scheduled Castes and Scheduled Tribes. Compared to other communities, the threshold level of education and skill development required for migration and the labor market among SCs and STs remain low. In the process of education-led development, these two communities lag behind others. The SC and ST households have no students enrolled in private unaided schools and their presence in higher and professional education is very limited. The average per capita yearly educational expenditure per student from ST and SC households (only Rs.375 and Rs. 971.53) is far below that of higher and backward castes (Rs.4103.03 and Rs. 3439.29 respectively) households (Jafar, 2018:100–101). Gradual withdrawal of the state and growth of the private sector (remittance-driven) in higher and professional education is likely to widen this gap in the coming years.

Historically, these two groups remain marginal or backward in education-led development; scholars identify them as 'outliers' of the so-called Kerala model of development (Kunhaman, 1985; Omvedt, 2006; Shyjan & Sunitha, 2009; Sivanandan, 1979; Yadu & Vijayasuryan, 2016). Popular policies including land reforms, decentralization, the Kudumbashree mission, or centrally sponsored flagship programs like MGNREGS have limited impact on their lives. At the state level, Kerala has an impressive record; it emerges as a model for other states but leaves these vulnerable communities on the margins. As education plays a central role in the migration-led development process, the low threshold of education among these two marginalized communities is likely to keep them as outliers of Kerala's development process for several years.

Migration-Induced Vulnerability: Alternate Narratives

The narratives on Kerala's migration experience have established its impact on upward social and economic mobility in the state while a few have explored its impact on families, a specific gender, age groups, and communities. Besides the success stories, there are several instances of unsuccessful events or their varied effects causing vulnerability. Our surveys identify many migrant households (with at least one member ever migrated out of state) but notice that many of them, especially in the coastal villages, have at least one family member as returned non-resident Indians. Most of them had migrated to Saudi Arabia as fishermen and returned due to the high risk involved in the job, low payment, legal problems or health issues, or issues related to the family. Many of them stayed only for a short period that was not long enough to earn anything and pay back the liabilities incurred during their migration (selling or mortgaging gold ornaments or documents of the property).

Following the success stories, the cost of migration has increased significantly. Prospective migrants take risky ways to generate the huge amount of money required for their travel, visa, job, and middlemen. Unfortunately, many of them get cheated by the recruiting agencies and middlemen or could not find jobs that suit their qualifications and are left with no choice other than to take a lower-grade job for recovering the financial liability incurred in migration. The institutional mechanisms, especially due to the gaps in legal measures – in both India and host countries – are often so weak to address many of these issues and leave their rehabilitation unresolved. Instead of strengthening upward socio-economic mobility, these instances suggest that migration can also function as a source of vulnerability or multiple forms of liability. These issues may be used to highlight some of the parallel narratives on Kerala's migration model and call for a closer look into the way some are left behind or fail to make it as successful migrants.

Concluding Remarks

Kerala's development experience, especially its remarkable progress in social and human development with the active intervention of the state and sociopolitical process has been widely discussed in the development literature. Education plays a critical role in the process of migration and remittance-driven development that Kerala has experienced in recent decades. The migration of workers and the inflow of their remittances have an impact on almost all spheres of Malayalee life. Compared to its positive effects on the upward socio-economic mobility of migrants and their families and success stories, its varied effect on specific regions, social groups/ communities remain under-explored for various reasons. The difference in the quality of human capital formation, access to physical and social capital, skillsets, opportunities that emerge in the labor markets outside the state, etc., influence the way a community or group participates in the process of migration. In this process, those groups with better human capital endowments may manage to reduce the risk involved in their migration and migrate successfully.

This chapter tries to revisit the larger model and attempts to highlight some micro evidence and highlight the role of local factors in shaping the new pattern. The paper focuses on the way certain socio-economic groups are left out of this larger model and its implications on the nature of migration-led development in the state. In some sense, the exclusion of marginalized communities (SCs and STs) and limited participation from other vulnerable groups from this model indicate that they remain outliers of Kerala's development.

Given the limited scope of the chapter, it leaves many areas where the migration of workers and the inflow of their remittances have specific roles.

This includes the cost of living and lifestyle, health status and health-care requirements, changes in the land price and real estate dynamics, housing, and other areas. They play critical roles in transforming Kerala through its culture, the functions of religious organizations, voluntary organizations, and other groups involved in philanthropy. Tapping the resources and expertise of the returned migrants and addressing issues related to their rehabilitation, employment, health, and other social security measures remain a challenge. The study understands the importance of effective policy intervention in these areas and strategies to reduce the gap in the quality of life that derives from this pattern of development.

Note

1 The author would like to acknowledge the support received from NIAS Bangalore, CSD Hyderabad, and ICSSR New Delhi for conducting the studies mentioned. The usual disclaimers apply.

References

Aravindan, K.P., & Menon R.V.G. (Eds.) (2010). *A snapshot of Kerala: Life and thought of the Malayalee people*. Thrissur: Kerala Sastra Sahitya Parishad

CDS (2005). *Human development report 2005 Kerala. Centre for Development Studies. Prepared for Government of Kerala*. Thiruvananthapuram: State Planning Board

Chakraborty, A. (2005). Kerala's changing development narratives. *Economic and Political Weekly*, *40*(6), 541–547

Chakraborty, P., Chakraborty, L., Nath, H.K.A. & Mitra, S. (2010). *Financing human development in Kerala: Issues and challenges. Draft report for comments*, New Delhi: National Institute of Public Finance and Policy

George, K.K., & Kumar, N.A. (1999). *What is wrong with Kerala's education system?* Working Paper No.3, Kochi: Centre for Socio-economic & Environmental Studies

Jafar, K. (2013). Reservation and women's political freedom: Candidates' experience from three gram panchayats in Kerala, India. *Social Change*, *43*(1), 79–97

Jafar, K. (2018). *Education, migration and human development: Kerala experience*. Jaipur: Rawat Publications

Joseph, K.V. (1988). *Migration and economic development of Kerala*. Delhi: Mittal Publications

Kannan, K.P. (1990). Kerala economy at the crossroads? *Economic and Political Weekly*, 25(35/36), 1951–1956

Kannan, K.P. (2005). Kerala's turnaround in growth: Role of social development, remittances and reform. *Economic and Political Weekly*, 40(6), 548–554

Kannan, K.P., & Hari, K.S. (2002). Kerala's Gulf connection: Remittances and their macroeconomic impact. In K.C. Zachariah, K.P. Kannan, & S.I. Rajan (Eds.), *Kerala's Gulf connection: CDS studies on international labour migration from Kerala state in India* (pp. 199–230). Thiruvananthapuram: Centre for Development Studies

Kannan, K.P., & Pushpangadan, K., (1988). Agricultural stagnation in Kerala: An exploratory analysis. *Economic and Political Weekly*, *23*(39), A120–A128

Kunhaman, M. (1985). The tribal economy of Kerala: An intra-regional analysis. *Economic and Political Weekly*, 20(11), 466–474

Mathew, E.T. (1997). *Employment and unemployment in Kerala: Some neglected aspects*. New Delhi: Sage Publications

Mathew, E.T. (1999). Educated unemployment in Kerala: Incidence, causes and policy implications, In B.A. Prakash (Ed), *Kerala's economic development: Issues and problems* (pp. 94–115). New Delhi: Sage Publications

Mathew, P.M. (2005). Kerala's 'turnaround in growth': A note. *Economic and Political Weekly*, *40*(30), 3287–3289

Nair, M.K.S. (1999a). Emerging trends in labour shortage in Kerala agriculture. In B.A. Prakash (Ed), *Kerala's economic development: Issues and problems* (pp. 220–241). New Delhi: Sage Publications

Nair, M.K.S. (1999b). Labour shortage in a labour surplus economy? A study of the rural labour market in Kerala. In M.A. Oommen (Ed.), *Rethinking Development: Kerala's Development Experience* (pp 247–268). Volume 2. Institute of Social Sciences, New Delhi: Concept Publishing Company

Nambiar, A.C.K. (1995). *The socio-economic conditions of Gulf migrants*. New Delhi: Commonwealth Publishers

Omvedt, G. (2006). Kerala is part of India: The Kerala model of development, Dalits and globalisation. In J. Tharamangalam (Ed.), *Kerala: The paradox of Public Action and Development* (pp. 188–214). New Delhi: Orient Longman

Oommen, M.A. (2008a). Capabilities, reform and the Kerala model. Paper presented at the Annual Conference of Human Development and Capability Association, New Delhi, 10–13 September

Pelletier, A. (2011). Household remittance, inequality and poverty: Evidence from the state of Kerala. In S.I. Rajan, & M. Percot, (Eds.), *Dynamics of Indian Migration: Historical and Current Perspectives* (pp. 378–417). New Delhi: Routledge

Pradhan, J.P., & Abraham, V. (2002). Does human development policy matter for economic growth? Evidence from Indian states. *South Asia Economic Journal*, *3*(1), 77–93

Prakash, B.A. (1988). *Educated unemployment in Kerala: Some observations based on a field study*. Working Paper 224. Thiruvananthapuram: Centre for Development Studies

Prakash, B.A. (1998). Gulf migration and its economic impact: The Kerala experience. *Economic and Political Weekly*, 33(50), 3209–3213

Prakash, B.A. (1999). The economic impact of migration to the Gulf. In B.A. Prakash (Ed.), *Kerala's Economic Development: Issues and Problems* (pp. 134–149). New Delhi: Sage Publications

Rajan S.I. & Kumar, P. (2010). Historical overview of International migration. In S.I. Rajan (Ed.), *India Migration Report 2010: Governance and Labour Migration* (pp. 1–29). New Delhi: Routledge

Rajan S.I., & Kumar, P., (2011). A long haul: Revisiting international migration from India during the 19th and 20th centuries. In D. Narayana and R. Mahadevan (Eds.), *Shaping India: Economic Change in Historical Perspective* (pp. 295–319). New Delhi: Routledge

Ranis, G., Stewart, F., & Ramiez, A. (2011). Economic growth and human development. In S. Fukuda-Parr & A.K.S. Kumar (Eds.), *Handbook of Human Development: Concepts, Measures, and Policies* (pp. 61–84). New Delhi: Oxford University Press

Shyjan, D., & Sunitha, A.S., (2009). Changing phases of Kerala's development experience and the exclusion of scheduled tribes: Towards an explanation. *Artha Vijnana*, *51*(4), 340–359

Sivanandan, P. (1979). Caste, class and economic opportunity in Kerala: An empirical analysis. *Economic and Political Weekly*, 14(7/8), 475–480

Subrahmanian, K.K. (1990). Development paradox in Kerala: Analysis of industrial stagnation. *Economic and Political Weekly*, 25(37), 2053–2055+2057–2058

Sunny, J., Parida, J.K., & Azurudeen, M. (2020). Remittances, Investment and New Emigration Trends in Kerala. *Review of Development and Change*, *25*(1), 5–29

Yadu, C.R., & Vijayasuryan, C.K. (2016). Triple exclusion of Dalits in land ownership in Kerala' *Social Change*, *46*(3), 1–16

Zachariah, K.C., Mathew, E.T., & Rajan, S.I. (2002). Migration patterns and their socio-economics, In K.C. Zachariah, K.P. Kannan and S.I Rajan (Eds.), *Kerala's Gulf Connection: CDS Studies on International Labour Migration from Kerala State in India* (pp. 13–45). Thiruvananthapuram: Centre for Development Studies

Zachariah, K.C., Mathew, E.T., & Rajan, S.I., (2003). *Dynamics of migration in Kerala: Dimensions, differentials and consequences*. New Delhi: Orient Longman

13 Culture as a Determinant of Goan Migration to the Gulf

Sonal Thakker

Introduction

People all around the world leave their homes in search of a better life, to meet their necessities, and to provide for their families (Cohen & Sirkeci, 2011). Male migration has become a way of life in certain cultures, and to use Van Gennep's idea, it can be compared with "rites of passage" for young men when they start on a voyage overseas, breaking the umbilical cord with their family, birthplace, friends, and neighborhood community. A calculated risk is taken by weighing the costs involved to travel overseas, and the probable rewards, and then a decision is made to embark on a journey which is perceived as something that will alleviate them from a life which is mundane, routine, and having negligible scope for social and material advancement.

In general, migration is understood as a long- or short-term geographic movement of people, whether permanent or temporary, in search of improved quality of life and employment opportunities. Since it is popularly believed that most of the migration to foreign lands takes place due to economic reasons, earlier studies primarily stressed monetary considerations as a motivating stimulus, as such scant attention was paid to the dominant sociocultural influence existing in society. There are few studies which have focused on the cultural milieu as a decisive factor and a driving force exerting a powerful influence on the migration of young men who are not gainfully employed in their hometowns.

Objectives

To make an analysis of the different sociocultural contexts which provide an impetus to the practice of migration as a prelude to understanding Goan migration to the Gulf. This paper seeks to explore the "migration culture" that exists in some societies, focusing on the cultural attitudes and social patterns that determine and motivate people in certain societies to migrate.

DOI: 10.4324/9781003369370-17

Methodology

In many cultures, migration is seen as a natural part of life, and I have looked at a few examples where movement is a norm. This research is mostly based on secondary data gleaned from a thorough assessment of literature on the sociocultural elements that have a significant impact on migration.

Background of Migration

Many experts have noted that men migrating without their families were seen as an aberration and only resorted to moving in extreme instances. Such men were perceived as eccentric since it appeared anomalous to move so far away to seek a livelihood without the unit of one's family where the division of labor provided succor and support for each other. In 1934 a farmer in Shantou, China, asked "Why should any individual take upon himself all the risks of travelling abroad to seek a livelihood?" As migration is so common, one of the most pressing questions is why men are eager to move overseas for work despite the numerous dangers they must face. Similarly, Adam Smith remarked "of all the luggage, man is the most difficult to transport", implying that most men dislike being out of their comfort zone.

Taft and Robbins (1955: 3) observed men on the move are frequently of more immediate value than dormant and inactive men". Such males were frequently labeled with opprobrious terms like "tramp" and "globe-trotter". "At certain times in European history, persons on the move were viewed as vagrants, as such socially undesirable and vulnerable to prosecution" (Cox, 1976: 144). These disparaging remarks dissuaded the mobility of single men to a large extent, and they kept up with social conventions in fear of being belittled and sometimes even rebuked by the community. Often moral pressure was imposed on young men branding them as "wanderers" and chided for not being firmly rooted in their family and birthplace.

This perception, however, is no longer valid. Millions of individuals have traveled around the world in search of work, whether skilled or unskilled. This has resulted in significant financial gains which are visible through improved lifestyles and life chances of subsequent generations.

The scarcity factor in hometowns and villages, as well as the prospect of improving their economic status and the possibility of landing a profitable job, are all highly appealing, and as a result, people migrate to bring in the coveted resources. The following account includes various illustrations of migration as a way of life in some societies.

Man's Role – "Provider" – Demonstrate "Maturity" and "Masculinity"

A man is expected to be a "provider", and there is a lot of social pressure on him to do so during his adolescent years. Young males, who are impressionable and susceptible, seek inspiration from their surroundings to meet this expectation. This takes us to the often-overlooked role of culture in migration decisions.

As pointed out by Gulati (1993: 14) in Kerala, "this willingness to 'jump' has resulted in practically all able-bodied young men from families with a member in West Asia having their passports ready, so that they can go at a moment's notice".

According to the Human Development Report (2009) "For many young people across the world, spending time abroad is regarded a natural part of life experience, and migration represents a step to adulthood", thus migration was "a means of alleviating a family's social status in the local society". The report cites field studies from Jordan, Pakistan, Thailand, Nigeria, and Vietnam, where the migration of men is a norm. This has resulted in the formation of a "migration culture", in which "international migration is connected with personal, social, and material success, while staying at home is associated with failure".

Many boys may have felt compelled to "follow the path" laid down by their predecessors to demonstrate their "manhood" and "maturity" by bringing in the desired economic resources. Cohen & Sirkeci, (2011: 89) note "Young men often mark their growth and pending adulthood through migration". "Migration is a rite of passage", according to Bakewell (2009), in a study in West Africa of some communities in Mali, Mauritania, and Senegal (Ba et al. 2008 cited in HDR, 2009: 81). Osella and Osella (1999; 2000) reported similar findings, stating that "migration is connected to the life-cycle strategy" and signals the "transition between adolescence and adulthood".

According to Watkins (2003), young Pakistani men from the Pakhtun tribal region migrate to the Gulf to "accumulate capital and become 'householders' back in their country". Further, "their stories of hardship appear to be part of the maturation process".

In the Sonike hamlet of Kounda in Mali, Jonsson (2007, cited in HDR, 2009: 81) observes that "movement distinguishes males and females". Men who are not independent are referred to as "immature youngsters", and women frequently refer to them as *tenes*, which means "glued together". Young men who have grown up in a culture that encourages migration are motivated by the desire to prove their masculinity.

According to Thakkilapati (2013), "individuals who remain in rural regions are believed to lack motivation, be failed attempted migrants, or dejected returnees" when compared to those who have migrated from Rural Andhra Pradesh. Those who moved were able to support their families financially and "help develop their rural hometowns".

In another study, Osella and Osella (2003) found a fascinating link between money and masculinity in the migration of men from Kerala, India. Migration to the Gulf entails not only escaping unemployment, but also elevating *payyanmar* (immature youths) from *payyanhood* (young immature status) to householder status. This has demonstrated their worth in terms of marriage, fatherhood, and being a "provider". However, the "accumulation and display of cash" is the primary requirement for achieving such an important position. As a result, they maintain their reputation among the villagers.

The habit of moving abroad from Goa is the result of a migration culture that has permeated the Goan cultural milieu. According to Mascarenhas (2011: 257), "individuals have personal and vicarious experience of marriage through separation in a migration-oriented society". As a result, marital partnerships with overseas migrants are seen more favorably because they are regarded as prestigious and provide certainty of a secure financial future. Often a man is rejected if he is working in a private enterprise, and a Gulf suitor is considered more eligible. With few public sector job openings, men prefer to work abroad, where they can improve not just their economic status, but also their marriage prospects.

The studies above show how the villagers, as well as their family and peers, impose normative expectations on young men. We note a migration trend in various cultures. It is thought to be the next logical step following late adolescence, and it is a cultural expectation (Thakker, 2015). A man is expected to fulfill his role as a provider for his family. This obligation makes men more mobile in the quest of raising their status. As a result, we can deduce that some cultures actively promote migration.

Migration as a Community Norm

The relative wage disparities between the host and home countries have enticed young men to travel abroad. According to Taft and Robbins (1955: 18), migration frequently takes on the characteristics of a "public frenzy" or a local custom, and recall "certain towns of Poland and Italy were at one point depopulated of their young blood". Furthermore, "entire nations have grown to rely on the remittances sent home by immigrants", resulting in men being literally "exchanged for goods". As the social network expands, the culture can develop its own self-sustaining momentum (HDR, 2009). The concept of a "migration-oriented society" was developed by Philipott's research of migration in Montserrat (1968, quoted in Mascarenhas, 2011: 11–12).

However, according to a study by Adhikari (2011: 171), migration is discouraged in some cultures. He draws attention to Nepalese cultural practices and beliefs, which are anti-migration. The monarchy and ruling elites' primary idea was rooted in "nationalism", which was generally defined as *bir* or brave people. The king and feudal aristocracy constructed a maxim that the Nepalese were valiant people who lived in pride despite their poverty. The ruling class believed that if Nepalese were forced to work in menial jobs in other nations, it would reflect badly on the country (ibid.: 181–182). As a result, migration was forbidden and vigorously opposed in Nepali society.

Traditional View of Goan Migration

The traditional view of Goan migration was that it was an unavoidable result or a desperate act of escape from a doomed situation. Some Goans considered Goa a primitive place, where one could do nothing to improve one's own standing. It was broadly assumed that the most capable Goans should be encouraged to view migration as a natural path and to take advantage of it as soon as possible (Cunha, J: 226 cited in GMS, 2008: 21).

Carvalho (2010: 3) describes the goal of a Goan pursuing money abroad and claims that young Goan males consider their condition in Goa to be hopeless. They were pessimistic and believe "nothing good can come from vegetating in the villages". They nurtured the belief that life in their dung-floored houses is unproductive, and they dream of a better life beyond the confines of their villages.

Mascarenhas (1990: 246) points out, "a potential migrant's perception was that Goa offered no chance of finding a 'good' job". This discouraged them from quitting their safe positions abroad and deterred them from returning to Goa to start a business. They also lacked business skills and were unwilling to accept the risks that such ventures demanded. As a result, they opted to stay and work abroad to assure a steady income. Furthermore, Goans saw physical labor as insignificant and degrading. Also, because tourism-related employment is seasonal, Goan males choose to travel abroad.

Post-Decolonization Scenario

With the British departure from India in 1947, Goans who had been hired in large numbers by the British enterprises lost their jobs, causing them to return home from 1948 to 1959 (Mascarenhas cited in GMS, 2008: 26). Also, many Goans who had gone to British Africa in pursuit of work were compelled to return to Goa in the late nineteenth century when the colonies reverted to indigenous sovereignty in the 1960s. Only a few Goans opted to remain in the country, while others relocated to Australia, America, Canada, the United Kingdom, New Zealand, and other countries (Fernandes, 2007: 46).

Post-Liberation Scenario

After the liberation of Goa in 1961 the trend of migration continued. The migratory pattern shifted in the 1960s and 1970s. People moved to the Gulf countries, where petroleum mining had taken off. Although many Goans began migrating to the Middle East in the early decades of the twentieth century, the advent of commercial oil drilling in the 1970s and 1980s attracted a bigger number of Goans (Gracias, 2007: 107; Rodrigues, 2002: 180). This resulted in high demand for blue-collar workers with limited qualifications.

However, Goans who travel to the Gulf countries cannot settle there and eventually return to Goa at the time of retirement.

Derogatory Mindset Towards Gulf Migrants

According to Gracias (2007: 108) the early Goans who went to the Gulf were despised by the upper classes and referred to derisively as *Gulfies* or *Kuwaitkars*. Carvalho mentions (2010: 116) "Goan society turned against the *Gulfkar*", a man working in the Gulf was caricatured as "someone who dressed gaudily, wore too much gold, spent conspicuously, but remained illiterate and unrefined". She goes on to say that the term *Gulfie* has a connotation of contempt; and very often ridiculed by Goans because it rhymed with "hippy" (a bohemian cultural trend of foreigners in Goa in the 1970s) and "shippy" (seaman). Similarly, "the *tarvotti* (seaman) had at one time been acknowledged as a worthy role model to aspire to and then subsequently diminished by ridicule".

However, Carvalho (2010: 118) adds, "From the mid-1980s, when people of the middle and higher classes began flocking to the region, attracted by its affluence, this demeaning mindset began to alter". Rodrigues (2002: 180) observes that the *bhatcars* (landlords) and persons of Portuguese descent, who once looked down upon them with disregard and "labeled them *Bombaistas* or *Mumoicares*" (Goans who went to Mumbai which was a part of British India), also started seeking employment overseas.

Fernandes (2007: 41–42) offers an interesting remark on a migrant being "labeled" based on which country he was employed. A Goan working in a Middle Eastern country is recognized back home by the country's colloquial name. For example, if a Goan was working in Bahrain, he was known as *Barinkar* or *Barinvalo*. Those laboring in Kuwait were referred to as *Kuvetkars*. However, until the 1960s, a Goan was known by a colloquial term – *Basurkar* – regardless of which Gulf country he worked in, because Basra, city in Iraq, was the first Middle Eastern country to which Goans traveled, and the term persisted for a long time.

Glory, Glitter, and Glamor of Gulf Migrants

International migrants usually amplified their newfound socio-economic position and they often indulged in grandiose exhibition of wealth. As a result of meeting people from diverse cultures, they had acquired refined tastes and their mannerisms appeared classy (Gomes, 1987: 361; 1996: 366). Their social etiquette made them "stand apart" at social gatherings. Wearing a tuxedo, shiny leather boots, gold ornaments, and reeking of perfume gave them a distinct edge over the ones who did not migrate. Thus, overseas migration resulted in enormous changes in their families' economic and social circumstances. Those who had once been from the lowest social strata had made it "big" in distant places, with the advantages trickling down to the family. This fueled the aspiration of young men in the villages to flock to the Gulf in huge numbers. As a result of the glory, glitter, and glamorous lifestyle of the family members, there was also an altered perception and attitude toward the Gulf migrants.

Remittances and Conspicuous Consumption

The remittances allowed immigrants' families to maintain a high level of living by allowing them to purchase luxury items such as silk and fine cotton garments, wines, liqueurs, beer, and cigars (GMS, 2008). With newly constructed residences, contemporary technologies, and surplus funds, remittances in Goa have had a positive impact on the standard of living (Larsen, 1998: 272). The volume and variety of material artifacts in Goa rose because of commodities' remittance. Electronic gadgets and household appliances were sent as gifts. The increased consumerism and lifestyle of migrants and their families reflected the improved economic situation (Mascarenhas, 1990: 250–251). Having a lot of disposable cash, the families indulged in conspicuous consumption and spent extravagantly during celebration of birthdays, weddings, village feasts, and festivals.

Reverse Snobbery

The migrants who had been subjected to an unflattering and hostile attitude had later begun to pander in reverse snobbery. Gomes (1996: 366) writes in his book *Village Goa*, return migrants refused to drink country liquors and despised those who did not migrate, referring to them as "less fortunate fellow villagers and plain rustics". They preferred to converse in the English language and showed contempt towards the local language. After achieving success, their entire demeanor was haughty. They bragged about the skills and refined taste that they acquired overseas.

Gulf Migrants – Role Models and Reference Group

It is a human tendency to look up to successful people as role models and worthy of emulation. "Others could be motivated by their accomplishments because they effectively functioned as reference group" Mascarenhas (1990: 246). Young males who want a better life and a stable income look up to returning migrants, want to imitate them, and thereby replicate their achievements. Almost every town has a few heroes who regale the villagers with tales of bravado, tenacity, and determination in a distant land, often exaggerating the favorable outcomes and disguising the trials and tribulations of the early days (Thakker, 2015).

When a person achieves upward mobility because of migration, other villagers, regardless of religion, consider seeking his help. "New movers and potential migrants turn to friends and family for support. Migrants follow paths to their destinations that have been mapped out over time and with the help of previous movers" (Cohen & Sirkeci 2011: 116). Larsen (1998: 263) observes "the allure of metropolitan adventure and the apparent ease with which they could find work enticed young and capable men from their communities". They derived encouragement from vacationing migrants' stories who recounted anecdotes about their life and work abroad. This created significant stimuli to induce peers and juniors to migrate.

Migrant Men Perceived as "Heroes"

Among the migrant Catholic Goans, "families have grown accustomed to the absence of fathers and saw them as heroes, harbingers of gifts, entertainment, and remote authority figures" Mascarenhas (2011: 257). Women hold their migrant spouses in high esteem and praise their migrant husbands for "performing their role as breadwinners of the household". As a result, there is no resentment due to staying apart for long durations because it is viewed as a normal part of life. There are many villages in Salcete Taluka of south Goa where there are cases of not only intragenerational mobility but also intergenerational mobility. As a result of a variety of historical and cultural circumstances, migration has primarily occurred from the territory's Christian population.

GMS (2008) findings show that emigrants from Goa are spread over 43 countries, with 56 percent working in the Gulf, 13 percent in Europe, 11 percent in South and Southeast Asia, 10 percent in North America, and 7 percent working on cruise ships and merchant ships. In the last decade and a half there has been an increase in the number of Goans procuring a Portuguese passport. The rationale for this is that obtaining a Portugal document will offer them easy access to European countries where they are now looking for better remunerative work.

Conclusion

This strong desire to "move overseas solely" and especially to the Gulf, has led to a trend among Goan youngsters to pursue tourism and hospitality-related employment such as working in travel agencies, airports, hotels, or on cruise ships, all of which pay well. As a result, there is a kind of anticipatory socialization to be prepared with the necessary skills and be prepared to take a "jump" when the opportunity to travel overseas arises. As a result, migration has become a way of life in Goa, and become a habitual trend.

References

Adhikari, J. (2011). Nepal. In Kelegama, S. (Ed.), *Migration, remittances and development in South Asia*. New Delhi: Sage Publications.

Carvalho, S. (2010). *Into the diaspora wilderness*. Goa: Goa 1556 & Broadway Publishing House.
Cohen, J. H., & Sirkeci, I. (2011). *Cultures of migration: The global nature of contemporary mobility*. Austin: University of Texas Press.
Cox, P. R. (1976). *Demography*. (5th ed). London: Cambridge University Press.
Fernandes, D. (2007). *Domnic's Goa*. Goa: Abbe Faria Productions.
Goa Migration Study Report. (2008). Department of NRI Affairs. Government of Goa.
Gomes, O. J. F. (1996). *Village Goa*. (2nd. Ed.) New Delhi: S. Chand & Co. Pvt. Ltd.
Gomes, O. J. F. (1987). *Village Goa*. New Delhi: S. Chand & Co. Pvt. Ltd.
Gracias, F. S. (October, 2007). Goans away from Goa: Out -migration to the Middle East. In *Parmal*, Vol. 6. Porvorim: Goa Heritage Action Group.
Gulati, L. (1983). Male migration to the Middle East and the impact on the family: Some evidences from Kerala. *Economic and Political Weekly*, *18*, 52–53.
———. (1993). *In the absence of their men: The impact of male migration on women*. New Delhi: Sage Publications.
Human Development Report. (2009). *Overcoming barriers: Human mobility and development*. New York: UNDP.
Larsen, K. (1998). *Faces of Goa*. New Delhi: Gyan Publishing House.
Mascarenhas, S. K. (1990). International migration: Its development, reproduction, and economic impact on Goa up to 1961. In De' Souza, T. R. (Ed.), *Goa through the ages: An economic history. (Vol. II.)*. New Delhi: Concept Publishing Co.
———. (2011). *Colonialism, migration and the international Catholic Goan community* (p. 1556). Goa: Saligao
Osella, F., & Osella, C. (2003). Migration, money, masculinity in Kerala. *Journal of the Royal Anthropological Institute*, *6*(1), 117–133.
Rodrigues, M. L. & Bravo, D. C. (2002). Goa: Four decades of freedom. In Cabral, M. (Ed.), *Redefining horizons*. Panaji, Goa: Department of Information and Publicity.
Taft, D. R., & Robbins, R. (1955). *International migrations: The immigrant in the modern world*. USA: The Ronald Press Co.
Thakker, S. (2015). *Migration and family dynamics in Goa*. (Unpublished Ph. D Thesis Submitted to Goa University).
Thakkilapati, S. (2013). Rather than drink milk and run one can drink water and rest. In Proceedings from the Human Migration in South Asia: Patterns, Development and Challenges, Goa.
Watkins, F. (2003). Save there, eat here: Migrant households and community identity among Pakhtuns in Pakistan. In *Contributions to Indian Sociology. Vol. VIII.*

14 Migration from Manipur's Pangal Community to the Gulf Countries

A Case Study

Md. Chingiz Khan

Introduction

It is evident that the term "migration" principally means a permanent or semi-permanent change of residence. While concerning the difference between external and internal migration in any state, it is pointed out that there is no clear-cut peculiarity between the two but by observing closely, the difference is there in terms of phenomenon, culture, and way of functioning. It is perhaps said that there is no restriction placed upon the distance of the move or upon the voluntary or involuntary nature of the act. So, a move across the hall from one place to another place is considered as much an act of migration as a move from the North East Indian states particularly Manipur to the various capital cities of the Gulf countries especially the cities of Saudi Arabia and Kuwait though, undoubtedly, the initiation and consequences of such moves are vastly different (Lee, 1966). Till now, it is certainty that around 15–20 Pangals have got permanent citizenship.

Before exploring the case study of the Pangals migration in the Gulf countries, there are different terms that need to be understood while discussing the migration of Manipuris to the Gulf countries, particularly in Saudi Arabia and its neighboring areas. The term "immigration" is the process of people moving from one country to another with the motive of staying there permanently. The two terms "in-migration" and "out-migration" mean the process of people moving from one area to another within their own country. Both the terms have the same process but in different directions. Some scholars defined the term "in-migration" as the process of people moving into a new area in their country to live there permanently. Furthermore, another term "out-migration" is the process of people moving out of an area in their country to move to another area in their country permanently. Most people used to prefer migration because they would like to have a standard life in a new place for employment regardless of expenses or other rationales.

Some well-known scholars have given several opinions regarding the process and procedures, reasons, and motives of migration in the world. First of all, it is a complex process and, therefore, it is unfeasible that one

DOI: 10.4324/9781003369370-18

theory can explore and examine all the events involved in it. The study related to causal factors of migration can be traced back to classical economic development theory and according to E.G. Ravenstein, who worked voluminously on migration, it is said that "It is considered to be a mechanism that establishes regional spatial-economic equilibrium" (Ravenstein, 1885; Ravenstein, 1889). Those persons who are willing to study the process and procedure of migration have to identify the factors involved in it. There are different models theorized by some well-known scholars to explain the factors involved. In 1885, E.G. Ravenstein in his study of the "laws of migration" attempted firstly to theorize migration. Based on the data of birthplace, Ravenstein identified the aforementioned laws concerning inter-county migration. Through these laws, Ravenstein elucidated the key areas on which the future of migration research would largely be based. He opined emphatically on major factors that influenced migration and highlighted the importance of the distance of the place of origin and destination, and the direction of migration as being seen largely from a primarily agricultural region to a region of relatively flourishing commerce and industry (Ravenstein, 1885; Ravenstein, 1889).

His laws of migration are furnished in the following points:

1. Most migration is over short distances.
2. Migration occurs in steps.
3. Long-range migrants usually move to urban areas.
4. Each migration produces a movement in the opposite direction.
5. Rural dwellers are more migratory than urban dwellers.
6. Within their own country, females are more migratory than males, but males are more migratory over long distances.
7. Most migrants are adults.
8. Large towns grow more by migration than by natural increase.
9. Migration increases with economic development.
10. Migration is mostly due to economic causes.

Everett Lee (Lee, 1966) remolded Ravenstein's theory emphasizing internal (or push) factors. He focused on the impeding effects of distance, physical and political barriers, and the presence of dependents on migration. He was the first scholar to point out the impact of age, gender, and social class on the responsiveness to push-pull factors. Since then, several theories have been developed which treat international patterns of migration on their own terms, but these too are variants of the push-pull theory.

The other theories relating to migration are given as: The neo-classical economic theory of migration has its historical roots in models of development (Arthur, 1954). This theory describes rural-urban migration to be caused by geographic differences in the supply and demand for labor, wage differentials between rural and urban areas, and an army of "under-employed" rural labor in agriculture. In the Lewis model, the underdeveloped economy consists of two sectors: A traditional, overpopulated, rural subsistence sector characterized by zero marginal labor productivity – a situation that permits Lewis to classify the surplus labor in the sense that it can be withdrawn from the traditional agricultural sector without any loss of output and a high-productivity, modern, urban industrial sector into which labor from the subsistence sector is gradually transferred. The primary focus of the model is on both the process of labor transfer and the growth of output and employment in the modern sector. Both labor transfer and modern sector employment growth are brought about by output expansion in that sector (*Ibid.*). Some of the other theories of migration are given as the Harris-Todaro model (Harris and Todaro, 1970), Stark and Bloom model (Stark and Bloom, 1985), etc. Though there are many models to explain the process of migration, it needs to be pondered and explored how far these models are applicable in the context of migration of Pangals to the metropolitan cities in Saudi Arabia such as Makkah, Madinah, Jeddah, etc. and nearby countries including Kuwait and the United Arab Emirates.

Methodology

The methodology adopted in this paper is based on both primary and secondary sources. It is a documentary in nature. It involved the closer study of some interviews of scholars, workers, laborers, and bureaucrats who moved to metropolitan cities like Jeddah, Makkah, Madinah, Dubai, Riyadh, etc. and worked there. As there is a lacuna of literature for this study, some selected personal interviews of persons who studied in Jamia Millia Islamia (JMI), Aligarh Muslim University (AMU), University of Delhi (DU), etc. and worked in different places of Saudi Arabia and its adjoining areas such as Oman, Kuwait, etc. are taken. Apart from the above-mentioned documents, some secondary sources of information like published research papers in various journals, websites, and articles published in newspapers, books, edited books, etc., are used.

Pangal Migration to Saudi Arabia

It is evident that in terms of absolute numbers, barring 1999, Saudi Arabia attracted the largest number of Indian laborers (Irudaya, 2014). Some of the states like Kerala, Tamil Nadu, and Andhra Pradesh have the largest numbers of emigrants in the world. While considering the State-wise Figures of Workers Granted Emigration Clearance ECNR Endorsements during the Years 1997–2000, it is found that the state of Manipur had seven workers only in 1997 (Ministry of Labour, 2002; Jain, 2005). The Pangal community started settling in Manipur during the early period of the seventeenth century in the reign of King Khagemba (1597–1652 CE) though there are many "fictitious" claims of their settlement by some local scholars before the seventeenth century (Khan, 2014a; 2014b; 2015;

2016; 2019; 2021). They have contributed economically, politically, socially, and culturally on a large scale in the state itself. One of the crucial historical episodic events is the *Chahi Taret Khuntakpa* (Seven Years Devastation 1819–1826 CE). This dreadful incident paved the way for the large migration of Manipuris including Pangals in different sectors of India like Assam, Tripura, and countries like Bangladesh. It is evident that the journey of settlement of Pangals in the Gulf countries began in the early middle of the twentieth century though there was migration in Saudi Arabia in the early period of the nineteenth century in accordance with oral traditions. There are several "push" and "pull" factors for the migration of Pangals in different areas of the Gulf countries especially in the different cities of Saudi Arabia like Makkah, Madinah, Jeddah, etc. like the other counterpart communities of Manipur such as Meitei/Meetei, some sections of tribes since the middle of the twentieth century. Why they were migrating to the different cities of Saudi Arabia and its neighboring areas needs to be paid attention to. Some of the pivotal reasons are given in the following:

1. Jeddah, Makkah, Riyadh, Madinah, and other places in Saudi Arabia act as sources of business and economic centers for those who came from far-off regions especially the northeast regions of India with special reference to Manipur.
2. Such places become affordable for the earning of their livelihood.
3. It becomes an easily accessible place for job employment seekers and other economic factors.
4. Furthermore, one of the crucial reasons is that the law and order situation in Manipur was not good at all times as this state of Manipur is prone to insurgency. The AFSPA 1958 is still in existence in different parts of Manipur. This factor impacted the Manipuri people that include the Pangal community of Manipur. Such an unavoidable reason plays a crucial role in their migration to the Gulf countries especially in the cities of Jeddah, Makkah, Madinah, Riyadh, and other adjoining areas.
5. Some cities of Saudi Arabia like Makkah, Madinah, etc. are considered as the pilgrimage site of every Muslim in the world including the Manipuri Muslims annually. It is theologically mentioned by every Muslim that "if someone is performing Hajj or Umrah there, his or her sins would be forgiven".

Noor Rahman Sheikh, a career diplomat and the first Indian Foreign Service (IFS) from amongst Pangals and Meiteis/Meeteis (General and OBCs) from the valley, who is currently the Joint Secretary (Economic Diplomacy), Ministry of External Affairs (MEA), Govt of India, New Delhi is of the opinion regarding the migration of Pangals in the Gulf countries particularly in Saudi Arabia that

> The Pangals from Manipur and Cachar started migrating to Saudi Arabia in the 1960s. Many of them numbering about 20 took Saudi citizenship. It is understood that the first one from Manipur to migrate and obtain Saudi citizenship was Haji Jaffar from Sangaiyumpham, Thoubal District. Pangals' migration took place in Saudi Arabia for boosting up their economic status and accessing some facilities for their social improvement in connection with health infrastructure, education, etc. There are doctors, professors, engineers, nurses, workers and labourers who are working in different sectors/places of Saudi Arabia. While he was working as the Consul General of India in Jeddah, Saudi Arabia, he was able to help many Indians including Manipuris to return to India during the time of the labor crisis and Covid-19 pandemic by facilitating passport/visa extension, supplying food, and arranging lodging for them, etc. (Noor Rahman Sheikh, personal communication, 10 April 2021).

Furthermore, it is worthwhile mentioning that some Manipuri Pangals joined different educational institutes in Saudi Arabia in the 2000s. For instance, firstly, in 2006, Dr. M. Naziruddin Khan from Lilong who worked earlier at the King Saud University is currently teaching in the Department of Physics, Islamic University in Madinah. Later on, some of the Pangals started migrating and working in different universities, colleges, schools, and companies. He is of the opinion that

> In 1990s, some medical doctors and engineers from the Pangal community migrated and worked in various hospitals and institutes in Saudi Arabia. In recent times, some girls also from the Pangal community migrated in the country and worked as Nurse in Hospitals and other various medical institutes of the country. In addition, it is pointed out that most of the Pangals who migrated before 2000s in Saudi Arabia worked as supervisor, technician, salesman, waiter, waitress and driver, etc., with the exception of few countable numbers of medical doctors in medical companies and engineers in skill related companies
>
> (Dr. M. Naziruddin Khan, personal communication, 24 April 2021).

Pangal Migration in Oman, Jordan, the UAE, Qatar, Bahrain, and Kuwait

We could not find much evidence regarding the migration of Pangals to the above-mentioned countries except the UAE and Kuwait. In the early part of the twentieth century, it is suggested that some Pangals started migrating to Kuwait on account of the fact that there Kuwaiti dinar had highest currency value as compared to the others, lots of job opportunities were there, as well as a shortage of labor in the country. They would like to earn

Table 14.1 List of Pangals from Manipur who are working in different sectors including universities, colleges, schools, hospitals, and companies of different cities of Saudi Arabia

(a) At university/college/school			
Sl No	**Name of the person**	**Permanent address**	**University/college/school**
1	Dr. M. Naziruddin Khan	Lilong, Thoubal District	University
2	Dr. Noorjahan Begum	Hatta, Imphal East	College
3	Dr. M. Shahabuddin Shah	Phouden, Thoubal	University
4	Dr. Sania	Kwakta, Bishnupur	University
5	Dr. Mohd. Aslam Khan	Lilong, Thoubal	University
6	Amir Banu	Hatta, Imphal East	College
7	Wahida Rahman	Kshetrigao, Imphal East	College
8	Shahidur Rahman	Mayang Imphal Bengoon, Imphal West	School
(b) At hospitals and medical institutes of Saudi Arabia			
Sl No	**Name of the person**	**Permanent address**	
1	Dr Syed Burhanuddin	Lilong, Thoubal District (Left Saudi Arabia)	
2	Dr Shaheed	Hatta, Imphal East	
3	Dr Sureiya	Hatta, Imphal East	
4	Dr Atiqur Rahman	Kshetrigao, Imphal East	
5	Dr Fatima	Hatta, Imphal East (Left Saudi Arabia)	
6	Dr Mustaque	Lilong, Thoubal District (Left Saudi Arabia)	
7	(L) Nasiruddin Pharmacist	Lilong, Thoubal District	
8	Dr Salam	Lilong, Thoubal District (Left Saudi Arabia)	
(c) At the nursing institutes of Saudi Arabia			
Sl No	**Name of the Person**	**Permanent address**	
1	Shehnaz Sheikh	Keikhu, Imphal East	
2	Muhsina Sultana	Keikhu, Imphal East	
3	Sajina	Lilong, Thoubal District	
4	Rizwani Zahir	Kshetrigao, Imphal East	

(d) At the engineering sectors of Saudi Arabia

Sl No	Name of the person	Permanent address
1	Nasir Khan	Lilong, Thoubal District
2	Mohd. Shakir	Golapati, Imphal East (Left Saudi Arabia)
3	Mujibur Rahaman	Lilong, Thoubal District (Left Saudi Arabia)
4	Mohammad Ajmal Ahamed	Yairipok Tulihal Mayai Leikai, Thoubal District

(e) Companies

Sl No	Name of the person	Permanent address
1	Lasker	Lilong, Thoubal District (Left Saudi Arabia)
2	Sahir Khan	Irong Cheshaba, Kakching District
3	Zakir Hussain	Paobitek, Imphal West
4	Mansoor Ali	Dewlahland, Imphal East
5	Iftikar Jalali	Kshetrigao, Imphal East
6	Maqbul Hussain	Lilong, Thoubal District
7	Roashan Ali	Kshetrigao, Imphal East
8	Farooq Ahmed	Lilong, Thoubal District
9	Kabir Hussain Nadwi	Lilong, Thoubal District
10	Jameel	Keirao, Imphal East
11	Omar Atta	Kshetrigao, Imphal East
12	Haji Gani (L)	Kairang, Imphal East
14	Tombi	Kshetrigao, Imphal East (Left Saudi Arabia)
15	Hasim (L)	Kshetrigao, Imphal East
16	Ahmad Khan	Hafiz Hatta, Imphal East (Left Saudi Arabia)
17	MA Rahman	Paobitek, Imphal West (Left Saudi Arabia)
18	Azad Komol	Yairipok, Imphal East (Left Saudi Arabia)
19	Sirajuddin	Mayang Imphal Bengoon, Imphal West (Left Saudi Arabia)
20	Mukaram	Kshetrigao, Imphal East (Left Saudi Arabia)
21	Haji Samad (L)	Irong Cheshaba, Thoubal District (Left Saudi Arabia)
22	Sariyat	Kshetrigao, Imphal East (Left Saudi Arabia)
23	Yakub	Mayang Imphal Bengoon, Imphal West (Left Saudi Arabia)
24	Adalat	Kshetrigao, Imphal East (Left Saudi Arabia)

(Continued)

Table 14.1 (Continued)

25	M. V. Fakar	Lilong, Thoubal District (Left Saudi Arabia)
26	Shahabuddin	Mayang Imphal Bengoon, Imphal West
27	Aziz	Yairipok, Imphal East
28	Abdul Kalam	Yairipok, Imphal East
29	Basir	Yairipok, Imphal East
30	Majid	Mayang Imphal Bengoon, Imphal West
31	Ziaur Rahman (L)	Mayang Imphal Bengoon, Imphal West
32	Wahidur Rahman	Lilong, Thoubal District
33	Abdul Gani	Irong Cheshaba, Thoubal District
34	Rahimuddin	Lilong, Thoubal District
35	Mujibur	Paobitek, Imphal West
36	Azad	Mayang Imphal Bengoon, Imphal West
37	Mishauddin	Mayang Imphal Bengoon, Imphal West
38	Askar	Mayang Imphal Bengoon, Imphal West
39	Rahman	Mayang Imphal Bengoon, Imphal West
40	Mohd Akbar Khan	Yairipok Ningthounai, Thoubal District (Left Saudi Arabia)

Source: Information given by Dr. M. Naziruddin Khan on 24 April, 2021.

some opportunities that may perhaps create a good environment for them. Besides, there are many substantial reasons for the migration of Manipuris particularly Muslims to the different cities of the country itself. Based on the available information, it is evident that till now around 20 Manipuri Pangals are working in different capacities of the various cities of Kuwait. Why Pangals migrated to such a country in the last decade is because of the following reasons:

1. Based on the interview of some persons working in Kuwait, it is suggested that they are of the opinion that they would like to explore new advanced areas and would like to stay in the peaceful areas as they are fed up with congested areas. Earlier they worked in different sectors of India that include Manipal Hospital and Columbia Asia Referral Hospital, Karnataka (Khulakpam Sabir Ahmed, personal communication, 10 August, 2020), and JK Tyre and Industries Ltd., New Delhi for many years (IMPACT TV Diaspora program, 2018). This is one of the basic reasons for the task of migration in Kuwait.
2. In addition, other commendable reasons are that they would like to access the good environment over there. Hoping for a good salary as compared to that of Indian companies and hospitals is one of the pivotal reasons that lead the way for their migration to Kuwait. It is worth mentioning that Kuwait is a far more advanced country than India when considering imports from Kuwait to India such as crude oil petroleum, economy, and other factors (Azhar, 2012). Furthermore, there is some sense of belonging in terms of culture being felt amongst the Manipuri Pangals. Every Manipuri Muslim considers Saudi Arabia and other neighboring regions that include Kuwait as important in the sense that such places are strongly considered one of the sacred places of their religion. What is the underlying essence here is that they feel a sense of belonging there as their culture is similar to the culture of Kuwait people.
3. There are some other Manipuris belonging to other faiths such as Tribals – around seven in number – in different hotels and companies of Kuwait. One of the interviewers says that "some of the Kuwaitis used to prefer and welcome Muslims rather than other religious communities" (Khulakpam Sabir Ahmed, personal communication, 10 August, 2020).

Some of the Pangals who are working in different areas of the Gulf countries are given in Table 14.1 and Table 14.2.

Conclusion

The preceding analytical study of the migration from Manipur's Pangal community to the different places of the Gulf countries, especially Saudi

Table 14.2 Number of Manipuris who are working in companies, pharmacies, hotels, and offices belonging to the UAE

Sl No	*Name of the person*	*Permanent address*
1	SM Sahir	Lilong, Thoubal District
2	SK. Aslam Shah	Lilong, Thoubal District
3	Samih Azad	Yairipok, Imphal East
4	Anzar	Yairipok, Imphal East
5	Mujibur Rahaman	Yairipok, Imphal East
6	Milan	Oinam, Imphal West
7	Bicky	Sagolband, Imphal West
8	Bigyan	Sagolband, Imphal West
9	Mustakim	Yairipok, Imphal East
10	Sharif	Yairipok, Imphal East
11	Nawaz	Yairipok, Imphal East
12	Wasim	Lilong, Thoubal District
13	Taju	Lilong, Thoubal District
14	Farooque	Lilong, Thoubal District
15	Grace	Ukhrul, Ukhrul District
16	Yamila	Ukhrul, Ukhrul District
17	Themi	Ukhrul, Ukhrul District
18	Edi	Yairipok, Imphal East
19	Nazir	Keibung, Thoubal District

Source: Information given by Dr. M. Naziruddin Khan on 24 April, 2021.

Arabia and Kuwait, suggests that the migration started many centuries ago. Though it has been a gradual process, it shows that socio-economic reasons were one of the major drivers behind the phenomenon. There are also many Manipuris including Pangals and tribes who migrated to the Gulf countries. Some of them got permanent citizenship in Saudi Arabia. It is historically witnessed that around 15-20 Pangals got permanent citizenship in Saudi Arabia. Such migration takes place due to job opportunities, exploration of rich countries, opportunities for accessing higher currency value, etc. There are some secondary reasons like religio-cultural affinities with the country while considering the migration of Pangals in the Gulf countries.

Acknowledgements

First of all, I would like to thank my supervisor Prof. Najaf Haider immensely for his great inputs, timely guidance and thoughtful comments for the improvement of this chapter. Moreover, I am extremely thankful to Dr. M. Naziruddin Khan, Prof. Yogesh Sharma, Khullakpam Sabir Ahmed, Noor Rahman Sheikh, Dr. Imtiyaj Khan, Dr. Khalid Khan, Mohd Mustapha and Dr. Habibullah Qaeser for providing me with some insightful information and suggestions for the improvement of this chapter. I am grateful to those who gave me permission for interviews and quoting their statements in this chapter.

Funding

I have not received any funding for the research, authorship, and publication of this chapter.

Conflict of Interest

This chapter has no conflict of interest.

References

Arthur, L. W. (1954). Economic development with unlimited supplies of labour. *Manchester School of Economic and Social Studies*, 22, 139–91.

Harris, J. R., & Todaro, M. P. (1970). Migration, unemployment and development: A two-sector analysis. *The American Economic Review*, *60* (1), 126–42.

Impact TV (02 May 2018). *Manipuri Abroad Diaspora Speak on 02 May 2018*. (Video). You Tube. https://www.youtube.com/watch?v=Ruc1p6aIPMk

Irudaya, S. Rajan (2014). Emigration from Kerala, Andhra Pradesh and Tamil Nadu: A mapping of surveys on international labour migration from India. Migrant Forum in Asia, 15.

Jain, P. C. (2005). Indian migration to the gulf countries: Past and present. *India Quarterly*, *61*(2), 50–81.

Khan, M. C. (2014a). The origin of Manipuri Muslims. *Indian History Congress* (IHC) JNU, 1–11. (Unpublished).

Khan, M. C. (2014b). Socio-cultural and religious facets of Manipuri Muslims during the 17th and 18th centuries. *International Journal of Research*, *1* (8), 1451–1482.

Khan, M. C. (2015). *The Formation of Muslim Community in Manipur during the 17th and 18th Centuries*. Jawaharlal Nehru University (Unpublished M. Phil Dissertation).

Khan, M. C.. (2016). Settlement and migration of Muslims in northeast India with special reference to Manipur. *The Quarterly Review of Historical Studies*, *LVI* (1& 2), 31–53.

Khan, M. C. (2019). The origin of Manipuri Muslims during the seventeenth and eighteenth centuries. *Thon'g*, 1, 13–18.

Khan, M. C. (2021). The inclusion of minorities in the changing dynamics of education. In P. K. Choudhury, & G. S. Suresh Babu (Eds.), *Contextualising Educational Studies in India: Research, Policy and Practices* (pp. 91–110). Routledge Publications.

Lee, E. S. (1966). A theory of migration. *Demography*, *3* (1), 47–57.

Ministry of Labour, Government of India. (2002). *Annual Report*, 135.

Ravenstein, E. G. (1885). The laws of migration. *Journal of the Statistical Society of London*, *48* (2), 167–235.

Ravenstein, E. G. (1889). The laws of migration. *Journal of the Royal Statistical Society*, *52* (2), 241–305.

Stark, O., & Bloom, D. E. (1985). The new economics of labour migration. *The American Economic Review*, *75* (2), 173–78.

15 Migration in Kerala

Prospects and Challenges with Special Reference to Return Migration

Baby Kizhakkekalam and Jyothi KK

Introduction

Migration is an international phenomenon which may be classified as internal, international, voluntary, or forced. People may migrate on grounds of employment or governments may encourage it as a means to solve the problems of unemployment. Migration of people from one country to another is known as "international migration", whereas migration of people within the country is known as "internal migration". Voluntary migration is usually undertaken in search of a better life but forced migration includes expulsion of people during war and the transfer of slaves or prisoners. At the beginning, international migration was mostly motivated by non-economic factors. However, the recent international migration has been motivated mainly by economic factors such as the prospects of earning higher wages and income from abroad. Globalization has definitely increased the demand for workers from the countries in order to sustain national economies known as "economic migrants". These individuals are generally from impoverished developing countries migrating to obtain sufficient income for survival. This income is usually sent home to family members in the form of "remittances". Migration has vast socio-economic and cultural implications both in the origin and in the destination countries. The importance of international migration has increased especially due to the huge foreign remittances involved in these migrations.

Significance of the Study

Foreign remittances can be regarded as the largest source of external finance in developing countries after Foreign Direct Investment (FDI) and it does help these countries to raise foreign exchange earnings which in turn increases the creditworthiness of these countries for external borrowing. Workers are actually scared not only of the threat of the virus but also the economic effects of the slowdown faced by the Gulf economy, which largely depends on oil and related activities. The number of available jobs goes on shrinking. Moreover, the migrants who have returned to Kerala for breaks/

DOI: 10.4324/9781003369370-19

holidays are stuck and are in danger of losing their livelihoods. The prevailing situation halted large infrastructure projects in the Gulf, and caused oil prices to fall drastically. As the Gulf is facing a severe economic crisis, it may not recruit migrants any more in the near future. This will seriously affect Kerala's economy and migrants' livelihoods the hardest. Migrants are running out of money and are not in a position to go out for work. In some cases, workers are not even provided with adequate financial support for food or rent. Thus, the unavoidable return of non-resident Keralites (NRKs) will be a blow as far as the Kerala economy is concerned. On the one hand, there is loss of remittances, and, on the other hand, the economy has returning workers adding to the state's unemployed for an undefined period. In this situation, Kerala is not in a position to provide employment opportunities for the returning migrants.

Objective and Methodology

The paper is descriptive in nature and based on the objectives: to study the problems and prospects of migration in the Kerala economy and to trace the overall impact of return migration of Keralite prior to the COVID-19 pandemic, and to verify the economic impact on the Kerala economy. The study is based on secondary data collected from published sources and websites.

Analysis and Discussion

Indian Diaspora in the Gulf Cooperation Council (GCC) Countries

GCC countries which include Bahrain, Kuwait, Oman, Qatar, Saudi Arabia, and the United Arab Emirates are one of the best known migrant corridors in the world. These six countries not only attract migrant workers from India but also from other South and Southast Asian countries Indian diaspora is found to be significant among all these migrant communities living in the Gulf countries. Indian population has been spread almost all over the world and created significant diaspora. According to the recent estimate prepared by Ministry of Overseas India Affairs (MOIA), Indian emigrants constituted about 30 million in 130 countries. Out of these almost six million Indian migrant workers have been engaged in various kinds of jobs in these six GCC countries. Indians in the UAE constitute the largest part of the population of the country.

International Migration in Kerala

Migration became the single most dynamic factor in the development scenario of Kerala economy during the last quarter of twentieth century. Migration in Kerala, which began with demographic expansion, won't end with demographic contraction. The migration of Keralites to the Gulf countries which

Table 15.1 Indian Diaspora (million)

Name of GCC country	*Indian Diaspora (million)*
Saudi Arabia	2.5
UAE	3.5
Kuwait	1.45
Oman	2.3
Bahrain	1.3
Qatar	0.92
Total	11.97

Source: MOIA estimation 2018.

started in 1973 has continuously increased thereafter. Even if we have a vast theoretical literature on the topic of migration, the sum and substance of the theoretical arguments regarding the reason for migration can be better explained by pull and push factors that are responsible for the process of migration. A combined effect of these two factors has created a favorable situation for the movement of workers from Kerala to the Gulf countries. Push factors compelled job seekers to move from their own origin to some other places. The Kerala economy that has certain unique indicators which include a high density of population, low and declining work participation rates, high rates of unemployment, stagnant agriculture and backward industrial sector, low per capita domestic product etc. forced Keralites to migrate to the Gulf countries. Pull factors are those conditions in the host countries which attract people to those countries. The structural changes that occurred in the Gulf region due to rise in oil prices provided new opportunities for employment, better income, and future prospects etc. are some of the pull factors which motivated Keralites to the Gulf countries. The number of Kerala emigrants living abroad in 2020 is estimated to be about 35 lakhs, up from 24 lakhs in 2014, 22.8 lakhs in 2011, and 13.6 lakhs in 1998. Most of the emigrants in Kerala were very careful in saving as much as possible out of their earnings and transferring the savings home either by periodical remittances through banks or by carrying savings with them in cash or in the form of goods during their visits to home on leave or through illegal channels.

Country of Destination of Migrants from Kerala

Table 15.2 portrays the details regarding the country of destination of the migrant Keralites which reveals that UAE became the largest host to provide destination to about 39.13% of the migrants from Kerala followed by Saudi Arabia (22.97%), Qatar (8.75%), and Oman (8.59%). It can also be observed from the table that Gulf countries which include UAE, Saudi Arabia, Oman, Kuwait, Bahrain, and Qatar became the major destination for migrants from Kerala.

Table 15.2 Number of migrants from Kerala (2018)

Country of destination	*Number of migrants from Kerala (2019)*	%
UAE	830254	39.13
Saudi Arabia	487484	22.97
Oman	182168	8.59
Kuwait	127120	5.99
Bahrain	81153	3.82
Qatar	185573	8.75
USA	46535	2.19
Canada	15323	0.72
United Kingdom	38023	1.79
Africa	5657	0.27
Singapore	12485	0.59
Maldives	6243	0.29
Malaysia	11350	0.53
Australia/New Zealand	30078	1.42
Other Countries	62441	2.94
Total	2121887	100

Source: Kerala migration survey (S. Irudaya Rajan, K C Zachariah 2019).

District-Wise Distribution of Migrants from Kerala

District-wise distribution of migrants from Kerala reveals that of the 14 districts, the highest percentage of migrants was contributed by Malappuram District (19.13%) followed by Kannur (11.77%) and Thrissur (11.36%). The lowest percentage was contributed by Wayanad (1.44%), followed by Idukki (1.55%), and Ernakulam (2.52%).

Interstate Migration in Kerala

Interstate migrant workers have become an indispensable part of the state's economy. What we find in Kerala is that human resources from Kerala both skilled and semiskilled migrants to different countries which can be attributed to the educational attainment in Kerala. The educated youth are not willing to do menial jobs thereby leading to the inflow of migrant workers from other states to Kerala in large quantities. Today almost all the sectors that require physical labor are dependent on migrant workers. The recent trend in the employment sector in the state shows a large inflow of migrant workers from other states such as West Bengal, Bihar, Odisha, Uttar Pradesh, Chhattisgarh, Jharkhand etc. besides the neighboring states. It can be observed from Table 15.3 that the highest percentage of migrant workers are from West Bengal (41.39%) followed by Assam (14.36), Odisha (10.73%), and Bihar (10.13%).

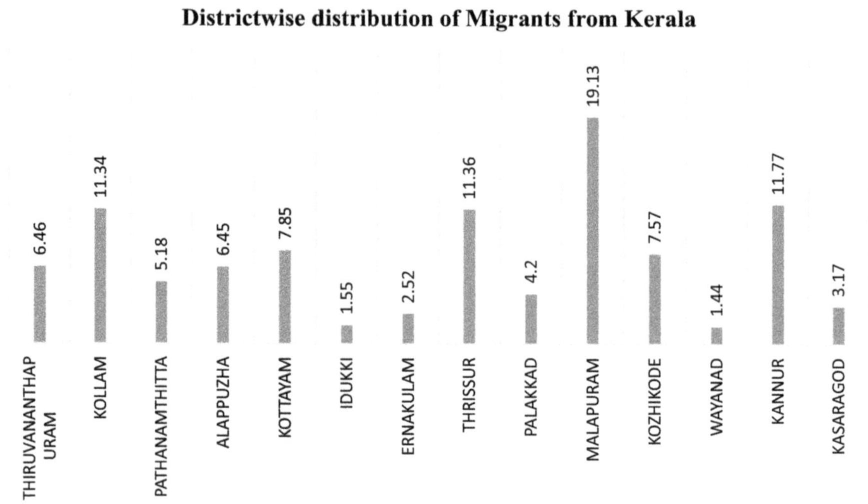

Figure 15.1 District-wise distribution of migrants from Kerala Source: Kerala Migration Survey (S. Irudaya Rajan, K C Zachariah 2019)

Table 15.3 Interstate migration in Kerala

State	*Migrant workers*
Assam	14.36
Bihar	10.13
Andhra Pradesh	0.48
Jharkhand	4.80
Karnataka	1.87
Madhya Pradesh	0.83
Odisha	10.73
Rajasthan	0.64
Tamil Nadu	9.01
Uttar Pradesh	3.79
West Bengal	41.39
Others	1.97

Source: Economic Review 2019

Distribution of Migrant Workers across Districts

The distribution of district-wise migrant workers in the State shows that Ernakulum has the highest proportion of 21% followed by Kozhikode and Thrissur. These migrant workers are engaged in different areas such as agriculture, construction, hotels and restaurants, manufacturing and trade. Also 60%of the migrant workers is engaged in the construction sectors, 8%in

Table 15.4 Distribution of migrant workers across districts

District	*% of migrant workers*
Kasaragod	2.92
Kannur	6.35
Wayanad	2.45
Kozhikode	10.33
Malappuram	6.24
Palakkad	5.33
Thrissur	9.43
Ernakulam	21.19
Idukki	4.04
Kottayam	5.07
Alappuzha	6.68
Pathanamthitta	5.41
Kollam	5.50
Thiruvananthapuram	9.06

Source: Economic Review Kerala Planning Board 2019.

manufacturing, 7%hotels and restaurants, 2%each trade and agriculture, and the remaining 23%engaged in other activities.

As far as the interstate migrants of Kerala were concerned, Kerala was able to ensure food and shelter to workers to a certain extent during lockdown period while the rest of the states were struggling to address the distress of migrant workers to arrest the COVID-19 pandemic. Kerala is also known for the welfare of interstate migrant workers it receives even if the state was suffering from the bad impact on remittances due to return migration during the pandemic.

Findings

Return Migration in Kerala

As of 2018, there are 8.5 million non-resident Indians (NRIs) working in the Gulf countries (Ministry of External Affairs 2018). The Indian expatriate community in the Gulf consists of domestic workers and unskilled labor employed in construction companies, municipalities, and agricultural farms. This labor contributes 70% of the diaspora. Skilled and semi-skilled workers – doctors, engineers, and accountants employed in government and private sectors, and businessmen – contribute between 20% and 30% of the diaspora workforce, and domestic workers comprise around 5% of the diaspora population (Khadria 2007). Majority of the Indian community in the GCC is from the southern states of Kerala viz. Andhra Pradesh, and Tamil Nadu. The remaining belong to Uttar Pradesh, Gujarat, Maharashtra, Goa, Punjab, Bihar, and Rajasthan.

Non-resident Keralites do play a crucial role in the development of the state of Kerala. However, return migration is showing an increasing trend over the last few years. According to Kerala Migration Survey 2018, the number of return emigrants is estimated to be 12.950 lakh which forms about 60%of the number of emigrants. Return migration became the focus area of researchers and policymakers as a socio-economic and political issue worldwide. No doubt Kerala has a long history of migration as a major exporter of the workforce to Gulf countries since 1970s, but it has a major portion of return migrants too. The state-wise distribution of return migrants in India shows that Kerala has nearly 50% of these return migrants. This has increased further by the crisis created during the COVID -19 pandemic.

Return Migration Prior the COVID-19 Pandemic

The COVID-19 pandemic has led to the loss of livelihood for many Indian migrants working abroad. The COVID-19 pandemic that originated in the Chinese city of Wuhan has spread to nearly every country across the globe, leading to numerous lockdowns, and closure of most international borders. In view of the threat of the spread of infection owing to migration, India closed its international borders in March 2020 as an attempt to "flatten the curve" and localize the spread of the virus. However, this sudden announcement sparked a chaotic rush among Indian migrant workers abroad, especially in countries in the Gulf, to return home amidst concerns of mandatory quarantine, cancellation of flights, and the loss of livelihood.

The COVID-19 pandemic forced around 8.7 lakh migrants from Kerala to return home, most of them from the Gulf. A majority of 5.67 lakh cited job loss as the reason for it, as per official data. The data from the Non-Resident Keralites Affairs (NORKA) department showed that 8.37% of Keralites who came back from other parts of the country also revealed loss of work as the reason for their return. The second biggest reason cited by the returnees (2.08 lakh) was their job visas. The rest include senior citizens, or children, and family members of migrants.

Migrant workers of low-income groups in the Gulf are mostly excluded from social security and health insurance even if they faced a number of health risks, such as poor living conditions, work in hazardous sectors, such as construction and oil and gas, and the associated exploitation, exacerbates existing health risks. Many migrants also work in the service sectors, including hospitality, which requires frequent exposure or proximity to both. Lower-income migrants generally tend to possess lower levels of education and language skills, inadequate access to information on health rights and benefits, and cultural sensitivities, which affect their ability to address their health conditions during a normal migratory process, thereby exacerbating their condition during cross-society pandemics. Workers were scared not only of the threat of the virus but also the economic effects of the slowdown experienced in the Gulf economy, which largely relies on oil and related activities. The number of available jobs goes on shrinking. Moreover, the migrants who have returned to Kerala for breaks/holidays are stuck and are in danger of losing their livelihoods. The prevailing situation halted large infrastructure projects in the Gulf, and caused the oil prices to fall drastically. As the Gulf is facing a severe economic crisis, it may not recruit migrants in the near future. This, no doubt, hit Kerala's economy and migrants' livelihoods the hardest.

Conclusion

The phenomenon of migration is not individual. The pandemic and the consequences of lockdown have had apparent impacts on remittances to Kerala from Gulf countries and an unemployment crisis among NRKs. Kerala has to supplement the expected drop in remittances with other income. Kerala has to consider these returning workers as an opportunity as their skill sets can be mobilized in sectors suffering from a shortage of human resources. Furthermore, enhancing the skills of returning migrants may also contribute to further international migration to new destinations or to the Gulf itself. There is a possibility that for a short span of time, return migration, and economic integration policies pertaining to returning NRKs may lose their relevance. However, this situation can be viewed as an opportunity to address the problems presently occurring in the state. However, more significant impact will unfold over the coming months. Only then we will be able to see how far Kerala's remittance economy has been hit by this pandemic. Even though the Kerala government has created medical facilities for returning NRKs, it will need to do more to overcome financial difficulties due to the loss of livelihoods.

References

Irudaya Rajan, S., & Zachariah, K. C. (2019). Emigration and remittances: New evidences from the Kerala migration survey, 2018," Working Papers id:12989, eSocialSciences.

Migration-Census of India, censusindia.gov.in

Mohan, A. C. (February 2017). Migration to Kerala: Issues and Challenges. *Indian Journal of Research*, 6(2).

Saikia, D. (December 2015). Migrant workers in Kerala: A study on their socio economic conditions. *SSRN Electronic Journal*, *11*(2), 29–43.

Sreejith, P. M., & Dr. Sreejith, S. (2021). Report on socio-economic impact of COVID 19 on migrant workers with reference to Kerala state. *Journal of Contemporary Issues in Business and Government*, *27*(1), P-ISSN: 2204-1990; E-ISSN: 1323-6903

Websites

https://indianexpress.com/article/india/covid-effect-8-4-lakh-migrants-back-in-k

https://indianexpress.com/article/india/covid-effect-8-4-lakh-migrants-back-in-kerala-from-abroad-5-5-lakh-lost-their-jobs-7136016/

https://keralaeconomy.com/admin/pdfs/Paper%20on%20COVID19%20sept%2
https://rbidocs.rbi.org.in/rdocs/Publications/PDFs/03CH_271020206C458AE36
https://thewire.in/labour/kerala-migrant-nri-return-job-loss-covid-19
https://www.gift.res.in/ofk_im/publish/GIFT_Report_Economic_and_Fiscal_Sho
https://www.prsindia.org/theprsblog/migration-india-and-impact-lockdown-mig
https://www.researchgate.net/publication/345401196_Migration_and_reverse_
https://www.routedmagazine.com/return-to-kerala-gulf

Part IV

Gulf Migration

Gender and Literature

16 Indian Female Migrant Workers and Human Rights Violations in the Gulf

A Case Study of Kuwait

Naziya Naweed

Introduction

By virtue of being human, every individual is entitled to certain inalienable rights irrespective of their caste, creed, race, sex, commonly termed human rights. The violation of such rights is often marked as an encroachment on their identity as individuals. Because of their sex, women have always been on the receiving end and face severe restrictions by societal hierarchies. Therefore, the study focus is to situate Indian female migrants in the context of the gendered division of labor that leads them in an environment of abuse and exploitation. Women experience gendered division of labor by working in lower-paying and less desirable jobs with less favourable working conditions and lack of redress mechanism to fight for their rights.

Talking about the status of Indian migrant women is in no way different from women's positions worldwide. But lucrative job opportunities in the world have attracted them to overcome their struggles. On similar lines, the discovery of oil in the Gulf region and its viable jobs opportunities attracted skilled workers from abroad. Soon, the wave of Indian migration, both skilled and semi-skilled, to the Gulf region started with a significant proportion of the female labor force. Moreover, seeking such employment opportunities was perceived to escape such oppression. In this background, the paper highlights the human rights violations faced by the Indian female migrant workforce working in the Gulf. To make it more organised, Kuwait becomes the focus of the study. The data has been collected from sources, ranging from an array of research papers documented in journals, books, newspaper reports, and reports prepared by Human Rights Watch, IOM, and United Nations Human Rights.

Historically, Indian females have migrated to the Gulf region as nannies and tutors from British times. Lately, the presence of the female workforce has been diversified in the service sector. The attraction of Indian female migrants towards the domestic sector is predominant. Indian female migrants are prominent in sectors like health care such as doctors, nurses, and in education (Kanchana, 2016). Employment in the Gulf is regulated through Kafala system. The system, unique to the Gulf countries, has its

DOI: 10.4324/9781003369370-21

implications for foreign workers. All foreign workers in the Gulf are subject to the coercive and exploitative mechanism of the system, which include limiting labor supply and restricting labor mobility.

On this front, therefore, these kinds of restrictions, exploitation, and discrimination faced by the female domestic workers in the region are noteworthy, which creates a problem for the host country and raises Indian government concerns for its population. The study explore the term exploitation and the position of the Human Rights to the female migrant workers in Kuwait. Consequently, the study also highlights the measures undertaken by the Indian government from time to time in ameliorating their vulnerabilities. The study also put forth salient findings and challenges for the policymakers to improve Indian female migrant workers' conditions.

Gender Dimension of Migration and the Position of the Human Rights

The interplay of gender with migration is meted out against female migrant workers at different levels and results in diverse types of discrimination; see Table 16.1.

In terms of the gender and migration intersection of female migrant workers in Kuwait, we can see that women experience exploitation in the realm of sex (women are considered inferior as compared to their male counterparts),occupation (low-paid jobs), wages (difference in the pay scale for the similar role), nationality (considering foreigners in the host territory

Table 16.1 Gender and migration: intersection

Sl. No	*Level*	*Discrimination*
1	Sex	Women workers vis-à-vis men workers
2	Race	Color and ethnicity: in labor market situations where the principle of "equal treatment and opportunities" is not applied, mainly in the case of women migrant workers belonging to a certain ethnic or racial group vis-à-vis the racial or ethnic origin of the majority of the population
3	Occupation	Performing jobs where they are not formally considered workers
4	Wages	Performing jobs where the principle of "equal pay for equal work" is not applied
5	Nationality	Foreign workers vis-à-vis nationals
6	Migration status	Undocumented vis-à-vis documented

Source: Women and men migrant workers: Moving towards equal rights and opportunities. International Labour Organization. Retrieved from https://www.ilo.org/wcmsp5/groups/public/@dgreports/@gender/documents/publication/wcms_101118.pdf.

as compared to the local nationals) and migration status (most of the women are recruited as undocumented laborers in domestic sectors).

Based on these ground levels of discrimination, migrant workers, both men and women, are often victims of exploitation and abuse in the country of destination. They are subjected to a harsh working environment, poor hygiene, long and tedious working hours, irregular payments and a lack of medical facilities, to name a few. Because of their gender, women are often employed in irregular and unregulated jobs that leave them at the door of vulnerabilities and exploitation. They often become the victim of abuse, psychological, physical and sexual, and they are deprived of the right to family reunification. Moreover, "large numbers of them can also often find themselves excluded from legal employment when arriving as spouses of temporary workers" ("Women and men migrant workers", n.d, para. 11).

According to the International Labor Organization,

> a very important reason for women migrant workers' vulnerability is that the jobs they find are mainly concentrated in the informal economy and are thus not covered or only partially covered by the labor legislation and social security and welfare provisions of the country of destination.
>
> (Lean Lim, Landuyt, Ebisui, Kawar, & Ameratunga, 2003, p. 11)

The women migrant workers are often not legally entitled to the standards and protection accorded to nationals or other migrant workers. Similarly, the labor inspection authorities do not monitor their situation, and thus they do not have access to the labor courts. This exclusion helps to account for the poor working conditions of women migrant workers:

> The most serious issue relating to the legal and contextual presence of foreign female domestic workers [...] is the fact that they do not fall under labor laws and regulations [...] The immediate implication of such a regulation is the denial of such rights as limited working hours, weekly or yearly holidays, and end-of-work compensation. The only regulation foreign female domestic workers fall under is the immigration law, which considers them more from a State-controlled perspective, a security perspective than from a developmental or human perspective.
>
> (Sabban, 2002, p.34)

In most cases, the abuses and exploitation against women migrant workers happen in an "invisible labor market" where it is difficult to identify the migrant's vulnerabilities compared to their male counterparts. Women are subjected to abuses like wage theft, restrictive mobility, absence of freedom, seizure of documents, long working hours coupled with inadequate housing facilities and sexual exploitation ("Women and men migrant workers", n.d.).

The gender intersection with migration is equally linked with the position of human rights. Therefore, it becomes necessary to look at it closely with the gendered exploitation. If we talk about what constitutes exploitation, there is a lack of consensus and "no legal definition" of the term. Exploitation is of different kinds like labor, non-labor exploitation, including sexual exploitation, forced labor, trafficking and exploitation during irregular migration process as in the case of smugglers. Abuse and violence experienced by these groups constitute exploitation (Global Migration Group, 2013). The Global Migration Group (GMG), in their publication entitled "International Migration and Human Rights Challenges and Opportunities on the Threshold of the 60th Anniversary of the Universal Declaration of Human Rights", mentioned that human rights are universal to all humans from birth. Thus, they maintain that

> Human rights are not a matter of choice, but are legal obligations under international treaties which bind all governments that have accepted them. Human rights should, therefore, be an integral dimension of the design, implementation, monitoring and evaluation of migration policies and programmes. Moreover, respect for the rights of migrants is essential to maximize the potential benefits and positive contributions of migrants to development. Indeed, respect for the rights of migrants contributes to the economic and social development in both sending and receiving countries.
>
> (Global Migration Group, 2008, p. 99)

Thus, on the basis of this, the question of exploitation stems in human rights. A human rights-based approach to migration is grounded on International Human Rights legislation. Under the legislation, all migrants, regardless of their migration status, have the right to have their human rights recognized, safeguarded, and thoroughly enjoyed (Hujo, 2019).

Some of the significant International Framework for the Protection of Women Migrant Workers is composed of International Convention on the Protection of the Rights of All Migrant Workers and Members of Their Families, 1990. This convention applicable to all migrant workers irrespective of any division based on sex, race, colour, language and religion etc. However, the convention also elucidates different articles referring to different aspect of migrant rights. It was adopted by General Assembly resolution 45/158 of 18 December 1990 (United Nations Human Rights, n.d., p.2).

In terms of numbers, 47 state parties have ratified the convention, and 20 states have been the signatories. But out of the total, none of the six economies of the Gulf Cooperation Council states, together with Kuwait, have signed and ratified the United Nations Convention on the Rights of all Migrant Workers and Their Families (Rafel, 2019).

Table 16.2 International conventions ratified by Kuwait

Convention name	*Ratification status*
International Labour Organization (ILO) Migration for Employment Convention (Revised), 1949 (No. 97)	Not ratified
United Nations Convention relating to the Status of Refugees, 1951	Not ratified
United Nations Convention relating to the Status of Stateless Persons, 1954	Not ratified
United Nations Convention on the Reduction of Statelessness, 1961	Not ratified
ILO Migrant Workers (Supplementary Provisions) Convention, 1975 (No. 143)	Not ratified
United Nations Convention on the Rights of the Child, 1989	Ratified in 1991
International Convention on the Protection of the Rights of All Migrant Workers and Members of Their Families (ICRMW), 1990	Not ratified

Source: IOM (2020, p. 2).

Second, important convention is the United Nations Special Rapporteur on the Human Rights of migrants. The mandate was created in 1999 aimed at providing adequate protection to the vulnerability exposed by women, children etc., considering the gendered dimension of migration while formulating recommendations for their redressal (United Nations Human Rights, n.d., para.4).

The above conventions are considered noteworthy for the protection of migrant workers in the host territory; irrespective of these in place, Kuwait, among all the other member countries of the GCC, has not ratified some of the essential legal frameworks.

Thus, the following is the status of Kuwait's international standards and fulfillment of migrants' rights, as per ILO estimates, 2018 see Table 16.2.

Irrespective of the treaties and laws in place, responses to migrant exploitation based on human rights might be enhanced when exploitation is prevented, a course of justice is provided, migrants are protected and safeguarded against the exploiters, and a structure for collaboration is established (Global Migration Group, 2013).

Indian Female Migrant Workers in Kuwait

As an oil-dominating kingdom, Kuwait has always relied on a foreign workforce. The Indian female labor force started to migrate to seek lucrative employment opportunities, support their families and children back home and to run away from the societal oppression that they face in their home country. Speaking primarily in terms of female migrant laborers in the Gulf, according to the 2016 statistics, there are around 3.77 million domestic workers hosted by the economies of the Gulf, out of which 1.65 million are

Table 16.3 Number of domestic workers in the GCC countries by sex (2016)

Sl. No.	*Country*	*Female*	*Male*	*Total population*
1	Bahrain	67,000	44,000	1,11,000
2	Kuwait	3,46,000	3,32,000	6,78,000
3	Oman	1,48,000	48,000	1,96,000
4	Qatar	1,08,000	66,000	1,74,000
6	Saudi Arabia	7,59,000	15,44,000	23,03,000
7	UAE	2,19,000	87,000	3,06,000
	Total GCC	16,47,000	21,21,000	37,68,000

Source: Tayah and Assaf (2018), p. 17.

female migrant workers (Tayah & Assaf 2018). Above are the numbers of domestic workers in the GCC region based on sex; see table 16.3.

Based on the data, out of 37,68,000 domestic workers in the GCC countries, female domestic workers constitute the second largest in Kuwait with a total number of 3,46,000 after Saudi Arabia with the highest number, around 15,44,000 female domestic workers. In fact, "migrant domestic workers provide indispensable services to the countries where they go, contributing to the wealth of ageing societies and the sustainability of these countries' welfare and employment systems" (Migrant Domestic Workers (Labor Migration), n.d., para 3).

According to the data calculated by the Kuwait Central Statistical Bureau, Labor Market Information System, from 2015 to 2017, the total number of domestic workers in Kuwait increased from 655,389 to 677,622 with an annual increase of 1.7%. However, the share of female domestic workers declined from 376,684 to 345,721 in 2017, constituting -4.2 % (Tayah & Assaf 2018).

Regarding the female migrant workforce, it can be argued that women migrant workers from India, Indonesia, Sri Lanka and Nepal constitute the most significant proportion of the female workforce in Kuwait and other GCC countries see Table 16.4.

As per the data, Indian female migrants are top in the category of domestic migrant workers in Kuwait, the reason for their pull towards the Gulf has been driven by economic support for their family, children, and business back in their home country (Human Rights Watch, 2010).

As per the 2019 statistics issued by the Embassy of India in Kuwait, Indian nationals constitute 10 lakhs, with 7.5 lakh Indian males as against only 2.5 lakh Indian females (Indian Community, n.d.) see Table 16.5.

There are around 90, 000 Indian female domestic workers working in Kuwait (Correspondent, 2019). They are working as skilled and semi-skilled and unskilled laborers. Mainly, the region attracts migrant laborers from different countries of Asia and Africa and are primarily employed in different sectors as construction workers, housemaids, nurses, etc. (Kuwait | The Life of Overseas Migrant Workers, 2020).

Table 16.4 Top five labor-sending countries for domestic workers (2017)

	Percentage (%)		*Number*	
Nationality	*Total*	*Female*	*Total*	*Female*
India	43.0	19.6	2,91,572	67,876
Philippines	24.1	47.1	1,63,531	1,62,691
Bangladesh	12.0	0.3	81,170	1,130
Sri Lanka	10.0	14.7	67,451	50,904
Nepal	3.6	6.6	23,377	22,703

Source: Tayah and Assaf (2018). The percentage share is out of 100; however, the original data include countries like Ethiopia, Madagascar, Ghana, Indonesia, Côte d'Ivoire, and others.

Table 16.5 Employment breakdown of Indian nationals in Kuwait

Deployment	*Numbers*
Private sectors, like construction workers, technicians, engineers, doctors, chartered accountants, IT experts, etc.	5.23 lakh Indians
Dependents, such as spouses/children	1.16 lakh Indians
Students	60,000 Indians
Domestic workers, like drivers, gardeners, cleaners, nannies, cooks, and housemaids	3.27 lakh Indians
Kuwaiti Government: As nurses, engineers in National Oil Companies, and scientists	28,000 Indians

Source: Embassy of India, Kuwait.

> In the current context, the asymmetric distribution of a small but educated migrant workforce centred around desirable and high-earning positions, and a large population of low-skilled, poorly educated and poorly paid overseas workers, employed in construction or domestic work, creates a modern caste system where low-skilled workers are limited to vulnerable job categories and are open to exploitation, whereas high-skilled employees enjoy the full benefits of Kuwaiti society. This differentiation between migrants and expats is inherently instilled in Kuwaiti labor relations.
>
> (Kuwait | The Life of Overseas Migrant Workers, 2020, p.4)

Approximately, "ninety per cent of Kuwaiti households employ domestic workers, resulting in 620,000 migrant domestic workers in the country, mostly women, forming 21.9 per cent of the workforce" (Staff, 2018, para 2). The majority of these workers have been subjected to abuse. However, according to the Human Rights Watch, despite the reform undertaken to restructure the Kuwaiti labor law, the rules have still been weaker in terms of enforcement mechanisms and not working in accordance to provide adequate facilities to the overseas migrant workers. The condition of women migrant workers becomes more nuanced due to their confinement within the Kuwaiti employer's home. So, these women migrant workers have to face double hardship in terms of earning to support their families and to meeting the abuse at their employer's hand (Kuwait | The Life of Overseas Migrant Workers, 2020).

An apt example is an increase in the demand for domestic workers in the GCC region, and mainly they constitute an important segment of the workforce in Kuwait and Saudi Arabia. However, the percentage share of women as independent workers has increased. They became a focal point of migration research and led to the coining of the word "feminisation of migration" by the United Nations. The very presence of the female migrant workers in these industries renders them to abuse, as they primarily operate in low skilled employment jobs. Women's mobility is considered a measure to break the shackles of marginalized societal hierarchies and pursue their dream in the distant land. Mostly, the Indian female workforce belongs to the Indian states of Andhra Pradesh, Kerala and Tamil Nadu. There is no question that migrant workers, particularly women, are significant developmental actors for origin and destination. Still, they have fallen into a vicious circle of exploitation and abuse in the host territory as well.

The claim that women domestic workers, and Indian women in particular have been exploited and their human rights violated, can be discern from the cases below.

The National Domestic Workers Movement (Non-Government Organisations (NGO's)) has rescued three Indian female migrant workers working in a domestic sector in the Gulf. These three women were trafficked to Kuwait and demanded Rs. 1.65 lakhs by the trafficked agent if they wished to return home. The women faced abuse from hostages and physical and verbal abuse (Indian Domestic Workers Rescued from Kuwait, 2019 and Kuttappan, 2020).

Among the three, one of the rescued migrant workers, Vasantha Mani, recalled her experienced and argued:

> I was made to work for 16-20 hours a day. They promised to pay me Rs 40,000 for working at one house, but I was made to work at two big houses and paid only Rs 20,000. She [...] was provided by her employers only one filling meal a day. They would give me only coffee decoction in the morning. I'll get my lunch only by late noon, by when I would be dizzy and tired.
>
> (Indian Domestic Workers Rescued from Kuwait, para. 2)

Another rescuer from Kuwait, Amudhavalli, further argued; "her employers and agent in Kuwait made her sign in four blank papers before she left and strip-searched her before they let her out. It was humiliating. They factory-reset my phone, so that I do not bring any evidence of abuse. They hit me so hard that nearly a week later I still feel pain and my hands and legs still shiver all the time" (Indian Domestic Workers Rescued from Kuwait, para. 6).

Thus, the above revelations highlight the severity of the situation and second the claim that the condition of female migrants is not right in Kuwait. Therefore, they urge the Government of India and Ministry to External Affairs to act decisively on this matter and rescue other trapped Indian female migrant workers in Kuwait.

However, on the contrary, according to the officials from the National Domestic Workers Movement, the efforts of the Indian states have been inadequate. The government further argues:

> that they neither have the authority to rescue women from their employers nor have the proof to do that. It is a double-edged sword. But Indian citizens continue to be trafficked in Middle Eastern countries in this legal loophole. The country needs to pass the Immigration Act drafted last year and provide respite for these victims.
>
> (Indian Domestic Workers Rescued from Kuwait, para 9)

Still, the truth remains that these populations are subjected to abuse and exploitation, thus remaining vulnerable to violence. The migrant workers do not have adequate legal protection and a redressal mechanism to gain assistance and guidance, and therefore subjected to mistreatment and forced deportation. As, Kuwait is not signatory to the International Convention on the Protection of the Rights of All Migrant Workers and Members of Their Families, 1990 and United Nations Special Rapporteur on the human rights of migrants.

If we explore the status of female migrant workers, the data reveals the fact that women, firstly, due to their gender, are a victim of abuse and violence; secondly, they are not provided with the redress mechanism to fight for their rights as well as they are not allowed to form trade unions thus depriving them of authority, thirdly, they are unable to safeguard and secure their rights in host land, i.e. Kuwait and lastly irrespective of the MoU's signed between both the region a cooperative structure has not been established that guarantees that the rights of the migrant would not be violated further.

The kingdom of Kuwait, in 2015, adopted Law No. 68 to meet the lacunae in the regulation of domestic workers (Kuwait Society for Human Rights, 2019). Kuwait undertook reforms that allowed migrant workers to transfer their scholarship without the approval of their employer; however, the provision of such reforms did not apply to the migrants employed in the domestic sector jobs (World Report 2019: Rights Trends in Kuwait, 2019). Some of the measures adopted by the Kuwait National assembly were:

> law granting domestic workers the right to a weekly day off, 30 days of annual paid leave, a 12-hour working day with rest, and an end-of-service benefit of one month salary for each year of work at the end of the contract, among other rights. In 2016 and 2017, the Interior Ministry passed implementing regulations for the law, and mandated that employers must pay overtime compensation. The ministry also issued a decree establishing a minimum wage of KD60 (US$200) for domestic workers.
>
> (World Report 2019: Rights Trends in Kuwait, 2019)

The reform laws grant provisions such as one day off per week, 30 days of annual paid leave, 12-hour workdays with rest, and overtime compensation to the workers and their employer. However, the law does not guarantee that the safety precautions of the domestic workers will be adequately taken into consideration (Staff, 2018).

The law is necessary to empower laborers by granting them labor rights. Irrespective of the law in place, the status of women has not improved. Due to factors like fear; and the language barrier (inability to speak Arabic), the presence of the Kafala system works detrimentally for the domestic workers when to highlighting their plight and seeking redressal; therefore, the role played by the Kuwait administration can play an important role in safeguarding the interest of the migrant population in the host territory as they are an important catalytic force in the development of their economies. Some measures like issuing severe penalties against the kafeel or the recruiting agencies, creating help portals or helplines, weekly monitoring and inspection of the site are some of the steps that can help the migrant worker to live a decent life without fear and intimidation in the host territory (Kuwait Society for Human Rights, 2019).

Rather, the dynastic rule of the al- Sabah family maintains that the power distribution in Kuwait remained confined mainly to the chosen representative by the family, in which migrant workers are not accounted for citizenship rights. The states, including Kuwait, work on the "rentier economy", but in legality, the citizenship law has left migrant workers and their adequate representation in the legal domain. The reason cited for the neglect of the migrant workers in the Kuwaiti legal system of citizenship is that they are a citizen of Kuwait. The very existence of the matter debarred the migrant workers from any redressal mechanism to fight for their rights and freedom. Simultaneously, migrant workers are not provided with adequate rights and duties, including the right to education, health care facilities and shelter. The absence of these constitutes a violation of the Universal Declaration of Human Rights of 1947 and puts the migrant laborers, including female migrant workers, into an abusive relationship (Rafel, 2019).

The well-known *Kafala* system (a form of sponsorship) is widespread in the Gulf. However, the system was enacted in Kuwait in 1959. The Alien Residence Law of Kuwait has led to developing this discriminatory system for migrant workers (Human Rights Watch, 2010). Under this system, the migrant workers are placed under a kafeel or sponsor and are dependent on them for Kuwait's economic and social needs. The system also restricts migrant freedom to move and leave their place of employment, such as their passports being confiscated and being debarred from seeking other employment avenues. On the other hand, the practice was prohibited in 2007. In contrast, the conditions of migrant domestic workers residing in national host homes have been more subordinate to other migrant workers (Rafel, 2019).

> The 1964 Labor Law has excluded all domestic workers from protections offered by Kuwaiti labor laws, such as the minimum wage, paid sick leave and paid holidays, despite Kuwait ratifying in 1966 the International Labor Organisation's (ILO) Convention No. 111 relating to Discrimination in Respect of Employment and Occupation.
>
> (Rafel, 2019, para. 5)

Further,

> the system falls under the jurisdiction of interior ministries, rather than labor ministries, workers have no protection under the host country's labor law. This leaves them vulnerable to exploitation and denies them such rights as the ability to enter a labor dispute process or join a union.
>
> (Robinson, 2021)

Irrespective of the provision of law, the Kuwait constitution echoes non-discrimination provisions based on the notion of citizenship. Instead, it is not the case; the migrant workers are far away from this provision. The Kuwaiti authorities have been unsympathetic to migrants concerns and issues. The economic challenges are also quite rampant and create hurdles for the migrant and their families. The lack of citizenship of the migrant workers also creates hurdles for the migrant labor and places them at the lower level of the hierarchy. In a study conducted by the scholar Mitchell, the migrant workers in Kuwait are divided based on their status as whites, non-white foreigners, Arabs and "riffraff". But Rafel, 2019, has added domestic workers as the fifth category in the list. The types are based on how migrant workers are treated in the Kuwaiti economy. The abolishment of slavery in Kuwait in 1968 has not led to the decline of forced labor. The position of migrant workers will not improve unless and until the sponsorship system is reformed and the legal mechanism is available to them at their disposal (Rafel, 2019).

However, the demographic composition of the labors has changed, "a shift from Arab nationals to South Asian nationals" (Godfrey, M., Ruhs M., Shah, N, and Smith M., 2004). But, today, due to the workforce nationalization policy initiated by the Gulf states, particularly by Kuwait, the system works detrimental to the recruitments of foreign nationals into the Gulf economy. The introduction of the Expat Quota bill in June 2020 is a prime example. The bill put a cap on the Indian population not exceeding 15% in the region (Kodoth, n.d.). Moreover, with the COVID-19 pandemic surfacing, the world has also seen a huge impact on the migrant population worldwide. The pandemic has also hard hit the Indian migrants in the Gulf region with the issue of wage theft, non-payment of dues, job loss, and the ability to return to their home country. Kuwait has a total population of 4.3 million, out of which three million are composed of migrant workers (Nair, 2020). Along with COVID-19, the receding oil prices in the Gulf region can also impact foreign nationals' composition as there is a danger of economic implications on the welfare of the Indian Diaspora in the region (Mitra & Kasliwal, 2020).

Indian Government Response

The Indian emigration policy has not been welcoming towards the lower-skilled workers. The Indian female lower-skilled workers have to face the "double sword" due to their sex and discriminatory treatment of the Indian state (Kanchana, 2016). One of the essential regulations covering emigration is the Emigration Act of 1983, which regulates the recruitment process of unskilled laborers. Two elements constitute a critical aspect of the act, namely emigration clearance and regulation of the recruitment; the latter involves the licensed recruiting agents (Kanchana, 2016). As a "proactive stance", the Indian government introduced the "age criterion" for gendered migration in the wake of abuses reported by overseas Indians in the 1990s. Also, the "restrictive migration policies have reduced the possibilities for regular and legal migration for females, forcing them to adopt risky processes to migrate" (Thimothy & Sasikumar, 2012).

The Ministry of Overseas Indian Affairs sets out the recruitment process with a recruitment agent playing a proactive role and registered under the ministry. However, the case of illegal recruiters is also not hidden. However, through the proper channels, the Gulf demand for labor is met by the recruiting agencies located in India. After that, they help the Indian candidate get permission to work in the host land. By law, the Indian government has set an age limit for women to migrate below 30 years of age for working as domestic workers; instead, now more women have been migrating through illegal ways and often, women are forced or trafficked. They are subjected to abuse and exploitation (Shree, 2011).

In the Kuwait context, the domestic workers also approach the recruitment agencies in their home countries that help them with migration to the host country. Often the lack of state of origin response and steps to protect the national before and during the migration process left the migrant with limited information about their rights and freedom. Simultaneously, they are prey to illegal ways and some corrupt officials and recruiting agencies. On their arrival in Kuwait, such migrants find themselves helpless in foreign territory without any legal protection at their hands (Human Rights Watch, 2010). Moreover, the situation of women migrant workers becomes graver due to the absence of labor laws for domestic workers in the GCC countries in general and Kuwait in particular (Shree, 2011).

Based on the data released by the Indian government for the year spanning 2016–2019, India has received 77,155 complaints of labor abuse from the Gulf region. The migrant laborers reported their grievances to the embassies and consulates in the six countries (for more details about the percentage, see Table 16.6) (India: Govt. Records 77,155 Labour Abuse Allegations, 2019).

As per the above data, labor abuses are experienced highest by the migrant workers in Saudi Arabia, followed by Kuwait and Oman. Approximately, in 2019, 9,771 complaints of torture were recorded alone, on the issues of late payment of wages, labor rights' violation including lack of health care facilities, to name a few (India: Govt. Records 77,155 Labour Abuse Allegations, 2019). In the words of External Affairs Minister S Jaishankar:

> As per the information given by Missions and Posts in the Gulf countries, as on 30.6.2019, Kuwait tops the list with the highest number of complaints (2377). While 2244 complaints were registered from Saudi Arabia, as many as 1764 complaints were from Oman. Around 1477 and 1459 complaints came from the United Arab Emirates and Qatar

Table 16.6 Percentage of complaints from the six regions of GCC

GCC country	%
Saudi Arabia	36
Kuwait	19
Oman	15
Qatar	14
UAE	13
Bahrain	3
Total	100

Source: India: Govt. Records 77,155 Labour Abuse Allegations (2019).

> respectively. However, only 450 complaints of torture were filed from Bahrain.
>
> (ANI, 2019)

According to a report published in *The Hindu Business Line*, "the Ministry had stated that the Indian Missions in Gulf countries receive many complaints, but compared to the proportion of Indian workers in Gulf countries, such complaints are 'marginal'" (Jadhav, 2019, para. 7). The answer was in response to the question asked in the Lok Sabha asked on July 10 about the abuse of migrant labor.

The report further states that the Indian Missions consider factors like illegal migration, unscrupulous agents, economic and financial challenges of employers, disputes with sponsors or companies, and violation of local laws as the main reason for the rise of abuse in the countries of destination (Jadhav, 2019).

Similarly, in the host country, according to the data gathered by the Kuwait Society for Human Rights, "a non-governmental body aimed at protecting and promoting human rights in Kuwait in accordance with international standards" (Kuwait Society for Human Rights, n.d.). The NGO has a working number to aid the labor working in different sectors; thus, their hotline for labor consultation and complaints registered 4758 query calls in 2018 to enquire about general labor laws and complaints related to finance and passport retrieval. Regarding employment in the domestic sector, the NGO noted that 363 complaints were registered by domestic workers (Kuwait Society for Human Rights, 2019).

In response to the complaints received, the Indian government has issued advisory for Indian workers in Kuwait to seek employment opportunities and awareness about their rights so that they won't face any exploitation and abuse in the host country (Advisory for Indian Workers in Kuwait, n.d.). Simultaneously, the role of Indian Diplomatic Missions and Embassy stationed in Kuwait can be an instrumental in highlighting the plight of female migrant workers and help them to fight for their rights and duties.

The Indian government has undertaken recent initiative to protect Migrant workers in Kuwait. The Indian cabinet has approved Memorandum of Understanding (MoU) between India and Kuwait for cooperation on the recruitment of domestic workers. According to a report published by The Hindu (2019); "The MoU provides a structured framework for cooperation on domestic workers related matters and provides strengthened safeguards for Indian domestic workers including female workers deployed in Kuwait" (Correspondent, 2019, para 3).

Some of the salient features of the MoU are (a) its validity for five years with automatic renewal provision, (b) setting up a joint committee to look into the implantation. The government hoped that the MoU will facilitate mutual cooperation between India and Kuwait on matters related to domestic workers (Cabinet Approves Memorandum of Understanding between India and Kuwait, 2019).

Concluding Section: Salient findings and Future Challenges

The Indian female migrant workers in Kuwait play an important role along with their male counterparts in the developmental process of the home country through remittance transfer. Yet, their position in the domestic sector remains vulnerable as the female domestic workers are recruited through both the official channel versus private recruiters.

Even though these agreements between the host and home countries have been put in place, the challenge is in their enforcement, especially in the context of the domestic service sector. Although the Indian government is more vigilant regarding protecting the Indian female workforce in Kuwait, more stringent laws are needed to curb ill practices and recruiting agencies hiring an undocumented female workforce.

Workers' rights need to be made more aware, and ongoing monitoring of bilateral agreements is necessary. Therefore, the onus lies on the government to undertake measures to facilitate the concerns of the female domestic workers. Therefore, there is a need for a sounder policy catering to the different aspects of migrant needs and concerns in the host and the home country

Regarding Kuwait's labor laws, it can be argued that there are fewer provisions for domestic workers. The domestic worker legislation falls short by failing to create a compliance mechanism, such as household working conditions inspections. Moreover, the legislation does not allow for punishment for employers confiscating passports or failing to provide sufficient accommodation, sustenance needs and leisure time. "Migrant domestic workers remain vulnerable to abuse and exploitation and can be arrested for 'absconding' from an employer largely because of the Kafala system, which ties their visas to their employers" (World Report 2019: Rights Trends in Kuwait, 2019).

On the Indian side, the government can play an instrumental role in protecting the rights of the female migrant workers in the Gulf by working in collaboration with the diplomatic mission to document the rights-based abuse in the host territory. Similarly, during and post COVID-19, the Indian government intervention becomes necessary to protect and ensure the safety and well-being of its migrant communities in the world and, more specifically, in the Gulf region. But, the return migration from the Gulf region will pose an additional burden on the Indian economy, which is already struggling. Therefore, Indian policymakers should keep all these aspects in mind so that the Gulf returnee can again be re-integrated into the Indian economy.

References

Advisory for Indian Workers in Kuwait. (n.d.). Embassy of India. https://www.indembkwt.gov.in/advisory-for-Indian-workers-in-kuwait.php

ANI. (2019, July 17). *9771 Complaints of Torture Filed by Indian Workers in Gulf Countries in 2019, Says S Jaishankar.* Business Standard. https://www.business-standard.com/article/news-ani/9771-complaints-of-torture-filed-by-indian-workers-in-gulf-countries-in-2019-says-s-jaishankar-119071700709_1.html

Cabinet Approves Memorandum of Understanding between India and Kuwait for Cooperation on the Recruitment of Domestic Workers. (2019, January 23). PMIndia. https://www.pmindia.gov.in/en/news_updates/cabinet-approves-memorandum-of-understanding-between-india-and-kuwait-for-cooperation-on-the-recruitment-of-domestic-workers/

Correspondent, S. (2019, January 23). *Cabinet Approves India-Kuwait Pact on Domestic Workers.* The Hindu. https://www.thehindu.com/news/national/cabinet-approves-india-kuwait-pact-on-domestic-workers/article26072332.ece

Global Migration Group. (2008). *International Migration and Human Rights Challenges and Opportunities on the Threshold of the 60th Anniversary of the Universal Declaration of Human Rights.* Global Migration Group.

Global Migration Group. (2013). *Exploitation and Abuse of International Migrants, Particularly Those in an Irregular Situation: A Human Rights Approach.* Global Migration Group.

Godfrey, M., Ruhs, M., Shah, N., & Smith, M. (2004). Migrant domestic workers in Kuwait: Findings based on a field survey and additional research. In S. Esim & M. Smith (Eds.), *Gender and Migration in Arab States: The Case of Domestic Workers* (pp. 42–63). International Labor Organisation.

Hujo, K. (2019, May 16). *A Global Social Contract: New Steps towards a Rights-Based Approach to Migration Governance?* SAGE Journals. Retrieved December 17, 2021, from https://journals.sagepub.com/doi/full/10.1177/1468018119849232

Human Rights Watch. (2010, October). *Walls at Every Turn Abuse of Migrant Domestic Workers through Kuwait's Sponsorship System.* https://www.hrw.org/sites/default/files/reports/kuwait1010webwcover.pdf

India: Govt. Records 77,155 Labor Abuse Allegations by Migrant Workers in the Gulf between 2016–2019. (2019, July 19). Business and Human Rights Resource Centre. https://www.business-humanrights.org/en/latest-news/india-govt-records-77155-labor-abuse-allegations-by-migrant-workers-in-the-gulf-between-2016-2019/

Indian Community. (n.d.). Embassy of India. https://www.indembkwt.gov.in/Indian-community.php

Indian Domestic Workers Rescued from Kuwait Narrate Tales of Horror, Harassment. (2019, August 6). The New Indian Express. https://www.newindianexpress.com/states/tamil-nadu/2019/aug/06/indian-domestic-workers-rescued-from-kuwait-narrate-tales-of-horror-harassment-2014572.html

IOM. (2020, May). *Migration Governance Overview: The State of Kuwait.* IOM UN Migration. https://migrationdataportal.org/sites/default/files/2019-09/MGI%20Kuwait%20Report%20FINAL.pdf

Jadhav, R. (2019, July 17). *Saudi Arabia Tops Indian Gulf Workers' 'Victimisation' List*. MEA. @businessline. https://www.thehindubusinessline.com/news/saudi-arabia-tops-indian-gulf-workers-victimisation-list-mea/article28521417.ece

Kanchana, R. (2016). Are India's policies increasing the vulnerability of its female migrants in the Arab Gulf countries? In S. Irudya Rajan (ed.) *India Migration Report 2016: Gulf Migration* (pp. 112–127). Routledge.

Kodoth, P. (n.d.). *Women Domestic Workers and Nurses in India's Migration Policy: Problems and Recommendations*. University Practice Connect. https://practiceconnect.azimpremjiuniversity.edu.in/women-domestic-workers-and-nurses-in-indias-migration-policy-problems-and-recommendations/

Kuttappan, R. (2020, January 10). *Rs 1.5 Lakh Is Freedom Fee for Indian Domestic Workers in Kuwait*. The Lede. https://www.thelede.in/kerala/2020/01/10/rs-15-lakh-is-freedom-fee-for-indian-domestic-workers-in-kuwait

Kuwait. (2020, June 15). *The Life of Overseas Migrant Workers*. ECDHR. https://www.ecdhr.org/?p=948

Kuwait Society for Human Rights. (2019). *Kuwait's Commitment to the International Covenant on Economic, Social and Cultural Rights*. CESCR – UN Committee on Economic, Social and Cultural Rights. https://tbinternet.ohchr.org/Treaties/CESCR/Shared%20Documents/KWT/INT_CESCR_ICO_KWT_33694_E.pdf

Kuwait Society for Human Rights. (n.d.). *Kuwait Society for Human Rights*. Retrieved December 16, 2021, from http://www.kuwaithr.org/about/growing-objectives.html

Lean Lim, L., Landuyt, K., Ebisui, M., Kawar, M., &Ameratunga, S. (2003). *An Information Guide–Preventing Discrimination, Exploitation and Abuse of Women Migrant Workers*. ILO. http://www.ilo.org/Public/English/Employment/Gems/Advocacy/Protect.htm

Migrant Domestic Workers (Labor Migration). (n.d.). International Labor Organization. https://www.ilo.org/global/topics/labor-migration/policy-areas/migrant-domestic-workers/lang--en/index.htm

Mitra, A., &Kasliwal, R. (2020). *Twin Crises in the Gulf: Implications for India* (ORF Special Report No. 105, April 2020). Observer Research Foundation. https://www.orfonline.org/wp-content/uploads/2020/04/ORF_Special_Report_105_GulfCrises.pdf

Nair, S. (2020, July 24). *Indian Migrant Workers in Kuwait: Challenges and Opportunities for India*. Times Now. https://www.timesnownews.com/columns/article/indian-migrant-workers-in-kuwait-challenges-and-opportunities-for-india/626515

Rafel, R. J. (2019, February 13). *How Do You Solve a Problem Like Migrant Workers?* Asfar. https://www.asfar.org.uk/how-do-you-solve-a-problem-like-migrant-workers/

Robinson, K. (2021, March 23). *What Is the Kafala System?* Council on Foreign Relations. https://www.cfr.org/backgrounder/what-kafala-system

Sabban, R. (2002). *Migrant Women in the United Arab Emirates: The Case of Female Domestic Workers (GENPROM Working Paper No. 10, Series on Women and Migration)*. International Labor Office.

Shree, M. (2011). Victimization of female Indian migrant workers in Gulf countries. In *First International Conference of the South Asian Society of Criminology and Victimology (SASCV), 15–17 January 2011, Jaipur, Rajasthan, India: SASCV 2011 Conference Proceedings* (p. 263). K. Jaishankar.

Staff, A. (2018, November 6). *Death of Ethiopian Domestic Worker in Kuwait Emphasizes the Dangers of Abuse for Migrant Workers.* Americans for Democracy & Human Rights in Bahrain. https://www.adhrb.org/2018/11/death-of-ethiopian-domestic-worker-in-kuwait-emphasizes-the-dangers-of-abuse-for-migrant-workers/

Tayah, M. J., & Assaf, H. (2018). The future of domestic work in the countries of the Gulf cooperation council. *Abu Dhabi Dialogue.* http://abudhabidialogue.org.ae/sites/default/files/document-library/2018%20ADD%20SOM%20-%20Future%20of%20Domestic%20Work%20Report%20-min.pdf

Thimothy, R., & Sasikumar, S. K. (2012). *Migration of Women Workers from South Asia to the Gulf.* VV Giri National Labor Institute.

United Nations Human Rights. (n.d.). *About the Mandate of the Special Rapporteur on the Human Rights of Migrants.* Office of the United Nations High Commissioner for Human Rights (OHCHR). https://www.ohchr.org/Documents/ProfessionalInterest/cmw.pdf

United Nations Human Rights. (n.d.). *International Convention on the Protection of the Rights of All Migrant Workers and Members of Their Families.* Office of the United Nations High Commissioner for Human Rights (OHCHR). https://www.ohchr.org/Documents/ProfessionalInterest/cmw.pdf

Women and Men Migrant Workers: Moving Towards Equal Rights and Opportunities. International Labor Organization. Retrieved from https://www.ilo.org/wcmsp5/groups/public/@dgreports/@gender/documents/publication/wcms_101118.pdf

World Report 2019: Rights Trends in Kuwait. (2019, May 24). Human Rights Watch. https://www.hrw.org/world-report/2019/country-chapters/kuwait

17 Studies on Indian Migration to the Gulf Countries

A Review of Current Indian Literature

K Deepa

Introduction

Throughout history, Indians migrated to different parts of the world for many reasons. During the last few decades, a large number of Indians migrated to West Asia particularly the Gulf states for their livelihood that constitute an important part of the Arab population. They are engaged in every sphere of life ranging from white-collar jobs to laborers. The Indian Diaspora to the Arab Gulf states is now nearly a hundred years old. During the last 45 years, the numbers raised and are now settling down to a regular pattern.

Indians are among the most preferred communities in the Gulf region not only due to their expertise, but also because of their sense of discipline, and their law-abiding and peace-loving nature. Many Gulf countries have completed the phase of infrastructure development which needed a lot of manual labor. Now they are also focusing on knowledge-based industries. This increased the job prospects of white-collar workers in the Gulf region; another change in the pattern of Indian workers migrating to the Gulf countries is the geographical spread. India is the largest recipient of remittances globally, notably from the Gulf. In 2008, the Gulf replaced North America as the top source of remittances to India.

A large number of Indian expatriates working in the different Gulf countries attracted Indian scholars to explore more about the sociopolitical situation of the region. Trade has been the dominant factor in India's relationship with the Arab Gulf states, with the import of oil being a major component. This chapter will solely be based on the content analysis of books and research papers published in academic journals and magazines. PhD theses and MPhil dissertations completed in Indian universities in recent decades will also be reviewed. The chapter aims to review contemporary research conducted by Indian scholars on Gulf-based Indian expatriates.

The purpose of this chapter is to point out various themes and issues that have been taken up by academics and researchers for the last few decades in Indian universities and research centers. In a way, this will be a survey-type study focusing on how the issue of Indian expatriates has been observed by

DOI: 10.4324/9781003369370-22

scholars in various universities and academic institutions in India. It will also look into the different aspects that have attracted scholars during the period.

Indian Communities in the Arabian Peninsula

It is interesting to note that research on India's migration to the Gulf States has various dimensions. For example, the India–Arab historical links provide information about the settlement of Indians in the Gulf region during the medieval trade engagement between India and the Arab world. Indian trading communities settled in Iran, Oman, and also in Iraq in the earlier centuries. What were the patterns of business and commercial exchanges? How have the archival materials been explored by economic historians in this regard?

In this regard, there is much research that talks about the historical perspective of Indian migration to the Gulf states. For example, Kundan Kumar's book chapter on "Aspects of Indian Merchant Diaspora in the Arabian Peninsula during the British Period" deals with the existence of the Indian community in the Arabian Peninsula. This paper is based on the extent and gravity of the mobility of the Indian merchants operating from different locations in the region. The chapter highlighted the manner in which they functioned socially, economically, and culturally. The political dimension is also underlined. It may not be an exaggeration to assert that the Indian trading networks along with Indian traders were the most prominent actors in the Arabian Peninsula, concentrating and dominating almost all mercantile activities.

During the western domination of the 17th and 18th centuries, this peninsula was under colonial control and India had no commercial attractions to the Arab world. During this period, India was the central command of the British Empire; it's interesting to know how this Arab Islamic region attracted expatriates. However, major interest in the Gulf region started after these countries became free from the full control of the colonial power. For example, in the 1970s when oil revenues in the Gulf countries started to play the role in economic development activities, the Arab Gulf states invited Asian workers for their economic development programs. This was the incentive for researchers to focus on a region of oil-rich Gulf States that could provide job opportunities for unemployed young people of this country. Most of the researchers looked into the prospects of the job market both for unskilled and skilled people. Some basic assumptions prevailed in their writings: that India needed to make easy rules and regulations and free recruitment procedures for Indians to grab comparatively better employment and positions.[1]

As for the Indian labor force of the Arab Gulf states, it's interesting to see that a few particular communities have been attracted to the region for jobs and business purposes. Which communities have been given special focus in the research? R. L. Franklin in his book chapter titled "The Bohra community in Bahrain" says that ironically, it is the Muslim Bohras, rather than the Hindu Bhatias who are in the more delicate position in Bahraini society. Bhatias and Bohras differ from most other groups in the Indian population. At the caste or sub-sect level of identity, solidarity, and cultural differentiation, these groups do not constitute real "communities" in Bahrain (with the notable exception of the Sonis). However, whatever their orientations may have been in India, because these groups are unable to organize in Bahrain, such elements of identity and culture may be given only limited expression, and traditional solidarities are further discouraged. Of course, the individuals are not without options, and it is to these options – the compromises made, the other solidarities exploited, and the groups thus formed – that I now turn.[2]

Another book chapter by Prakash C. Jain talks about the Thattai Bhatia Community of Dubai. This chapter provides a sociocultural as well as the historical profile of the Thattai sindhi Bhatia community of Dubai, UAE. It included family-wise data on age, gender, education, and population in the UAE. The Thattai Bhatias made the UAE their adopted home and dedicated themselves to its leading role in the shaping and growth of the community. Its basic objective is the creation of a spirit of brotherhood and cooperation among its members and striving for the general improvement of the community, especially of its educational, financial, and sociocultural aspects. The Thattai sindhi Bhatia community derives its name from the city called Thatta, now in Pakistan. Bhatias trace their genealogy from the Chandravansi/Yaduvanshi Kshatrias.

T.L.S. Bhaskar's chapter "Protection of labor migrants at destination countries: a note on the Indian Community Welfare Fund" talks about the protection of Indian migrant workers in destination countries, especially in the Gulf which is the destination of most of India's unskilled migrant laborers.

> Protecting migrants' rights and providing requisite welfare, especially at destination countries, have become prominent measures in assessing the proactiveness of countries of origin (COO) like India in addressing the welfare concerns of migrant workers. The issue of welfare becomes even more critical to migrants who are on a temporary contract and have meager chance of becoming naturalized citizens of countries of destination (COD). This is true in the case of millions of labour migrants in the Gulf Cooperation Council (GCC).[3]

Another study by Patricia Uberoi discusses the internationalization of migration. The author says that

> a significant new development in the field of Indian family and kinship, and one which has so far barely been addressed in the sociology of

> India is the internationalization of the middle-class family. This paper analyses two popular Hindi films of the mid-1990s, *Dilwale Dulhania Le Jayenge* (DDLJ) and *Pardes*, that thematise the problems of transnational location in respect of courtship and marriage. The two films share a conservative agenda on the family, but differ in their assessment of the possibility of retaining Indian identity in Diaspora. DDLJ proposes that Indian family values are portability of retaining Indian identity in Diaspora. DDLJ proposes that Indian family values are portable assets, while Pardes suggests that the loss of cultural identity can be postponed but ultimately not avoided. These discrepant solutions mark out Indian popular cinema as an important site for engagement with the problems resulting from middle-class Diaspora, and for articulation of Indian identity in a globalised world.[4]

The book titled *Indian Diaspora in West Asia: A Reader*, edited by Prakash C. Jain is a collection of essays on the subject written by distinguished scholars during the past two decades or so. The essays highlight the past and the present of the Indian Diaspora in West Asia. The contemporary diaspora, unlike in other parts of the world, has been a discrete phenomenon temporary, short-term, shifting, and circulatory. Two major exceptions are Israel and Yemen where Indians have been permanently settled in sizeable numbers for the past several decades, and can be called "Diaspora" in the proper sense of the term. A few studies done on the Indian Diaspora in Israel and some of the articles, chapters, or book excerpts reproduced here in this volume remain an exception.[5]

Another book chapter by Prakash C. Jain highlights the salient features of Indian migration to West Asia from a cultural perspective. The article, besides discussing the cultural aspects of Indian migration to the Arab countries, makes an inquiry into the cultural issues related to the migration of Indian Jews to Israel.

> This paper discusses the salient features of the Indian migration to West Asia from a cultural perspective. It is argued that this migration pattern, though determined by cultural factors, particularly by religious affinity. Two major sub- region of Indian migration to West Asia are the Persian Gulf and Red Sea region countries and Israel. Whereas the share of Muslim migrants is high in case of the Gulf countries, Indian migration to Israel was dominated by the Indian Jews. In spite of India's historical relations with many countries of West Asia, the Indian Diaspora remained very small in size until very recently the main focus of the paper therefore would be on the migration, settlement and the consequent emergence of the Indian diaspora in the region in recent decades. Small communities of Indian traders called Baniyans existed in present day Iraq, Iran Oman, Yemen and Saudi Arabia in the seventeenth and eighteenth centuries. When the region came under the British influence

in the 19th century, Indian merchant communities flourished in a number of towns in the Gulf countries. The Indians served as bankers, importers and exporters customs farmers, agents for local merchants, government contractors, pearl-financiers etc. During the past few decades a large number of Indian entrepreneurs have migrated to various Gulf countries and are involved in a wide variety of business, commercial and professional activities.[6]

Prof. Anisur Rahman in his book chapter discusses the current status of Indian migrants to the Gulf and says that

> Indian Diaspora today constitutes an important socio-economic force in the World. The 1990s witnessed a structural shift in the market for expatriate labour in majority of the Gulf countries. There is a marked change in demand for skilled workers. There is a marked change in demand for skilled workers. There is a trend to hire more professionals and skilled workers. Some countries like the UAE in fact have imposed strict restrictions on the entry of unskilled workers. Indian Diaspora in the Gulf region is considered to be one of the significant components and are given due recognition. The rights of labour Diaspora in the Gulf region are not protected. They live in their own enclaves and cannot obtain citizenship, cannot even join trade unions. They are still deprived of social benefits and are excluded from participation in the political system. Since labour legislation and social security institutions are not yet fully developed in many countries of the Gulf region, the employment contract, to some extent, depends on the honesty and integrity on the part of employers in respect of the terms and conditions of the agreements.[7]

Ginu Zacharia Oommen's book chapter discusses the association of Kerala Christians to the Gulf region. He says that

> The socio-economic progress of the Syrian Christians of Kerala in general and the Syrian Church in particular, can be attributed to the booming oil economy of the Muslim countries in West Asia. The Syrian Christians of Kerala have a long association with West Asia since the Gulf countries opened its doors for this community for employment. In spite of nearly 50 years of the immigration of Syrian Christian into Kuwait, information pertaining to Syrian Christian communities in Gulf is very limited. This chapter wills also investigate the emerging role of women immigrants and the religious adaptation of the Syrian Christian youth in an oil-rich Islamic society like Kuwait. The socio-economic progress of the Syrian Christians of Kerala can be attributed to the booming oil economy of the GCC countries. The migration opportunity has consequently changed the status of women in Kerala to a great

> extent. The lack of interaction with the host nationals, social isolation, and economic anxiety has strengthened the religious orientation of the immigrants.[8]

Sajitha Beevi Karayil in her MPhil dissertation examines the influence of migration on India's GCC trade. She says:

> The study examines India's exports to the Gulf Co-operation Council (GCC) countries with a special focus on the influence of migration. An analysis of the trends in India-GCC exports shows a structural break in the beginning of the 90s and acceleration since then. The trade intensity indices show overrepresentation of the two in each other's markets, despite the fluctuations. Further, all the bilateral trade orientation ratios have been increasing systematically over the period of the study. Still, the export orientation of India towards GCC seems to have lower growth compared to the import orientation, at the aggregate level as well as at the level of individual countries. Among the GCC countries, the export intensity index of India with UAE shows the lowest growth, despite its comparatively higher level throughout the period.[9]

She further says:

> As an explanation for the growing orientation of India's exports towards the Gulf countries, she examines the demand pattern of these countries, as revealed by the import structure of GCC. This is particularly important in the context of the influence Of Indian migrants on the GCC imports, probably leading to preference similarity. A notable feature of India-GCC relations is that the largest expatriate Indian community is living in the Gulf. In view of the emerging literature on the positive link between migration and trade, the present study sought to examine the nexus between migration and trade in the concrete context of India-GCC trade. India-GCC trade being a major subset of the network of South-South trade, conclusions of the present study would be of some relevance for the South-South trade in general as also for India's export policy, particularly in the context of the influence of migration. Interestingly enough, as results clearly show, the presence of the Indian Diaspora is an important source of demand and hence growth of India's exports to the GCC.[10]

Living Conditions of Migrants in the Gulf

The researchers haven't paid much attention to the impact of NRIs in the country's social and economic aspects. There is a need to focus on the Diaspora life and experience of Indian expatriates, both males and females in the Gulf States. In this regard, some studies have highlighted this aspect.

For example, Saima Shahid in her M. Phil dissertation titled *Diasporic life and experience of Indian female expatriates in Dubai* highlighted

> a huge imbalance between the male and female populations in Dubai which contributes to the negative atmosphere of the city. Even as early as the mid- 1980s men made up 67 per cent of the total population, and today official reports indicate that over three quarters of Dubai's residents are male, moreover it is likely that the real proportion is even higher given the described census inconsistencies and exclusion of countless illegal immigrants working in Dubai, the majority of whom are male.[11]

Female Migration

Scholars have also focused on female migration to the Arab Gulf states. A joint research article of Deepika Varshney and Suman Lata says that

> Feminization of international migration is a global phenomenon. One of the most significant trends in migration has been the entry of women into migration streams. The percentage of women in the migrant population has been increasing in the post war period and now women comprise majority of international migrants. Female immigration in Asia has been estimated to be about 45 per cent to total immigrants.[12]

Another study of Marie Percot titled "Indian Nurses in the Gulf: Two Generations of Female Migration" is based largely on fieldwork in Gulf countries and in Kerala. This study

> focuses on female nurses from Kerala who have worked, are currently working or are preparing to work in Gulf countries. It examines in particular to what extent these women today aspire not only to a lucrative career abroad, but also to a new lifestyle in which traditional gender-based restrictions are replaced by increased and improved female agency and a focus on the nuclear family.[13]

Praveena Kodoth in her research paper raises the important aspect of structural violence against migrant workers and says that

> Indian emigration policy's emphasis on restrictions on the mobility of women domestic workers to the Middle East has created conditions in which they are subject to exploitation and abuse in the emigration process as well as in overseas employment. Indian policy has made way for unscrupulous recruiters, raided the costs of migration and reduced returns. It is underpinned not by economics but by a gendered, caste and class- based nationalism that regards the emigration of women domestic workers as degrading. In the Middle East, where the "kafala"

> system of sponsorship endows sponsors- employers with extraordinary powers over immigrant workers, the lack of support from Indian embassies reinforces structural violence. Push factors and the demonstration effect of previous migration motives women to disregard state regulation. Domestic workers survive multiple pressures, tolerate abuse and strive to gain the sponsor's patronage or defy the system with the help of social networks to tap the gains of informal/illegal employment.[14]

Impact of Migration on Gulf Society

There are few studies focusing on the impact of Asian migrants on the society and demographic changes in the region. For example, rising numbers of Asian expatriates have greatly affected the changing urbanization in a number of cities such as UAE and other Gulf countries have experienced a new demographic situation where local populations are greatly affected by the foreign labor force. The MPhil dissertation of Tarannum Raza titled "Dynamics of migration and urbanization in the Gulf region: with special reference to UAE" talks about the impact of migration on the UAE. She says that "it is generally observed that the Gulf Region have experienced rapid rate of urbanization and migration in the recent past especially after 1970 when oil added to their massive availability of wealth and capital".[15]

R. Chitra in her PhD thesis titled "Patterns of Migration in India: A Study with Special Reference to Gulf Migration" argues that 'the migration has contributed positively in terms of development and the flow of migrants' workers from all parts of the world to all directions is increasing. "India is a major player in the global workforce and it has the second largest overseas community with an estimated 25 million overseas Indians spread across in more than 11 countries in the world. The Gulf region has enjoyed a tremendously sustained growth in productivity over the last three decades. A major factor behind this productivity has been the easy availability of an educated skilled and the same time cheap workforce".[16]

Another important aspect is the impact of culture on both the local population and foreign workers. Interestingly, a number of studies in recent years have highlighted this from the cultural perspective. Ratheesh Radhakrishnan in his study titled "The Gulf in the imagination: Migration, Malayalam Cinema and Regional Identity" talks about the cultural impact of migrants.

> This article taking up for analysis the three-decade-long relationship between the economy influenced by the Gulf and Malayalam cinema, in its industrial and narrative context, argues that 'the Gulf' has been a significant point of reference for the imagining of a cultural identity in Kerala. It attempts to weave together three aspects- the development models that are in place, the economic conditions within which the film

> industry operates and the textual aspects of the films produced- to foreground the links between the economy, aesthetics and the imagining of regional identity.[17]

Another paper by Prakash C. Jain titled "Indian Migration to West Asia: A Cultural Perspective" highlights the salient features of Indian migration to West Asia from a cultural perspective. The article, besides discussing the cultural aspects of Indian migration to the Arab countries, makes an inquiry into the cultural issues related to the migration of Indian Jews to Israel. This paper discusses

> the salient features of the Indian migration to West Asia from a cultural perspective. It is argued that this migration pattern, though determined by cultural factors, particularly by religious affinity. Two major subregions of Indian migration to West Asia are the Persian Gulf and Red Sea region countries and Israel.[18]

S. Arasu in his MPhil dissertation discusses the relation between migration and urbanization in West Asia. He says that

> the analysis of this dissertation reveals that colonial impact, rural-urban migration and natural increase have been a combined force in the process of urbanization in the Third World countries. The rates of growth as well as the number of urban agglomerations are increasing rapidly. The emergence of medium cities *is* also a trend *in* the Third World now. In the Latin American countries, the level of urbanization is high but the rate of growth is declining where as in West Asian countries the rate of growth is higher and in Afro-Asian countries the rate of growth is the highest but with a very low level of urbanization. This shows that the urbanization is in African and Asian countries will be higher in future. Even though the evolution of cities in the West Asian countries started very early in history but only in the past four decades the urbanization has gained a higher momentum. In Kuwait, Bahrain, Israel, Lebanon, Qatar and Saudi Arabia the level of urbanization is more than 80 per cent. Yemen and Oman have very low of the same. The higher order cities have higher level of population concentration but at the same time the middle order cities are increasing number. Turkey is the only ·country where the primate cities are well distributed which is the sign of urban primacy. Whereas in other countries the primacy rate is very high which will lead to socio economic imbalance? As the migration of international labour declines, the rural-urban migration and natural increase have become the predominant factor of urbanization.[19]

Remittances and Development

In a number of studies, the researchers have shown that the role of expatriates has a deep impact on trade and commerce activities. This was in particularly seen in cases in China whose foreign population played vital roles in China's trade expansion in the global market. How has India been seen by the researchers in this area? Rajaram Panda in a research paper titled "Migration Remittance: The Emerging Scenario", published in *India Quarterly* said that

> Remittances are increasingly identified as golden eggs that contribute crucially to the foreign exchange earnings of many developing countries across the world. Governments and international agencies have recognized that remittances to the developing world are substantially greater than aid. Though the global flow of such remittances is in the vicinity of $150–200 billion, remittances to South Asia alone total perhaps $40–50 billion"[20]

R.B. Bhagat, Kunal Keshari, and Imtiyaz Ali in a joint research paper titled "Emigration and flow of remittances in India" said that

> the National Sample Survey Organization in India has collected information on emigration and remittances in its 64th round, for the first time, during 2007–2008 at the household level. It is estimated that 4.4 million Indians who are currently members of the households were living outside the country. The average amount of remittances during the last one year was INR 57 thousand (1US$ = 45 INR in 2007–2008). The paper shows a vast disparity in the levels of emigration across different states of India as well as per capita remittances sent by them. It also analyses the characteristics of emigrants, reasons of emigrations and the related policy issues.[21]

Another paper by Supriya Singh titled "Towards sociology of money and family in the Indian Diaspora" said that

> the linking of money, family and migration has become increasingly important with the rise in Indian remittances to US$ 21.7 billion in 2004, the largest number of remittances in the world. The economic importance of remittances has meant that they have primarily been studied as money flows resulting from direct migration. Some attention has been paid to their economic impact at the local, regional and national levels in India. In this article, I argue that sociologists and anthropologist have much to contribute to the study of remittances, as a social phenomenon linked to family and migration.[22]

It's interesting to note that after the globalization drive in both Asia and West Asian countries, there has been much policy change in the respective countries especially in the areas of labor reforms, wages, and working conditions for the workers. The NRIs have been much focused on India's policy perspective. In this regard the book chapter of Prakash C. Jain titled "Globalization and Indian Diaspora in West Asia and North Africa: Some Policy Implications" argued that in spite of the variable and at times contradictory effects of globalization processes – the movement of people, capital, and ideas – India has been successful in exploiting them to its economic advantage. According to him, not only are an ever-increasing number of Indians migrating abroad, particularly to the Gulf countries, the quantum of remittances, investment, and trade networking has also grown significantly. The bond between India and its Diaspora has given a new meaning and form to "Indianess" that is increasingly global.[23]

Anisur Rehman in his book chapter talks about the "Economic and Social Consequences of Indian Emigration to West Asia" and says that the main aim of his paper is to assess the economic and social consequences of Indian emigration to West Asia, especially the Gulf region. To fully understand these two dimensions an effort is made to trace the historical presence of the Indian community in the West Asian region which has always been strategically significant for India for a variety of reasons. An attempt is also made to examine the annual trends of Indian labor outflow as well as the volume of Indian emigrants present in this region during the last three decades. How it has affected the place of origins as well as the place of destinations are dealt with in this paper In what way remittances are benefiting India are also discussed. What the overall impact of the Gulf migration is also receives due attention in this paper. Finally, the working and living conditions of emigrant workers in the host countries are also examined with emigrants' demands and expectations from the Indian government. Possible solutions are given in this regard.[24]

On this notes, an edited book of Prakash C. Jain titled *Indian Diaspora in West Asia: A Reader* needs a special mention here. The book comprises 340 pages in a collection of essays on the subject written by distinguished scholars during the past two decades or so. The essays highlight the past and present of the Indian Diaspora in West Asia. The contemporary Indian Diaspora in West Asia, unlike in other parts of the worked, has been a discrete phenomenon temporary, short-term, shifting and "circulatory". Two major exceptions are Israel and Yemen where Indians have been permanently settled in sizeable numbers for the past several decades, and can be called "Diaspora" in the proper sense of the term. A few studies done on the Indian diaspora in Israel and some of the articles, chapters, or book excerpts reproduced here in this volume remain an exception.[25]

Stephen Castle discusses the relationship between migration and development and argues that

> The socio-economic change and human mobility are constantly interactive processes, so to ask whether migration or development comes first is nonsensical. Yet in both popular and political discourse it has become the conventional wisdom to argue that promoting economic development in the Global South has the potential to reduce migration to the North. This carries the clear implication that such migration is a "bad thing," and that poor people should stay put. In other words, the idea is that encouraging international migration now may help create conditions conducive to eliminating – or at least reducing – it in the future. This belief in the positive consequences of migration for development represents a reversal of dominant views prior to the 1990s according to which migration represented a loss of labor and human capital likely to hold back development of origin countries.[26]

The writer in his article mentions the views on migration.

> This article explores the processes and reasoning behind changing views on migration and development in the European Union and Asia, arguing that social, scientific and political discourses are often closely linked, and that this can have negative consequences both for the advancement of knowledge and for policy development. The article proposes an alternative view of human mobility as a normal part of social transformation processes. Migrating in search of better opportunities and greater human security is a way in which people can exercise agency to improve their livelihoods. Embedding migration studies in an analysis of contemporary social transformation processes can help overcome the frequent separation between migration research and mainstream social theory, and may contribute to improved international cooperation in the migration field.[27]

Gulf Return Migration

Return migration is a new phenomenon that is affecting the labor-exporting countries like India. Return migration is happening due to many reasons in the host countries and it is hitting India hard. Scholars are now started to look into this new phenomenon very carefully. Not many studies are available but a book titled *Gulf return migration and dilemmas of rehabilitation: Policy issues in India* by G. Gopa Kumar is very important in this regard. This book is an attempt to study the gravity of the problem of Gulf returnees to Kerala. He says

> the issue received attention among social scientists from 1996 onwards. But the gravity increases day by day demanding urgent solutions from policy makers. Although return migration to Gulf take place, the increasing presence of Gulf returnee in Kerala raises numerous questions, challenges and issues in policy making. More than a million Gulf returnees

are now identified in Kerala. They face the basic challenge of rehabilitation in the home state. What exactly is the role of government in addressing this issue? What are the tasks of political parties and civil society in helping these people? What will be the impact of this problem on Kerala's economy and polity? These are the major concerns of this work.[28]

Conclusion

The migration of Indians to the Arab Gulf states for a variety of reasons has been a very important and relevant subject for academics and policymakers in India because of the presence of a large number of Indians in the region. It is worth mentioning here that a considerable part of the Indian economy is based on the remittances sent by expatriates. The hosting countries also play an important role in providing jobs to Indians in different capacities and help India to minimize its unemployment burden. These factors have encouraged Indian academicians, scholars, and policymakers to study different aspects of Indian migration.

Indian scholars have extensively written on the various aspects of Indian Diaspora in the Gulf region because a huge number of Indians are engaged in the region; academics have started from a historical perspective of the subject up unto return migration. Most of the studies concentrate on the economic part of the migration and how the remittances are contributing to the Indian economy. Less importance has been given to the social living condition of the migrants, their contribution towards the hosting countries, and the issue of return migration. It is notable that the new research centers working in West Asia are now focusing more on the emerging issues that are linked to the migrant workers.

Notes

1 Kumar, Kundan (1999). Aspects of Indian Merchant Diaspora In The Arabian Peninsula During the British Period. In: Prakash C. Jain, Kundan Kumar (Ed.), *Indian Trade Diaspora in the Arabian Peninsula* (pp. 51–76). Delhi, New Academic Publishers.

2 Franklin, R.L. (1999). The Bohra Community in Bahrain. In: Prakash C. Jain, Kundan Kumar (eds.), *Indian Trade Diaspora in the Arabian Peninsula* (pp.192–211). Delhi, New Academic Publishers.

3 Bhaskar, T.L.S. (2017). Protection of labor migrants at destination countries: a note on the Indian Community Welfare Fund. In S Irudaya Rajan (Ed.), *India migration report 2016: Gulf migration* (pp. 133–145). New York, Routledge.

4 Uberoi, Patricia (1998, November). The Diaspora Comes Home: Disciplining Desire in DDLJ, *Contribution to Indian Sociology*, 32(2), 305–336.

5 Jain, Prakash C. (ed.). (2007). *Indian Diaspora in West Asia: A Reader*, New Delhi, Manohar Publisher and Distributers.

6 Jain, Prakash C. (2007). Indian Migration to West Asia: A Cultural Perspective. In: M.H.Ilias, P.J. Vincent (eds.), *India-West Asia Relations: Understanding Cultural Interplays,* (pp. 113–137). New Delhi, New Century Publications.

7 Rehman, Anisur (1999). Indian Labour Diaspora in the Gulf: An Overview. In: Prakash C. Jain, Kundan Kumar (eds.), *Indian Trade Diaspora in the Arabian Peninsula* (pp. 325–341) New Delhi, New Academic Publishers.
8 Oommen, Ginu Zacharia (1999). The Syrian Christians of Kerala in the GCC States. In: Prakash C. Jain, Kundan Kumar (eds.), *Indian Trade Diaspora in the Arabian Peninsula* (pp. 247–258). New Delhi, New Academic Publishers.
9 Karayil, Sajitha Beevi (2003). *India's Exports to the GCC and the Migration Trade Link* (Doctoral dissertation). Available from Shodhganga @INFLIBLET.
10 Ibid.
11 Saima, Shahid. (2012). *Diasporic Life and Experience of Indian female Expatriates in Dubai*, New Delhi, CWAS Jamia Millia Islamia (Doctoral dissertation).
12 Varshney, Deepika, & Lata Suman. (2014, March) Female Migration, Education and Occupational Development: A Geospatial Analysis of Asian Countries. *Environment and Urbanization Asia*, 5(1), 185–215.
13 Percot, Marie (2006, February). Indian Nurses in the Gulf: Two Generations of Female Migration. *South Asia Research*, 26(1), 41–62.
14 Kodoth, Praveena (2016, January). Structural Violence against Emigrant Domestic Workers and Survival in the Middle East: The Effects of Indian Emigration Policy. *Journal of Interdisciplinary Economics*, 28((1), 83–106.
15 Raza, Tarannum (2010). *Dynamics of Migration and Urbanization in the Gulf Region: with Special Reference to UAE*, New Delhi, CWAS, Jamia Millia Islamia (Doctoral dissertation).
16 Chitra, R. (2012). *Patterns of Migration in India: A Study with Special Reference to Gulf Migration* (Doctoral theses). Available from Shodhganga @INFLIBLET.
17 Radhakrishnan, Ratheesh (2009, May/August). The Gulf in the Imagination: Migration, Malayalam Cinema and Regional Identity. *Contributions to Indian Sociology*, 43(2), 217–245.
18 Jain, Prakash C. (2007). Indian Migration to West Asia: A Cultural Perspective. In: M.H.Ilias, P.J. Vincent (eds.), *India- West Asia Relations: Understanding Cultural Interplays* (pp. 113–137) New Delhi, New Century Publications.
19 Arasu, S. (1992). *International Migration and Urbanization in West Asia* (Doctoral dissertation). Available from Shodhganga @INFLIBLET
20 Panda, Rajaram (2009, April/June). Migration Remittances: The Emerging Scenario, *India Quarterly: A Journal of International Affairs*, 65(2), 167–183.
21 Bhagat, R.B., Keshari, Kunal, & Ali, Imtiyaz (2013, June). Emigration and Flow of Remittances in India, *Migration and Development*, 2(1), 93–105.
22 Singh, Supriya (2006, October). Towards a Sociology of Money and Family in the Indian Diaspora, *Contributions to Indian sociology*. 40(3), 375–398.
23 Jain, Prakash C. (2008). Globalisation and Indian Diaspora in West Asia and North Africa: Some Policy Implications. In: Anwar Alam (Ed.), *India and West Asia in the Era of Globalization* (pp161–187). New Delhi, New Century Publications.
24 Rehman, Anisur (2014). Economic and Social Consequences of Indian Emigration to West Asia. In: Fazal Mahmood, Rafiullah Azmi (eds.), *India-West Asia Economic Relations*, New Academic Publishers, New Delhi-2014, pp 66–82.
25 Jain, Prakash C. (ed.). (2007). *Indian Diaspora in West Asia: A Reader*, New Delhi, Manohar Publishers and Distributors.
26 Castles, Stephen. (2009, December). Development and Migration or Migration and Development: What Comes First?, *Asian and Pacific Migration Journal*, 18(4), 441–471.
27 Ibid
28 Kumar, G Gopa (2008). *Gulf Return Migration and Dilemmas of Rehabilitation: Policy Issues in India*. New Delhi, Icon Publications pvt. Ltd.

18 Indian "Guest Workers" in the Gulf

Discussing Deepak Unnikrishnan's Temporary People

Nitesh Narnolia and Mousam

Introduction

India is one of the largest contributors to the world's labor migration, be it skilled, semi-skilled, or unskilled. Among the various destinations for labor migration, the Gulf region has developed a particular interest of Indians. Indian labor migration to the Gulf can be traced to the period of Arab settlers. There were many Indian settlers in Arab countries who went either as businessmen or to seek employment or to escape instability at home at the time of the advent of Islam. The period from the seventh to the tenth century is considered the "golden age" of the Indo-Arab migration (Ahmad 1971). Thus, the Indian labor migration to the Gulf is not a new phenomenon; it can be traced back to the early 20th century in relation to the oil discovery in the region.

Emigration from India to the Gulf can be explored in three phases. The first phase can be considered till the mid-1990s during which considerable migration from India to the Gulf region took place owing to the oil boom and increasing employment opportunities. The late 1990s can be deliberated as the second phase. This saw a decline in Indian labor migration "due to restrictive immigration policies and localization policies to control the non-Arab population, as well as the completion of major projects and saturation of the labour market" (Chanda & Gupta 2018: 180). The next phase of migration, from 2000 to 2008, witnessed a resurrection in the demand for semi-skilled and unskilled workers in the Gulf region and the Indian government also promoted the international migration. Overall, there have been ups and downs in Indian labor migration to the Gulf region.

The immigrant laborers who have permission to work temporarily in the Gulf are called "guest workers". Indian workers also come into this category of guest workers. These guest workers experience exploitation, abuse, and hardship from their employees for a range of reasons. As these guest workers are not citizens of the Gulf countries, they have a limited number of rights to protect themselves. Human Rights Watch, an international organization, has explored the conditions of these guest workers in the Gulf region. They are overworked and underpaid in the Gulf countries and face

DOI: 10.4324/9781003369370-23

racial and religious discrimination in the workplace. As the guest workers are not citizens of the Gulf, so there were a very few laws to protect their rights. However, in 1990, the U.N. adopted some resolutions to protect guest workers, not only in the Gulf but also across the world. The International Convention on the Protection of the Rights of All Migrant Workers and Members of their Families, signed on 18 December 1990 (https://treaties.un.org/Pages/ViewDetails.aspx?src=IND&mtdsg_no=IV-13&chapter=4) and applies to 56 countries as of August 2021, emerged to protect the human rights of around 164 million guest workers across the world.

The guest workers in the Gulf have helped in the growth of the economy of that region, but their negative treatment brought the attention of the world towards the Gulf. The experiences of these guest workers have been depicted in fiction, especially by writers of Indian origin. One such novel is *Temporary People* (2017a) by Deepak Unnikrishnan – born to migrant laborers in the Gulf who grew up in Abu Dhabi (UAE). The present chapter attempts to understand the plight of the Indian guest workers in the Gulf region through a detailed discussion of Unnikrishnan's novel. In order to establish the background, the authors will first look into the history and recent trends of Indian labor migration to the Gulf.

Indian Labor Migration to the Gulf Region: Recent Trends

Labor migration from India carries a long history dating back approximately 200 years to the colonial period. Between the period of a hundred years from the mid-19th century to the mid-20th century (1840–1940), around 30 million Indians migrated to seek work, making India the largest country of labor migration (Mckeown 2004). In the late 20th century, such movement to the Gulf region became one of the largest in the world. Labor migration to the Gulf region originated in the mid-1920s when the Bahrain Petroleum and Kuwait Petroleum Companies were established. By 1950, approximately 800 Indian workers had migrated to seek work in these oil companies (Sasikumar 2019, 113). By the 1970s, with the establishment of the Organization of the Petroleum Exporting Countries (OPEC), labor migration from India to the Gulf region witnessed a sharp increase. Except for a phase in the late 1990s, (as discussed in the Introduction of this chapter), the overall trend of Indian labor migration to the Gulf has remained upwards. As shown in Figure 18.1, Indian migration from 1991 to 2000 witnessed fluctuations and a significant decrease towards the end of the decade.

This decrease in the late 1990s in Indian labor migration to the Gulf, saw a systematic increase in the first decade of the 21st century (as shown in Figure 18.2).

The second decade of the 21st century also witnessed a fluctuation in the labor migration from India. In the first half of the second decade, it continued to increase after a decrease in 2009–2010 (as shown in Figure 18.2), but

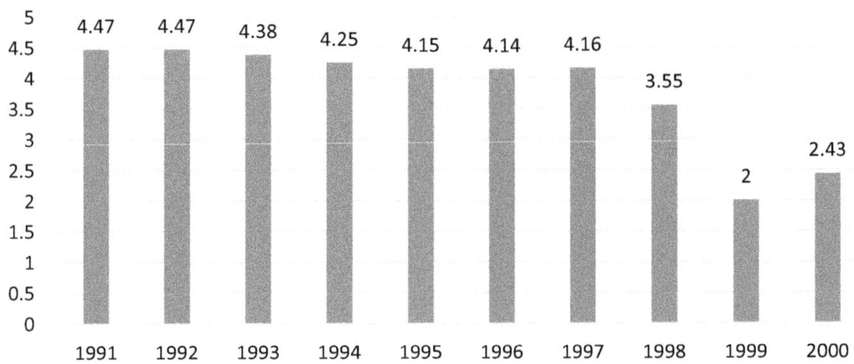

Figure 18.1 Number of emigration clearance to Indian laborers, 1991–2000. Source: Ministry of External Affairs.

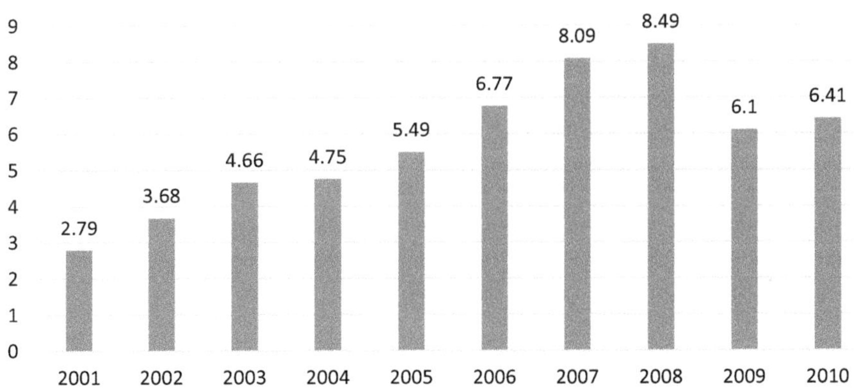

Figure 18.2 Number of emigration clearance to Indian laborers, 2001–2010. Source: Ministry of External Affairs.

it again decreased in the second half of the decade (as shown in Figure 18.3). According to the MEA's Annual Report 2016–2017, the decrease in labor migration is due to the "decline in crude oil prices and the resulting economic slowdown in the GCC countries" (MEA Annual Report 2016–2017).

India is an important source country for providing manpower in the Gulf region. Hence, through the limited yet clear data on the basis of the emigration clearances granted by the Protector of Emigrants, Government of India, the increasing trend of Indian labor migration in the Gulf can be easily established, especially in the last two decades. In 2013, nearly 13.3

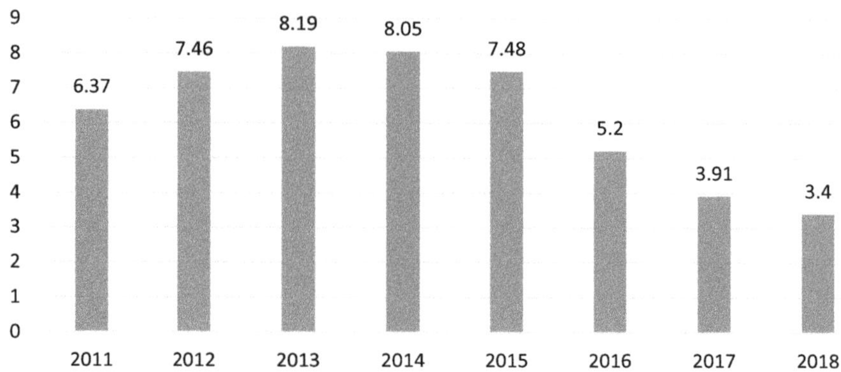

Figure 18.3 Number of emigration clearance to Indian laborers, 2011–2018. Source: Ministry of External Affairs.

million South Asian migrants were living in the Gulf region, which formed about 59% of total migrants living in the Gulf. Out of 13.3 million, India contributed 6.8 million migrants, which is 51% of South Asian migrants and 30% of all migrants in the Gulf region (Chanda & Gupta 2018, 181). This increasing trend led the Indian migrants in the Gulf region from 0.5 million in 1979 to 1.96 million in 1990, 2.7 million in 2000, 6.4 million in 2010, and 8.9 million in 2017 (UNDESA 2017). It is clear from the above-mentioned data that the Indian migrants' population in the Gulf region has remained roughly the same over time, though fluctuating. These constantly increasing and decreasing trends designate India's importance as a source of manpower for the Gulf region.

Despite a significant proportion of Indian laborers in the Gulf, they face difficulties at all levels of migration – while migrating from home to the host country, while staying in the host country, and also while returning to the home country. The present chapter is focused on the problems faced by the Indian migrants during their stay in the Gulf region, so let us look at some of these problems. The problems that migrants face in the Gulf are mostly derived from the *kafala* system (Chanda & Gupta 2018, 189) which allows the employers to confiscate the passports of laborers, poor working and living conditions, and awful salaries. The other problems that migrants face can be explained in the words of Chanda and Gupta,

> Workers are accommodated in ghetto-like labour camps that lack basic amenities such as drinking water and sanitation facilities. Lack of safety at the workplace is another concern. Accidents at construction sites are common, leading to a number of labourer deaths every year
>
> (Chanda & Gupta 189–190)

This already miserable life of Indian labor migrants become more miserable with their status as "guest workers". The status of guest workers doesn't make them eligible for citizenship and any other benefits. The recent trends show a decline in the number of these guest workers (as shown in Figure 18.3), which may be because of both a decline in crude oil prices and an upsurge in difficulties for the migrants in the Gulf. The Indian labor migrants in the Gulf are regulated by the *kafala* system which requires the workers to obtain direct sponsorship from employers in the Gulf to get work and residence. Andrew M. Gardner (2010) defines the system of *kafala* as the keystone of the inadequate relations between the nationals and the foreigners and says that:

> When a poor Indian family mortgages its productive assets, pulls children from school, and pawns the mother's jewelry to come up with the thousands of dollars it takes to send a son to the Gulf, only to have him face month after month of no pay and, finally, to be relegated to scrounging for illegal work, it may seem tragic for that family.
>
> (Gardner 68)

In this way, the labor migrants are completely dependent on their employers which increases the risk of physical and mental exploitation of the migrants without any possibility for legal help. Although the guest workers are the backbones of economy of the Gulf region, they are treated as secondary, and get no legal recognition. In spite of some laws in favor of these guest workers, they are not considered equal to the citizens of the Gulf. These guest workers and their plight are depicted in literature which situates them into a legal and public frame of recognition.

Thus, the recent trends of the Indian labor migrants in the Gulf illustrate that despite all the difficulties, the workers are eager to seek work in the Gulf as "guest workers" and this makes India and the Gulf the world's largest temporary migration corridor.

Indian "Guest Workers" in Unnikrishnan's *Temporary People*

In the Gulf region, foreign nationals are brought to construct and serve the monuments/buildings that touch the skyline, especially in Abu Dhabi and Dubai. This labor force is not given the option of citizenship, rather it is termed as "guest workers". Deepak Unnikrishnana's novel *Temporary People* (2017a) delves into the history and struggle of these guest workers in Abu Dhabi, the city where he grew up. Unnikrishnan interweaves 28 stories, including construction workers who shapeshift into luggage and escape a labor camp, a woman who stitches back together the bodies of the workers who have fallen from buildings under construction, and a man who grows ideal workers to live 12 years. Hence, the novel revolves around the stories of day-to-day life of the Indian migrant workers in the Gulf.

Born into migrant workers' family in the Gulf, Unnikrishnan has described Abu Dhabi as a city where citizenship is out of reach for migrant workers. In an interview with *The Guardian*, Unnikrishnan recalls:

> My father came in 1972 on a three-year work visa, which allowed you to sponsor spouses or children to join you. After 18, sons were on their own. To stay in Abu Dhabi as a young man, you had to find a job or enroll in university. Only unmarried daughters could stay on their parents' visas.
>
> But unlike in the US, where the H-1B work visas offer the possibility of a pathway towards permanent residency, no long-term option exists in the UAE for non-citizens. It a foreign loser loses his or her job or reaches retirement age, they need to leave, irrespective of how long they have lived in the country – or even if they were there.
>
> (Unnikrishnan 2017b)

This temporariness of "home" affects their lives as they remain uprooted throughout their lives. To be temporary is to be devoid of a home that can affect one's growth. It is from this perspective of temporariness that Unnikrishnan situates the question of migrant workers in the Gulf in his debut novel *Temporary People*. Unnikrishnan writes that temporariness is something that delves into one's psyche and situates him/her in a state of being or not being. This turns the work life in the Gulf into a spectral being, as Unnikrishnan writes:

> Once the last brick is laid, the glass spotless, the elevators functional, the plumbing operational, the laborers, every single one of them, begin to fade, before disappearing completely. Some believe the men become ghosts, haunting the facades they helped build.
>
> (Unnikrishnan 2017a, 03)

This novel discloses the life of migrants in the Gulf, who are ordained to be "temporary people" by law and order. The novel is divided into three parts – the first two parts contain nine stories each and the third has ten stories which are juxtaposed on the basis of seriousness. Some stories depict the existence and day-to-day life of migrant workers, while other stories represent the inconsistencies and irony of migrant life. The intact experience of Indian migrant workers in the Gulf is portrayed through short narratives of the wholeness of migrant life.

The stories by Unnikrishnan depict what life is like for the temporary people in the Gulf. The story "Gulf Return" describes how three men flee from a labor camp by transforming into a passport and a suitcase. The story represents the lifeless conditions of migrant workers through metaphor and simile. Another story, "Birds", represents a woman, named Anna who wanders around construction sites during the night to stitch the limbs back onto injured workers, making them whole again so that they can work again in the morning. If the limbs can't be stitched back, Anna would pray "until the man breathed his last" (Unnikrishnan 2017a, 09). Anna does not reveal her job of fixing the limbs of the workers and mentions that she is a careworker or a nurse in a hospital. She has left her children and pond fish to perform this job. Another person called Iqbal, who came to the Gulf to transform his life, falls from a building and states that "my family's with me; we all have wings. The sun's cold... we fly... they [birds] fly [as] their feet possess talons and they fly" (Unnikrishnan 2017a, 18). This horrific nature of Anna's job haunts her into her dreams but she is unable to escape.

In another story "Mussafah Grew People", the workers are grown like plants, inherently wired to live only a short term, though long enough to complete their tasks, assigned to them. Hence, the story blends the fact and fantasy to create fictional representation. In this story, three migrant workers from Kerala – Pinto, Tinot, and Vimto carry seeds to an island situated in the west of Dubai, which was ruled by Sultan Mo-Mo. There on the island, a group of researchers were trying to develop a miniature body with two limbs and a brain. These three migrants from Kerala were carrying the seeds for this project. Once they handed over the seeds, they were driven to the desert to die. Before indulging in this project, they were working as truck drivers in Dubai for six years. When they were informed to deliver the seeds to Musaffah for 600 dirhams a day, they found it beneficial and agreed to the job. But once they completed their assignment, they were given half the amount and driven to a desert to die. After wandering in the desert for a few days, they were handed over as desert survivors to the commander and they were housed inside shipping containers. Thus, this story represents the harsh reality of the Gulf region where there is no certainty for the migrant workers.

Another story, "Dog", depicts the temporariness of human life on earth. A dog remained alone after the demise of the last member of the family, so two siblings, a man and a woman, were recruited to look after the dog. The siblings were planning to sell their property and spilt their share, but incongruously the dog passed away first. It states:

> In two years the house would sell, the siblings would splinter, and men would show up with machines and saws, cut everything down, level the ground, destroy the dog, which became part of a tree, strip it all away, as though there had been no old lady, no house, no children, no tame parrots, no crows, no Botswana, no pickle, no Mathai, no dog, no life.
> (Unnikrishnan 2017a, 219)

Hence, Unnikrishnan's "chabters" (he writes "chabter" instead of "chapter" to give the narrative Arabic touch) attempt to preserve what has been left behind by the migrant workers. The above discussed stories familiarize readers to the life of Indian migrant workers in the Gulf through the Malayalee workers grown from seeds who rebel against their masters, through elevators that molest children and through mobile nurses who stitch the injured limbs of the workers, fallen from buildings under construction.

Conclusion

The Gulf region remains an important destination for Indian migrants, but their status remains questionable. Indian migrants, especially unskilled and semi-skilled workers, who are termed "guest workers" are subject to a number of abuses and exploitation in the Gulf region. The life of the "guest workers" in the Gulf is under threat which can be summed up in Elizabeth Jaeger's words:

> Living abroad, working in a country that will never accept you as an equal and doing jobs that are dangerous is a lifestyle many would shun if they had other opportunities. But sadly, many do not, and so they agree to less than favorable terms of employment that so that they and their families do not go hungry.
>
> (Jaeger 2017)

Unnikrishnan's novel depicts vivid images such as a passport with arms and a mustache running through an airport, roaches dressed as humans, a tongue jumping out of a teen's mouth, and words spilling onto the street which allow the readers to peep into the lives of each character. These stories arise empathy, despair and rage and loiter in the mind for a long time after reading them. This makes the reader delve into the lives of "guest workers" who live thousands of miles away, in challenging conditions. Indian migrants in the Gulf fall under the category of irregular migration, so they remain vulnerable to exploitation by the employers as they are not entitled to legal help there.

The novel traces various characters who neither live in their native land, nor in their hostland, rather they create something new for themselves. Without the legal citizenship of the Gulf, the migrant workers in Unnikrishnan's novel become global hobos, mingling in a kind of no man's land where they mutate from one identity to another, but they never find "home".

Thus, it can be argued here that Unnikrishnan pervades his novel with words and signs that depict a clear picture of the lives of Indian migrant workers in the Gulf. With this novel, *Temporary People*, the author, rather than exploring the inward subjectivity, intends to get access to the inner substance of these migrant workers which is inaccessible to us for the time being.

References

Ahmad, Maqbool S. (1971). "Indians in West Asia." in Anirudhha Gupta (ed.), *Indians Abroad: Asia and Africa*. New Delhi: Longmann.

Chanda, Rupa and Gupta, Pralok. (2018). "Indian Migration to the Gulf: Overview of Trends and Policy Initiatives by India." in Philippe Fargues and Nasra M. Shah (ed.), *Migration to the Gulf: Policies in Sending and Receiving Countries*. Cambridge: Gulf Labour Markets and Migration (GLMM) Programme, Gulf Research Center.

Gardner, Andrew M. (2010). *City of Strangers: Gulf Migration and the Indian Community in Bahrain*. Ithaca and London: Cornell University Press.

Jaeger, Elizabeth. (2017). "A Review of Temporary People by Deepak Unnikrishnan", *An International Journal of Contemporary Writing*. retrieved from https://www.theliteraryreview.org/book-review/a-review-of-temporary-people-by-deepak-unnikrishnan/.

Mckeown, Adam. (2004). "Global Migration 1846–1940", *Journal of World History*, Vol. 15, No. 2, pp. 155–189.

Ministry of External Affairs. *Annual Report, 2016–17*, Government of India.

Sasikumar, S. K. (2019). "Indian Labour Migration to the Gulf: Recent Trends, the Regulatory Environment and New Evidences on Migration Costs", *Productivity: A Quarterly Journal of the National Productivity Council*, Vol. 60, No. 2, pp. 111–125.

United Nations Department of Economic and Social Affairs (UNDESA). (2017). *International Migrant Stock: By Destination and Origin*, New York.

Unnikrishnan, Deepak. (2017a). *Temporary People*. Brooklyn, New York: Restless Books.

Unnikrishnan, Deepak. (2017b). "Abu Dhabi: The City Where Citizenship Is Not an Option", *The Guardian*, Dec. 13. retrieved from https://www.theguardian.com/cities/2017/dec/13/abu-dhabi-citizenship-uae-foreigner-visa-india.

Index

For Product Safety Concerns and Information please contact our EU representative GPSR@taylorandfrancis.com
Taylor & Francis Verlag GmbH, Kaufingerstraße 24, 80331 München, Germany

www.ingramcontent.com/pod-product-compliance
Ingram Content Group UK Ltd.
Pitfield, Milton Keynes, MK11 3LW, UK
UKHW020143200926
475702UK00005B/882
9781032307640